ROMANTIC INTIMACY

ROMANTIC INTIMACY

NANCY YOUSEF

Stanford University Press
Stanford, California

Stanford University Press
Stanford, California

© 2013 by the Board of Trustees of the Leland Stanford Junior University. All rights reserved.

This book has been published with the assistance of Baruch College, City University of New York.

Printed in the United States of America on acid-free, archival-quality paper

Library of Congress Cataloging-in-Publication Data

Yousef, Nancy, author.
  Romantic intimacy / Nancy Yousef.
  pages cm
  Includes bibliographical references and index.
  ISBN 978-0-8047-8609-6 (cloth : alk. paper)
  ISBN 978-0-8047-9944-7 (pbk. : alk. paper)
  ISBN 978-0-8047-8827-4 (electronic)
  1. English literature—18th century—History and criticism. 2. English literature—19th century—History and criticism. 3. English literature—Psychological aspects. 4. Intimacy (Psychology) in literature. 5. Romanticism—Europe. I. Title.
  PR447.Y68 2013
  820.9'145—dc23
2013011627

Typeset by Bruce Lundquist in 10/15 Minion

To my husband, Jonah, and my daughter, Silvia Luna

I share the suffering in him, in spite of the fact that his skin does not enclose my nerves. . . . His experience is mysterious, for it is something our faculty of reason can give no account of, and its grounds cannot be discovered on the path of experience. And yet it happens every day. . . . Every day it comes before our eyes, in single acts on a small scale.

Arthur Schopenhauer, *On the Basis of Morality*

I will receive from them not what they have, but what they are. They shall give me that which properly they cannot give, but which emanates from them. But they shall not hold me by any relations less subtle and pure. We will meet as though we met not, and part as though we parted not.

Ralph Waldo Emerson, "Friendship"

CONTENTS

ACKNOWLEDGMENTS

The long time that it has taken to complete this book has been enriched by the generosity of friends and colleagues. Isobel Armstrong, David Clark, David Collings, Frances Ferguson, Jacques Khalip, Jonathan Kramnick, Meredith McGill, Andrew Parker, Adam Potkay, and Orrin Wang each read portions of the manuscript. Thomas Pfau and William Galperin read and commented on the whole. I am grateful for the kindness, encouragement, and unstinting intelligence of their responses and for their energetic devotion to building and sustaining intellectual community. Ongoing conversations with these readers, as well as with Ian Balfour, John Brenkman, Mary McGlynn, and Joshua Wilner, never failed to challenge and to hearten. I am also grateful to interlocutors at Rutgers University, the Cogut Center at Brown University, and various conferences of the North American Society for the Study of Romanticism (NASSR) for thoughtful responses to presentation of this material.

Work on this project commenced during a year's leave at the National Humanities Center, a wonderful place that leaves no scholarly need unmet. Special thanks are due to Geoffrey Harpham, Kent Mulliken, the remarkable library staff, and my cohort of resident fellows for accommodating and sustaining a new mother at her work. An initial draft of the book was completed thanks to a Mellon fellowship at the Center for the Humanities of the City University of New York (CUNY). The interdisciplinary working group on emotion that I organized that year with Peter Liberman deepened my understanding of a topic with profound and unresolved implications across a range of fields. Between these important leave years, work on this project could not have progressed without the support of my union, the Professional Staff Congress, in the form of grants funded by their Research Foundation, and of Jeffrey Peck, dean at Baruch College, who has worked to create a context in which scholarship can flourish at a public institution.

At the CUNY Graduate Center, I benefited from the energy and passion students brought to a series of seminars on emotion, ethics, aesthetics, and psychoanalysis. Andrew Dicus, Anne McCarthy, Allison Powell, and Leila Walker were especially important interlocutors. My thanks are also due to Meechal Hoffman and Lindsay Lehman for research assistance.

The manuscript received a warm welcome from Emily-Jane Cohen at Stanford University Press. I am grateful for her intelligent and effective work and to her assistant, Emma Harper, for her careful stewardship of the project.

Many friends outside the academy have patiently tolerated what must have seemed to be baffling periods of inaccessibility and preoccupation while continuing to befriend me. My thanks to Michael Casey, Molly Finnerty, Maria-Elena Gonzalez, Peter Gordon, Vivien Greene, Oliver Herring, Kamron Keshtgar, Peter Krashes, Manlio Narici, Audrey Oster, Rachel Porter, Tara Sherman, and Susan Yelavich.

Jonah Siegel, my closest reader, brings his rigor and intelligence to bear on all my writing. I am deeply grateful for his companionship, his wit, and his daily gifts of kindness and encouragement. Along with so much else, our daughter, Silvia Luna, has taught me almost all I know about glee. This book took shape in their loving presence and with their collaboration.

. . .

A version of Chapter 1 first appeared in *ELH* 78:3 (2011): 609–633. Chapter 2 is a substantially altered version of a contribution to *Theory and Practice in the Eighteenth Century*, ed. Tina Lupton and Alex Dick (London: Pickering and Chatto, 2008), 193–210. A version of Chapter 5 first appeared in *European Romantic Review* 21:5 (2010): 653–672.

INTRODUCTION
Ethics, Literature, and the Forms of Encounter

Nothing is more fallacious than general laws for human feelings. The web of them is so fine-spun and so intricate that it is hardly possible for the most careful speculation to take up a single thread by itself and follow it through all the threads that cross it. And supposing it possible, what is the use of it? There does not exist in Nature a single unmixed feeling; along with every one of them there arise a thousand others simultaneously, the very smallest of which completely alters the first, so that exceptions on exceptions spring up which reeducate at last the supposed general law itself to the mere experience of a few individual cases.

Gotthold Ephraim Lessing, The Laocoon (1766)

The term "intimacy" (from the Latin *intimus*, "most inner") refers both to what is closely held and personal and to what is deeply shared with others. Intimacy designates the sphere of the inmost, of the private, and also the realm of cherished connection and association. Unexpressed thoughts and feelings are intimate, but my friend is also my intimate. She might have become intimate with a new lover (the euphemism for sexual intercourse is a usage coeval with modern meanings of the term going back to the late seventeenth and early eighteenth centuries) but also confide to me that they are not otherwise intimate with one another. Naming close forms of friendship, familiarity, and erotic entanglement, and also naming an intrinsic psychic inwardness, "intimacy" crystallizes a tension between sharing and enclosing as opposed imaginations of relational possibilities. The term designates, and thus to a degree attests to, a confidence that individuals can and do disclose to one another thoughts, feelings, and experiences, but it also pertains to, and thus intimates the foreboding or wish for, an inward region of irreducible privacy, a fated or perhaps willed withholding. In the habitual confluence of these conflicting convictions, ethical aspirations and epistemological anxieties are always intermingled, nowhere more obviously than in the eighteenth-century theories of moral sentiment—principally "sympathy"—which are the subject of the first part of this book, unless perhaps in the twentieth-century theories of psychoanalytic "empathy," which I address directly in the Coda.[1] My use of the term "intimacy" is meant to evoke the persistent tension between a confidence in the possibility of knowing and being known by others and an implicit commitment to existential privacy that is characteristic of these two discourses (each being, in its own period, a cultural locus for reflection on modes of relational experience). At the same time, my use of intimacy is meant to suspend this problematic in order to investigate, without reduplicating, symptomatic conflicts around the term "sympathy" and to hold in abeyance, as far as possible, the ethical and epistemic goal of mutual recognition that is always at stake in the imagination of intimacy as a form of sympathetic insight or achievement.

This is not, then, another book about the cultural and discursive ubiquity of sympathy in the eighteenth and early nineteenth centuries but rather an effort to recover the conflicting drives and urgencies involved in thinking about the emotional and cognitive possibilities of shared experience in the period. To consider these possibilities as forms of intimacy, rather than iterations of sympathy, will, I hope, help turn the axis of inquiry away from terms such as "identification," "imitation," and "recognition," all of which presuppose and anticipate precisely what is in question: an end or aim—be it perceptual, affective, or moral—for the contingent, evanescent, multitudinous forms of experience among others. Indeed, antecedent to the sympathetic demand for identification is the seemingly necessary presupposition that two subjectivities come upon one another, finding or failing to find what they have in common. To hold the aim of mutual recognition in suspension is, then, also to set aside the presupposition that determines that aim in advance and to begin to think about the ways that intimacy (at least in its romantic forms) might be generative of both personal and interpersonal experience. Subjectivities may be said to arise and take shape in the realm of encounter—a realm that no one (existentially speaking) ever stands outside of.

Unlike sympathy, intimacy need not, and rarely does, entail a symmetrical relationship between one and another; need not, and rarely does, involve the discovery of similitude between one and another. Yet insofar as intimacy, like sympathy, designates feeling for and with another, it also admits and discloses affective expectations and disappointments—from aversion to self-abasing admiration, from gratitude to resentment, from frustration to fascination—that involve neither mutuality nor reciprocity but that certainly must be counted among the many "fine-spun and intricate" threads of the web (to borrow Lessing's metaphor) that bind one to others.

To the degree that it signifies closeness (being close to, involved closely with), intimacy invites a lingering upon the phenomenal fact of proximity between persons—whether sustained over time, as in a familial relationship, or in the fleeting immediacy of an encounter with a stranger. As mere proximity, intimacy is without content: whatever comes to turn bare proximity into intimacy, into the feeling or sense of closeness, is left to be determined by the particular imaginative articulations of relation and encounter found in the works of philosophy, literature, and psychoanalysis brought together here. The irresistible teleology associated with sympathy, which seems inevitably to lead to querulous demands for intersubjective symmetry—be it the perception of similarity, the impression of equality, or the expectation of reciprocity—inevitably passes over or discounts moments and modes of relational experience that fall short of the aim but are not, thereby, failures or breakdowns of relationship—or even, perhaps, ethical or epistemic failures.[2] Becoming intimate may occasionally take the form of scrupulously mutual recognition, or involve a fantasy of its attainment, or occur only to evanesce in quickly successive and varied moments of social and interpersonal experience. More frequently, more typically, intimacy involves asymmetrical and nonreciprocal forms of relation, attention, and appreciation. And it is principally these forms of intimacy—undetermined by, but not indifferent to, the ideal of mutuality—that receive subtle and sustained attention in the romantic-era writing that occupies the central portion of this book.

The romantic elaboration of mid-eighteenth-century writing on sensibility in general, and sympathy in particular, has been amply demonstrated in scholarship now extending back two decades that has substantially enriched our understanding of how romanticism absorbs rather than supersedes or decisively breaks with Enlightenment culture. In the work of Frances Ferguson, Marshall Brown, Adela Pinch, and Julie Ellison (among others), the philosophical preoccupations and aesthetic forms of the romantic era involve both the persistence and transformation of areas of inquiry vital to the eighteenth century (including sociability, sensation and the senses, representation, and imagination).[3] James Chandler's recent study of the politics of sentiment not only takes for granted the importance of the Enlightenment legacy but also insists on the comparative dimension of that context, the important circulation of texts and ideas between England, France, and Germany, in order to account for the complex and multivalent connections between aesthetic and political theory in the romantic era.[4] *Romantic Intimacy* relies and draws upon these nuanced studies, but my particular aim is as much to estrange as to clarify the imbrication of ethics, epistemology, and emotion in the era's imagination of intersubjectivity—to engage with the dynamic, shifting forms of that imagination by amplifying and pressing implications that might be lost under the pressure of constructing a scrupulously contextualized historical narrative.

The claim advanced in this book is that romantic-era literature (represented here by the poetry of William Wordsworth and Samuel Taylor Coleridge and the fiction of Jane Austen) is exceptional in its simultaneous acknowledgment and suspension of the epistemic and ethical demands of sympathy, allowing a backward and forward glance toward certain impasses in Enlightenment thought that recur within psychoanalysis—in particular, the struggle to reconcile ideals of mutual feeling with equally compelling commitments to the idea of an incommunicable core of the self. The transformative romantic inheritance of Enlightenment sentimentalism does not dispel or resolve the paradox of intimacy, but it does so soften the hard opposing edges of solitary inwardness and interpersonal exposure as to make intelligible the notion that "the place where we live" (in the terms of one psychoanalyst) is "alone and yet in the presence of the other."[5] Whether this being-alone-together can be understood as holding relational possibilities that include, rather than evade, an ethics of recognition is a question that arises repeatedly and variously in the romantic-era texts at the center of this study.

SENTIMENTALISM
AND THE IMMEDIACY OF SYMPATHY

Among the most important terms in eighteenth-century British ethics, "sympathy" is at once ubiquitous and conceptually unstable. The task of estranging us from sympathy need not involve the discovery or incorporation of new material, but it does involve a willingness to resist imposing theoretical coherence prematurely. Even though identification, for example, is almost always associated with sympathy, the meanings and implications of both terms depend on unsettled and unsettling questions about perception, cognition, and feeling. Does sympathy presuppose identification, or is it synonymous with and simultaneous to identification, or is identification the effect of sympathetic feeling? Any effort to establish the relationship between identification and sympathy given this instability risks assuming that sympathy must entail a form of identification, when it is that very requirement that bears investigation. In my own return to sympathy in eighteenth-century philosophy (in the first three chapters of this book), I am less concerned with the ways identification is imagined to occur between persons than I am with the difficulties, yearnings, and hopes that shape this possibility into a psychological preconception and an ethical demand. Identification is to sympathy what "formal unity" and "crystalline purity" are to actual language for Ludwig Wittgenstein—a "preconceived idea" that can be removed only by rotating the "axis of reference" of our examination around "the fixed point of our real need."[6] In the terms of this study, the "problem" of sympathy may not be its failure to provide an adequate or satisfying account of identification but its exposure of the disquietudes shaping our demand for such an account.

Arguing against the egoistic premises of Hobbesian psychology, philosophers of moral sentiment such as Anthony Ashley Cooper (Third Earl of Shaftesbury), Francis Hutcheson, David Hume, and Adam Smith confidently adduce sympathy as the self-evident ground of social virtues, the affective root of "fellow feeling," "benevolence," and "humanity" (as an adjective). But just as Thomas Hobbes's hypothesis of an aggressive, relentless struggle for self-preservation driven by mutual fear is derived from a radically individualistic or atomistic theory of mind, so too the sentimentalist hypothesis of an instinctive sympathy binding individuals to one another requires epistemic grounding. Although egoism and sentimentalism present straightforwardly opposed views of basic human inclinations with far-ranging ramifications for the political and moral theories linked to them, it is vital to recognize that sentimentalism evolves within the same dominant empiricist paradigm of mind and psychology proposed by Hobbes and influentially elaborated by John Locke. Consequently, insofar as identification is the irreducible sympathetic insight—the other is like me—sentimentalist writing must imagine other human beings as exceptional objects of knowledge, somehow exempt from the mediations of sense, impression, perception, and ideation that split all other objects into (inaccessible) essences and (frequently unreliable) appearances.

The explicit moral interest of the sentimental defense of "human nature" against the indictment of egoism obscures the inveterate, recurrent, and variously ineffectual efforts to account for sympathy as an epistemological problem. In his important early twentieth-century study of sympathy, the phenomenologist Max Scheler begins by observing that "any kind of rejoicing or pity presupposes, in principle, some sort of knowledge of the fact, nature, and quality of experience in other people, just as the possibility of such knowledge presupposes, as its condition, the existence of other conscious beings."[7] Scheler's presupposition—"*knowledge* of the fact, nature, and quality of experience in other people"—underlies eighteenth-century theories as well, though it is also, crucially, unarticulated. Indeed, its articulation would introduce a kind of conceptual stutter, interrupting the affective *immediacy* that the sentimentalists typically emphasize. Francis Hutcheson, for example, writes of irresistible benevolent inclination as a "gravitational" pull toward others, and Hume imagines the urgency of sympathetic response as a swift, impulsive, thoughtless "flight" toward the other.[8] "No sooner are actions viewed, no sooner the human affections and passions discerned (and they are most of them as soon discerned as felt)," writes Shaftesbury, "than straight an inward eye distinguishes and sees the fair and shapely, the amiable and admirable, apart from the foul, the odious, or the despicable."[9] Discernment of others' affections arises effortlessly and instantly, by force of attraction (Hutcheson), by instinctive transport (Hume), by the supplemental sense of an "inward eye" (Shaftesbury). Even though such representations circumvent epistemological reflection, foreclosing questions about the reliability of perception and sense impressions that so preoccupy contemporaneous theories of knowledge, such preemptions do not so much dispel as displace the troubling implications of empiricism.

Sentimentalism attempts to shield the realm of intersubjectivity from the corrosive scrutiny directed at the inanimate things that typically figure as exemplary objects in empirical investigation of knowledge. The elaborate analysis of mental operations in Locke, for example, destabilizes the most straightforward experiential certainties. My child has left her toy ball in the hallway; all I "really" see (according to Locke) is a flat circle, and I infer its three-dimensional roundness. After putting the ball back in the toy box, I return to the books and papers on my desk; they "disappeared" from my sight when I turned away, but I presume their continued existence.[10] (Of course, entirely omitted from Locke's account, and of no value to his analysis of cognition, are the emotional contexts and cumulative experiences that embed the ball and the paper and the books within a dwelling I share. The ball I see now, for example, involves the habit of picking up after a child that, with the passage of time, leads to shrugging acceptance or ambivalent frustration at the persistent presence of objects underfoot. I return to the books and papers, ready, and sometimes unable, to take them up again after interruptions that I wish were merely matters of perceptual discontinuity.) Although the conclusions of the *Essay concerning Human Understanding* are not what Locke would admit to calling skeptical, a profound concession to skepticism is granted in his conclusion that our untroubled confidence in the existence of these ordinary material phenomena amounts only to *probability*, not certainty. If such an analysis estranges the ordinary, then the same can be said of sentimental certainty about sympathy. Hume, for example, imagines intersubjective accessibility as a harmonious transmission of feeling—"all the affections readily pass from one person to another, and beget correspondent movements in every human creature"—and a play of mutual reflection—"the minds of all men are mirrors to one another."[11] Such descriptions of how readily we discern one another's thoughts and feelings veer wildly toward certainty at precisely those points where we are, ordinarily, most liable to question our impressions and find ourselves most vulnerable to possible disjunctions between perception and judgment. Skepticism and sympathy are thus bound in a strangely complementary structure in eighteenth-century philosophical discourse, whereby the first generates an excessive anxiety about the accuracy and reliability of our apprehension of things and the second presumes an improbable confidence about our intimacy with other persons.

The confidence of sentimentalism and the anxiety of empiricism seem inversely related to their objects. Is it too much to suggest that a poem like Wordsworth's "Strange Fits of Passion" dramatizes an awareness of this peculiar inversion?[12] Making his way to his lover's cottage, the rider holds to the constancy of a visible object: "Upon the moon I fixed my eye" (9); "all the while, my eyes I kept / On the descending moon" (19–20). Sure of his way over "paths so dear to me" (12), he proceeds through the orchard and atop the hill until "behind the cottage roof / At once the bright moon dropped" (23–24), prompting the lover's "fond and wayward thought": "'O mercy!' to myself I cried, / 'If Lucy should be dead!'" (27–28). The moon's sudden disappearance, its dropping out of sight, is at once the immediate occasion, and retrospective figuration, of anxiety about the continued existence of the other. The problem of interrupted perception, which in Locke and Hume turns into a question about the persistence or continuity of things in the world, turns instead into a question of affective constancy. The thought "If Lucy should be dead" is "fond and wayward" not only because it is unmotivated by the occasion that prompts it—an errant superstitious association—but because it evokes the passion driving an existential uncertainty that, the poem proposes, belongs only to those who are fond. In its opening lines the poem invites, indeed insists, that its reader imagine listening in the mood of one who loves (but who, after all, does not love?) if she is to receive or share what it confides: the thought that "will slide / Into a lover's head" (26–27) is meant for "the lover's ear alone" (3). In the abrupt economy of its final line, the literal dread of loss—"If Lucy should be dead"—also figuratively implicates something like the passionate conflation of living and loving. Lucy's love might be dead; my love for her might be dead; her life is dear to me; she is as dear to me as life: such is the waywardness of fondness. And such are the estranging possibilities of passions that, even in such a whimsical form, represent disruptions of the genial emotional certainties of sentimentalism.

Insofar as sentimentalism openly sets itself against a Hobbesian analysis that effectively derives all forms of relational experience from fear, it is not surprising that familiar emotions associated with what we might call intersubjective anxiety—suspicion, dread, wariness, frustration, disappointment—would be unaccounted for in theories propounding the facility and normativity of sympathy.[13] Nor should it be surprising to find that these are the very emotions evoked in the melodramatic staging of doubts about material objects to which analysis drives the philosopher, and that Stanley Cavell has taught us to appreciate as intelligible versions of achingly familiar misgivings about our relations to others.[14] As straightforward as this philosophical misalignment of affect might seem—where anxiety is relegated to epistemology and confidence to sentimentally based ethics—insistence on the immediate self-evidence of sympathy displaces, but cannot altogether suppress, the affects it disowns.

The very effort to avoid explaining that Schelerian presupposition of sympathetic response—the *knowledge* of others entailed in pitying and rejoicing—only leaves unresolved the question of how feeling for others can be understood as a form of (re)cognition. This impasse cannot be averted—and would only be reduplicated—by imagining sympathy (among other feelings and affects) as a non- or precognitive sense. Although sympathy is conceptualized as a "natural affection" or "instinct" (as in Shaftesbury and Hume), that pseudo-anthropological category always serves and is subordinate to complex, speculative claims about ethical judgment. For all eighteenth-century theories of moral sense, sympathy necessarily entails a valuation of the other (as a fellow human being, as one like me, as one with whom I identify), the ethical implications of which are lost when relational experience is reduced to the automaticity of instinct. "A kind of mysterious instinct is *supposed* to reside in the soul that instantaneously discerns truth," observes Mary Wollstonecraft, but "we ought to beware of confounding mechanical instinctive sensations with emotions that reason deepens, and justly terms the feelings of *humanity*" if there is to be any meaningful distinction between virtue and "brutish affection."[15] In this postrevolutionary critique of sensibility, the thrust of Immanuel Kant's earlier call for a "pure moral philosophy, completely cleansed of everything that may be only empirical and that belongs to anthropology," is readily discerned.[16]

But the effort to distinguish the ethical substance and obligations of the recognition involved in sympathy from its dubious psychological grounds in affective immediacy still leaves open the question of epistemic discernment. In Shaftesbury, for example, as discussed in Chapter 1, response to others dissolves into a mere mood of responsiveness where what matters is that "our affections and passions are known to us . . . are certain" even if, and regardless of whether or not, "the objects on which they are employed . . . are realities or mere illusions."[17] Rousseau's response to the epistemic complexities and contradictions of sentimentalism, which is taken up in Chapter 2, involves a radical and unsustainable effort to invert the psychic inwardness that undermines the correspondence between sympathetic feeling and its ostensible object. The series of utopian works composed in the middle of his career (including *La Nouvelle Héloïse* [1761], *The Social Contract* [1762], and *Emile* [1762]) are unified by the task of imagining conditions that allow no social or existential space for the cultivation of privacy. Rousseau's communities of mutually transparent, openhearted confidants and citizens are designed to render sympathetic identification a matter of indubitable fact as well as irresistible feeling. The ethical implications of sympathy (including trust, fidelity, constancy, benevolence) are secured by, but also thereby contingent on, epistemological access to the thoughts and feelings of others—an access Rousseau imagines as constant mutual exposure, a transparency that discloses no hidden depths and effectively hollows out interiority. If this is an unsatisfying account—at once utopian and dystopian—of the conditions for intimacy and the ethical possibilities it might summon, we may also recognize in it an exhaustion of the effort to align knowledge of others with feeling for others.

Insofar as Shaftesbury's passional self-certainty seems to sever sympathy from its ostensible object, such "affective narcissism" has typically been understood as symptomatic of romantic lyric meditation and, more broadly, of romanticism's hypostasis of the imaginative faculty, its aesthetic investment in what we "half create" at the expense of what we "half perceive." Even Adela Pinch, who openly displaces the familiar charge of egotism so as to explore the "transindividual aspects of emotion" in Wordsworth's poetry, reverts to analysis of "deep inwardness," "self-absorption," and solitary "reverie" in her interpretation of "Strange Fits of Passion." Pinch lays stress on the self-reflexive "to myself I cried," suggesting that this penultimate line belies the promise of interpersonal confidence with which the poem begins. "By the end of the poem, the speaker seems to be his only audience," she notes, suggesting that this "self-quotation" retrospectively turns the "lover's ear" for whom the tale is destined into "his own ear."[18] The formal slippage from address to soliloquy is reinforced, thematically, by Wordsworth's excision of the original final stanza in which the speaker shares his tale with the beloved: "I told her this: her laughter light / Is ringing in my ears: / And when I think upon that night / My eyes are dim with tears." In omitting this stanza, Wordsworth gives "the speaker the last word . . . by removing [the lover's voice] from the poem" and thus refocuses attention on a "fundamental uncertainty about the basis for the speaker's fit."[19] I agree with Pinch that the excised final lines hint at, as if confirming, the anxious intimation of the lover's death, though this is by no means the only possibility. The odd temporal convergence of past and present tenses, as if to say her laughter is *still* ringing in my ears (still the lover's ears?) even as I think back to that night through the dim haze of tears (what De Quincey describes as the "humid light" of the emotions caught in poetry[20]), might as easily suggest the waning of the passion that motivated this "strange fit," or the demise of the intimacy that allows for such telling and such laughing, or the passage of time from that night "When she I lov'd, was strong and gay" to this other night when, implicitly, she is no longer so. But is it necessarily the case that, in omitting this ending, Wordsworth removes the lover's voice? And does the self-quotation ("to myself I cried") that concludes the final version necessarily exclude, or forget, the audience of lovers the poem initially invites? The answer to these questions is certainly yes if engagement with others is rigidly opposed to (inner) rumination.

What if the poem's themes of vulnerable confidence and confidential address are developed, refined, and revaluated in its ending rather than overturned? The self-reflexive lines of the final version more fitly uphold the poem's unity as an occasion of confiding between the lover who speaks and the lover who reads, sustaining the address by omitting reference to the past intimacy of disclosure and response (the "real" relationship between him who told and her who laughed) from which the reader is necessarily excluded. Moreover, the removal of any remotely tenuous connection between the speaker's anxiety and the reality of the object with which it is concerned effectively shifts the grounds upon which the passion becomes intelligible. The passion is known, is certain (to recall Shaftesbury's phrasing), but its contextual mooring is neither purely inward in the sense of indifferent to the reality or illusion of its object nor necessarily extrinsic in the sense of being verifiable by the real fate of the object. Rather, the self-absorbing grip of this passion is radically attenuated by the dramatic affective preoccupation with another that it evinces: the "to myself I cried" is less a self-reflexive self-quotation than it is an attestation of the beloved's power to elicit the subject, to engender passion and its utterance. And insofar as this recollection is meant for the "lover's ear," it appeals for its intelligibility to the reader's silent corroboration and assent to the compulsive and generative force of such psychic preoccupation. Such a reading depends on transmuting rigid oppositions between solitude and sociality, self-reflection and disclosure, inwardness and responsiveness so as not to fall back into sentimentalist impasses over the reality or illusion of feeling for others to which romantic lyric meditation offers a complex response.

INTERPRETING AFFECT, THEORIZING OTHER MINDS, AND THE PRACTICE OF SLOW READING

If eighteenth-century sentimentalism leaves open the question of intersubjective knowledge that it sought to foreclose by recourse to the immediacy of affective insight, it nevertheless bequeaths to later eras (including our own) a powerful valuation of emotion as bound up with and formative of response to others and as constitutive of relational experience. Nor does the particular feeling for others privileged by the term "sympathy" ever become detached from ethical discourses in which recognition of others is imagined in terms of identification, equality, and reciprocity. From this perspective, even Kant's radical break with sentimentalism remains consistent with the ethical aspirations of that influential school of thought, as the abstract recognition of others as ends in themselves transmutes sympathetic identification into a formalized acknowledgment of essential similitude and equal dignity. What I mean by this is that the epistemic and ethical resonances of sympathy are by no means exhausted or contained by imagining it to be a "mere" feeling. To understand Kantian "respect" (*Achtung*) as an important variant of sentimental sympathy is not to ignore Kant's distinction between pathological (*pathologisch*, in the literal sense of emotional) and moral incentives but rather to wrest the phenomenal possibilities of recognition from the rigidly nondynamic opposition between feeling and "reason" or "reflection" or "cognition" or (most recently "consciousness" itself) that typically pertains in discussions of sympathy.[21]

Those features of the emotions that Kant excludes from what he calls "moral feeling" (*moralische Gefühl*) (including embodiment, contingency, unreflective inclination, unwilled disposition) are precisely the features highly valued by currently influential theories of affect, so it is worth pausing briefly to address how my own treatment of mood, emotion, and affect—as I find these articulated and evoked in the texts under discussion—differs from these approaches. In a recent, remarkably lucid critical survey of the field, historian of science Ruth Leys points to the consistencies between theoretical claims about affect in the humanities and current conceptualization of the emotions in neuro- and cognitive science. What they share, she argues, "is a commitment to the idea that there is a gap between the subject's affects and its cognition or appraisal of the affective situation . . . such that cognition or thinking come 'too late' for reasons, beliefs, intentions, and meanings" to shape response.[22] Such a perspective, she suggests, can be maintained only by adhering to the "same false opposition between the mind and the body" that is ostensibly challenged by attention to affect as a "visceral," "bodily and autonomic," "non-conscious experience of intensity,"[23] or as an evolutionary inheritance and neurobiological substratum of conscious experience.[24] Hume seems to describe something like a physiology of affect when he writes that "the blood flows with a new tide; the heart is elevated," and the whole organism acquires a "new vigor" in the presence of a "rational and thinking being like ourselves."[25] It is as if sympathy is constituted out of bodily response, and the corresponding judgment that I am with a "rational and thinking being like myself" is either a precipitate of these physical effects or a redundant discursive formulation of their significance. Such moments in sentimentalist writing have tempted both literary critics and philosophers to claim strong correspondences between modern scientific investigations of affect, empathy, and "mind reading," on the one hand, and eighteenth-century hypotheses of sympathy, on the other. Surprisingly, within literary studies such interpretations have come to coexist with poststructuralist and historicist accounts of sentimental rhetoric that adhere to a strictly constructionist account of the emotions and therefore tend to emphasize the factitiousness of sympathy in the period: its specularity, its theatricality, its manneristic deployment of tears, blushes, sighs, palpitations.[26] Even though the attention to affect as a corporeal process involving bodily reaction and unconscious neural functions relies on scientific hypotheses of "basic emotions" that are historically and culturally constant (universal and innate mechanisms), this perspective has generally been taken to supplement rather than controvert analysis of emotion as the social, constructed, cultural determination, or "capture" of affect.[27] Both approaches belong to a wider poststructuralist (or sometimes posthumanist) decentering or displacement of "consciousness" and "mind" as loci of intention and agency, and in both cases, theoretical presuppositions shape, a priori, the object of study. If we already understand affect as a neurobiological function, and if we already understand emotion as a historically determined and culturally relative mode of subject formation, then sympathy will only ever be a particular articulation of these predetermined categories. Methodologically, however rich and rigorous a particular reading might be, the text in question inevitably offers an exemplification that affirms (or occasionally subverts) a conceptualization of emotion that is extrinsic to the formal and aesthetic specificity of the work at hand.[28] Textual interpretation can work toward an exposure of sympathy as a specific instantiation of "affect" or "emotion" but will leave those larger categories unmodified by its exegetical labors.

Eighteenth-century representations of sympathy might or might not be seen to correspond with, or anticipate, or be usefully illuminated by current research on "mirror neurons" (echoing Hume's proposal that the "minds of men are mirrors to one another"), but interdisciplinary efforts to align cultural studies with empirical findings tend to neglect the humanistic genealogy of contemporary scientific paradigms. There is instead a tendency to construe current scientific research on empathy in particular as "confirmations" of eighteenth-century theories that are also the cultural sources for the frameworks of inquiry that have played a significant part in these developments in evolutionary biology and cognitive psychology. Thus, for a philosopher like Jesse Prinz, committed to "us[ing] empirical findings to help adjudicate otherwise interminable philosophical debate," the preponderance of research indicating that "emotions are necessary for moral judgment" licenses an argument that "sentimentalism [as theorized by Hume] is true" while Kantian-inspired "normative ethical theories," if not altogether false, are "inaccurate" descriptions of ethical experience.[29] Similarly, Stephen Darwall (a less ardent empiricist than Prinz) argues that "Hume and Adam Smith correctly believed" sympathy "to be central to human thought and practice" because their "theoretical speculations" have been vindicated by "experimental psychology."[30] Darwall's defense of the primacy of sympathetic concern against a "metaphysical" commitment to "rational egoism" draws on experimental research on facial recognition, motor mimicry, and emotional simulation in support of eighteenth-century sentimental psychology.[31]

Recent work in so-called cognitive literary studies extends this reliance on the explanatory force of empirical findings and scientific experiment into rhetorical analysis and narrative theory. Thus, Blakey Vermeule concludes her recent study of emotional engagement with fictional characters by hailing the "growing movement towards understanding literary experience . . . as a human phenomenon that can be tested, measured, and defined in ever more precise terms."[32] Applying "theory of mind" (ToM) findings about the cognitive mechanisms involved in perceiving and interpreting the thoughts and feelings of other persons, Lisa Zunshine hypothesizes that "the novel, in particular, is implicated with our mind-reading ability to such a degree that . . . in its currently familiar shape it exists because we are creatures with ToM."[33] Alan Richardson is perhaps more circumspect in his engagement with contemporary work in the brain sciences—conceding that these fields are "not intrinsically superior to or more authoritative than the humanities"—but he also openly admits "hold[ing] a scientific world view as part of my basic intellectual equipment" and thus "accept[ing] unhesitatingly that 'the mind is what the brain does.'"[34] Ultimately, Richardson is clearly drawn to scientific "resolutions" to questions that, as Prinz puts it, have generated "interminable philosophical debate" as well as richly varied aesthetic treatment. "The traditional philosophical problem of other minds really isn't a problem," Richardson observes, because "according to ToM theory . . . human beings are adaptively designed . . . to search for and identify signs of intentionality, emotions and belief states in others."[35] From this perspective, the representations of "mind reading" and its failures in Jane Austen's narratives correspond with the (scientific) resolution to the "philosophical problem of other minds" rather than offer a complex aesthetic engagement with that very problem. The "intersubjective dramas" of Austen's fiction provide (and in some sense are reduced to) illustrative corroboration of current empirical findings about social cognition, so, although "the flexible medium of fictional representation and technique" allows for a "more holistic account" than the "necessarily limiting means of the controlled experiment," the aesthetic and the scientific are implicitly coextensive with one another—more or less precise or accurate studies of human behavior.[36] Concomitant with this attenuated regard for aesthetics as a distinct mode of cognition is a diminished account of the formal techniques and rhetorical elaboration specific to literary works. Thus, Paul Hernandi maintains that "there is no clear division between literary and non-literary signification," a contention Zunshine identifies as "an important tenet of [the] cognitive approach."[37]

My aim here is not so much to call this interdisciplinary effort into question but rather to more clearly delineate what I take to be at stake in eschewing the attention to brains and bodies so prevalent in recent work on affect and empathy that, like this book, is concerned with the forms and possibilities of relational experience. It does not suffice to note, though it is perhaps worth recalling, that the creeping reliance on scientific evidence in humanistic and cultural studies runs counter to the romantic era's own insistent articulations of the distinctive domain of literary and aesthetic attention. Wordsworth imagines the poet "at [the] side" of the scientist, making his discoveries "proper objects of the Poet's art" only *if* and *when* those discoveries "be manifestly and palpably material to us as enjoying and suffering beings."[38] Until that time, scientific knowledge "cleaves to us as a necessary part of our existence" unlike poetic knowledge, "slow to come to us," which "by no habitual and direct sympathy connect[s] us with our fellow-beings" (881). What Wordsworth might mean in suggesting that the sympathy shaped in poetry is nonhabitual and indirect matters in this study precisely because it at once incorporates and seems to rebuke the presumption of reliable, immediate sympathetic connection to others, which, in its own way, was the core hypothesis of sentimentalism as the psychological science of its time. The "other" knowledge of poetry, unlike the inescapable "unalienable" truths of science, may or may not become a "personal and individual acquisition," in which case we are free to forgo it, to leave our habits undisturbed. I take it that not acquiring the knowledge of poetry as Wordsworth conceives it here means forfeiting the indirect sympathy that connects us with our fellow beings. How audacious is this claim? Are we unconnected by "habitual and direct sympathy," or is it rather that the knowledge of connection with others that is not given but acquired, or attained, might itself be constitutive of new, strange, and arduous forms of connection? Wordsworth's claim hovers over the terms "sympathy," "connection," and "fellow-beings," at once assuming and obscuring their relationship to one another and their collective relation to a way of knowing that is neither necessary in itself nor necessarily shared ("a personal and individual acquisition"). To take heed of such confusion is, perhaps, not to be arrested in one's thought but to be slowed down in thought, given over to what might "come to us" by way of rhetorical intimation rather than conceptual cogency.

Insofar as theorists of affect, on the one hand, and enthusiasts for contemporary theories of mind reading, on the other, are alike liable to seek out instantiation of explanatory models in their objects of study, they will not have much patience for Wordsworth's ensnarling of the term "sympathy" with insistent yet obscure claims that poetry is a mode of knowledge that arrives (if it does) not immediately and habitually but slowly and indirectly, nor will they have much patience for my tendency to belabor and pursue the suggestive implications of Wordsworth's claims rather than to assimilate them to a clarifying theoretical or scientific framework.[39] As I noted earlier, this study does not aim to provide a historical account of variations in sentimental and romantic renderings of relational experience, but I do recognize and often rely on such accounts and can readily imagine amplifications and revisions of the readings offered here along historical lines. My insistence on the specificities and irresolutions involved in the effort to define and represent possibilities of intimacy between persons is, however, driven by something like an anxiety about missing the implications of the period's compulsive intellectual and aesthetic engagement with those possibilities, and thereby failing to make out the terms of readerly engagement elicited by the texts themselves. I attend, therefore, to the evocative rhetorical, figural, and conceptual discriminations that make "sympathy" (for example) so unstable and liable to subtle but consequential reinterpretation virtually *every* time it appears. This is not simply to say that Shaftesbury's use of sympathy differs from Hume's or Rousseau's (though that is certainly the case) but also that its appearance in a particular text (Hume's *Enquiry*, as distinct from his *Treatise*, for example; Wordsworth's "Old Cumberland Beggar," as distinct from *The Prelude* and the "Preface" to *Lyrical Ballads*) always compels a renewed effort to account for the otherwise undetermined responsiveness it names.

ROMANTIC INTIMACY

The emotions that recurrently arise in *Romantic Intimacy*—especially disappointment, respect, gratitude, appreciation, frustration, embarrassment—are ones that I am reluctant to label as either cognitive or precognitive precisely because the way these feelings or moods implicate or correlate with self-knowledge and knowledge of others is almost always at issue in their textual elaborations. These emotions are perhaps para-cognitive, shaping and being shaped by prior assumptions and reasoned expectations in a dynamic interplay that alternately defines and dissolves the conceptual boundaries between feeling and knowing.

Kant's account of "respect" is especially pertinent here. Insofar as it involves projections and intimations of one's own identity (as a rational being), respect might be imagined as the necessary precondition for recognition of others as ends in themselves, an implication Kant dreaded enough to repeatedly refute. "It could be objected that I only seek refuge, behind the word *respect*, in an obscure feeling [*dunkelen Gefühle*]," he writes in the *Groundwork of the Metaphysics of Morals*, "but though respect is a feeling . . . it is . . . a feeling *self-wrought* by means of a rational concept [*einen Vernunftbegriff selbstgewirktes Gefühle*]" and therefore distinct from all other feelings "which can be reduced to inclination or fear" (*GM*, 56; all emphases in the original unless otherwise noted). In the *Critique of Practical Reason*, Kant explains that "sensible feeling [*sinnliche Gefühl*] . . . is indeed the condition of that feeling we call respect, but the cause determining it lies in pure practical reason" (*CPR*, 201). At stake in the struggle to distinguish respect from other feelings is an effort to displace the immediacy of affective response (so important to the sentimentalists) with an alternative temporality of judgment that grants reason the determining, urgent role.[40] Thus, there is a concession to feeling in general as the condition for the possibility of respect but an insistence that the particular feeling of respect arises only with the cognition or consciousness of the moral law that commands respect. Respect is thus "the *effect* of the law on the subject, and not the *cause* of the law" (*GM*, 56); it is "produced solely by reason" and "seems to be solely at the disposal of reason" (*CPR*, 201–202); the affective form is wrought by rational content.

The wresting of respect from its underlying condition in feeling seems inextricably bound up with Kant's effort to subordinate respect for persons to respect for the law governing their relations. The transpersonal recognition of oneself and therefore others as ends in themselves is consistently invoked only to be insistently sublated. "*Respect* is directed only to persons, never to things" (*CPR*, 202) Kant specifies, but "any respect for a person is properly only respect for the law" (*GM*, 56). Nevertheless, insofar as the law we respect concerns the "idea of the *dignity* [*Würde*] of a rational being"—which necessarily entails a vision of "the relation of rational beings to one another" (*GM*, 84) and of all persons as equal to one another—it is clear that an identificatory recognition of others as essentially like oneself is embedded within, and perhaps even constitutive of, the concept of the moral law itself. In this sense, Kant's metaphysics of morals shares more with the ethics of alterity advanced by Emmanuel Levinas than might appear at first glance, and their points of convergence attest to the persistence, within modernity, of philosophical aspirations arising in the late Enlightenment. Like Kant's notion of the other as an end-in-herself, Levinas's principal figuration of the Other as the face is insistently nonphenomenal and immaterial. (Consider, as an instructive contrast, Wittgenstein's famous remark that "the human body is the best picture of the human soul" [178], an aphoristic distillation of the habitual responsiveness to others evinced by the myriad concrete instances compiled in the *Philosophical Investigations*.) In Levinas the encounter with the Other, which evokes the "epiphany" of my absolute responsibility, involves an obligation analogous to the self-imposed constraint of the moral law in Kant—as the later philosopher himself acknowledges. What "we catch sight of [in the face] seems suggested by the practical philosophy of Kant, to which we feel particularly close": this conceptual affinity certainly underlies the notion that "universality reigns as the presence of humanity in the eyes that look at me."[41] Levinasian "otherness" is, in a sense, shared. Bearing in mind that the eyes looking at me, like the face, are figures for irreducible alterity *and* universality at once, it is possible to see the immediacy of ethical revelation in Levinas as commensurate with the imperative force of respect in Kant.

The "look" of the other "appeals to my responsibility and consecrates my freedom as responsibility," writes Levinas; so too, for Kant, does recognition of the other's dignity. The Levinasian face may be taken as a proleptic reminder that the moral law in Kant cannot be fully abstracted from recognition (of the likeness and equality of rational beings); it inevitably bears some trace of persons. I do not mean to discount the clarity or efficacy of distinctions that Kant carefully draws but rather to emphasize the complex interdependence of terms within the exposition that aims to separate them. Even if respect involves a "rational determination," it cannot be wholly distilled from the capacity for emotion (what Kant elsewhere terms the "subjective conditions of receptiveness to the concept of duty" [*MM*, 528]) that is the necessary ground for its possibility. Even if "law" is understood as the proper object of respect, the formal abstraction cannot wholly elide the recognitions, projections, and identifications entailed in *seeing* others as ends in themselves, for these are necessarily antecedent to and implicit in respect for a law that enjoins us to treat others as ends in themselves.

So, for example, Kant reasons in *The Metaphysics of Morals* that "the *respect* I have for others or that another can require of me is . . . recognition [*Anerkennung*] of a *dignity* in other human beings" and it is by virtue of this recognition that I am "under obligation to acknowledge [*anzuerkennen*], in a practical way, the dignity of humanity in every other human being" (*MM*, 579).

In the terms of this study, what distinguishes Kantian respect from other modes of emotional proximity is not the rational determination that marks its most obvious rupture with moral sentimentalism but the insistence on equality and similitude that it shares with sentimentalism. It overcomes the epistemic impasse of sentimentalism—does my feeling for another comprise knowing another (to be like myself)?—by formalizing the intersubjective identifications and presumed reciprocities intrinsic to eighteenth-century sympathy. Moreover, Kantian respect includes mutuality as an ideal rather than an expectation; it anticipates rather than presupposes or ensures reciprocity and thereby decisively sets recognition on ethical grounds that abide no hesitations or anxieties concerning return. Where Rousseau's effort to establish a social contract required some account of how it is that "while I [am] scrupulously observing" the social law toward others, I can be "sure that all of them would observe it toward me," for Kant the very imagination that "a kingdom of ends is possible" enjoins me to "act as if" I am already a member without "count[ing] on every other to be faithful" to the same law (*GM*, 87).[42] Indeed, "even if there never have been actions arising from such pure sources [as respect for law], what is at issue is not whether this or that happened" but only "what ought to happen" (*GM*, 62). Acknowledgment and recognition of the humanity of others simultaneously presume and anticipate, but by no means account for or ensure, a reciprocal structure: although my "claim to respect" from others "*in turn* [binds me] to respect every other" (*MM*, 579), I am bound without, and regardless of, any prospect of return.

Against this ideal, or striving, or aspiration to dwell among others *as if* in the kingdom of ends, to cleave to "what ought to happen" between us, experience with others (all the "this or that" that might happen between persons) always risks disappointment. Almost everything I do with, and especially to, others is a relational failure when set against the perfect symmetry of mutual respect for one another's dignity. Kant himself concedes this implication in the surprisingly poignant concluding pages on friendship in *The Metaphysics of Morals*. Having earlier proposed that "by analogy with the physical world, *attraction* [*Anziehung*] and *repulsion* [*Abstoßung*] bind together rational beings (on earth)"

(*MM*, 568), Kant at first imagines friendship as the perfect balance between these opposing forces. "Mutual love [*Wechselliebe*] admonishes [us] constantly to *come closer* [*sich nähern*] to one another," while the respect we "owe one another" commands us to "*keep at a distance* [*in Abstande . . . erhalten*] from one another" (568). As "the union of two persons through equal mutual love and respect [*gleiche wechselseitige Liebe und Achtung*]," friendship "in its perfection" achieves and maintains the equilibrium between closeness and distance (584). As soon as this definition is ventured, and as its apparently necessary consequence, Kant withdraws its promise. "It is readily seen," he writes, that such friendship is "only an idea . . . unattainable in practice" because the relational structure of equality and mutuality turns out to be easily undermined by the dynamics of loving and respecting. The "equal balance [*das Ebenmaß die Gleichgewichts*] required for friendship" is threatened, for example, by anxiety that "if the *love* of one is stronger, he may . . . just because of this, forfeit something of the other's *respect*" (585); generosity might well be inspired by "equality [*Gleichheit*] in love" but will also corrode the grounds of mutual respect because one will now "see himself obviously a step lower in being under an obligation without being able to impose obligation in return" (586).

In an analysis to which I am otherwise indebted for its emphasis on the intersubjective structure of value in Kant, Christine Korsgaard nevertheless too quickly absorbs the "unattainable" perfection of friendship into familiar modes of relational experience in order to argue that "the territory of personal relations is continuous with moral territory" in his writings.[43] Thus, for Korsgaard, to regard another "as a *person*" in Kant's sense is "the distinctive element in the relation of adult human beings." "To accept promises, offer confidences, exchange vows, cooperate . . . have a conversation, make love, be friends, or get married" always already involves "reciprocity in some or all of its forms."[44] The difference between "personal as opposed to moral relations" concerns the "degree of reciprocity" achieved measured, implicitly, against the *telos* of "perfect reciprocity."[45] Thus, Korsgaard implicitly disowns the possibility that Kant's stress on equality and reciprocity between persons is so unyielding, so un(for)giving, as to degrade multifarious possibilities of relational experience that fall short of perfection.[46] It seems to me that we cannot discount the potentially despairing implications of Kant's unattainable relational perfection without also diminishing the force of what Cavell describes as the "aspirational" dimension of his thought.[47] On my reading, the territory between personal and moral relations in Kant may be continuous, but it is perilously rough and unmarked terrain where we promise and confide and befriend and marry in spite of finding no bearings or secure footing on the path of reciprocity. That such converse between us takes place even though the horizon of mutuality lies too distant to be discerned is what I take romantic-era writing to be struggling to account for and value.

If sentimental sympathy imagines an identification with others so complete and immediate as to effectively dissolve the distance between persons, the (mutual) identification of equal dignity at stake in Kantian respect can be sustained only at a distance. Between the affective fusion of sympathy and the remote regard of respect lies a realm of proximity—of mere coexistence with others, both familiars and strangers—that provides occasions for intimacy easily missed so long as equal mutual recognition between persons remains the privileged epistemic and ethical archetype of relational experience. The rendering of such occasions in all their affective, psychic, and social particularity, involving, as it does, the chastening eschewal of mutuality and reciprocity, becomes the special province of a range of romantic-era writing that at once assimilates and forsakes the affective confidence of sentimentalism and the moral idealism of Kantian respect. For example, the pressure Wordsworth places on the relationship between sympathy and charity in his many poems of encounter, explored in Chapter 3, involves a radical revaluation of the affective affinity Hume both affirms and disarticulates from the disinterested regard of justice. Sympathetic presumptions and aspirations are at once rendered and chastened in these poems that attend so carefully to the limits of recognition as a conceptual framework for understanding interest, withdrawal, responsiveness, and abstention as constitutive ethical orientations. The remarkable force of gratitude in Austen's *Pride and Prejudice*, which is the topic of Chapter 4, unsettles the possibility of a perfect (Kantian) union of mutual love and respect but, in so doing, also engenders a "good will" that precludes any expectation of reciprocity by bringing the welfare of the beloved into the ambit of one's wishes. Affective involvement is not threatened but occasioned by a willingness to receive, to offer thanks, free from the self-reflexive preoccupation of giving in return. If such an engagement fails to establish a marriage of equals, it nevertheless attends to the emotional and erotic possibilities of receptivity. In Chapter 5, the self-reflexivity of romantic lyric meditation discloses itself as sustained or held by the passive presence of another—quite literally in Coleridge's "Frost at Midnight," for example, where the "strange silence" that provokes the speaker wholly depends on the audible breath of the sleeping infant at his side. Solitude thus appears as a caesura in the otherwise uninterrupted rhythms of attendance on others rather than a clear break or escape from involvement with others.

Romantic intimacy takes form in moods of appreciation, gratitude, awkwardness, frustration, humiliation, and even indifference. I noted earlier that such attitudes or orientations at times define and at other times dissolve the boundaries between feeling and knowing. Their amplifications in lyric, poetic tale, and narrative allow for rhetorical elaborations and temporal stagings that stress the shifting dynamics of relational experience rather than the establishment of a relational structure. What transpires in the realm of proximity is rarely reciprocal, and what counts as recognition is rarely mutual.

The intersubjective asymmetries typical of romantic intimacy are not only radical (and perhaps radically amoral) in suspending equality (in the form of sympathetic affect or scrupulous respect) as a relational *telos*. They are also radical in their attention to thoughts and feelings that pass and fail to pass between persons rather than to exchanges of thought and feeling. In the complex phenomenology of intimate experience in romantic-era writing, proximity becomes the occasion for awareness of relational possibilities, for intersubjective traversals and encounters that are affectively and conceptually fluid precisely to the degree that they eschew the rigidity of epistemic and ethical demands for symmetry. What I am describing here is more akin to the insistent disclosure of "what we have always known" yet "been unable to notice," which Wittgenstein undertakes, than to the "asymmetry of the interpersonal" theorized by Levinas.[48] As I suggested previously, the impact of the face in Levinas and the responsibility it summons are not phenomenological occasions or events. By contrast, Wittgenstein's procedure in the *Philosophical Investigations*, which involves the accumulation of examples and the assemblage of what he calls "reminders" (§ 127), rather than theses or explanations, finds its ethical implications in exposing the myriad, familiar modes of responsiveness that at once constitute and evince a common "form of life." Romantic intimacy, like form of life, is not a structure but an unfolding of its conditions and implications.[49] As a practice, Wittgenstein's attention to the "*possibilities* of phenomena" (§ 90) bears affinities to the specificity and intensity with which romantic-era literature scrutinizes the varieties of our shared experience.

Romantic forms of intimacy involve dwelling in and on phenomenal grounds where sympathetic fellowship and mutual respect emerge as ideals, even occasionally as exceptional achievements, but never as stable, sustainable modes of relational experience. Attending to the phenomenological complexity of intimacy in romantic-era writing—especially in romantic lyric—requires what will at times seem an obstinate superseding of long-standing critical presuppositions about the metaphysical preoccupations of the poetry, as well as the historical elisions and ethical evasions taken to be symptomatic of "romantic ideology." It is perhaps premature to assert that many of these presuppositions are verging on obsolescence, but a growing body of recent work in romanticism has defined new areas of attention within the period by challenging the competing interpretive paradigms of poststructuralism and historicism. What much of this work has in common is an attention to rhetorical, formal, and phenomenal details that resist assimilation to theoretical meta-narratives that effectively attribute to the critic a kind of retrospective lucidity in exposing processes of social, psychic, and ideological formation obscured at the moment of their articulation. I engage with these revisionary approaches to the regnant topoi of romantic-era writing as they arise in connection to the problems posed by Wordsworthian charity in Chapter 3, by Austen's putative accommodations to social hierarchy in Chapter 4, and by the ostensibly foundational self-reflexivity of romantic lyric meditation in Chapter 5. Exemplary investigations by Frances Ferguson, Thomas Pfau, Mary Favret, and William Galperin, among others, advance a dynamic view of the relationship between aesthetic form, cultural discourse, and historical conditions, allowing the contradictory, multivalent, and dissenting strains within romanticism to emerge with new clarity and urgency.[50] In arguing that the boundaries between solitude and sociability, psychic and intrapsychic experience become permeable and labile under the pressure of romantic scrutiny, I have drawn on these highly generative revaluations of how romantic-era writing constructs, deconstructs, and creatively and variously articulates the possibilities of affective, ethical, political, and civic experience in the period.

. . .

The prevailing mood out of which romantic forms of intimacy become articulated involves no more and no less than palpable proximity—whether this occurs literally, as in coming upon a stranger, resting on the arm of a lover, shrinking from a rebuke, heeding an entreaty, or whether this proximity is subsumed, as it were, into psychic preoccupation or reverie. In that sense, these forms evince the irreducible "phenomenal fact," as Martin Heidegger puts it, that "the world is always the one I share with Others" even when "no Other is present at hand or perceived."[51] In Heidegger's suggestive discussion of "everyday, average Being-with-one-another," the environmental presence of others entails an understanding that is existentially prior to recognition and that is overlooked by the philosophical impulse to establish the grounds of recognition. "In characterizing the encountering of Others . . . does one not start by marking out and isolating the 'I' so that one must then seek some way of getting over to the Others from this isolated subject?" Heidegger asks (154). His remarks on empathy bear on eighteenth-century theories of sympathy as well. Empathy is "supposed, as it were to provide the first ontological bridge from one's own subject . . . to the other subject," but the presupposition "fails to hold" because the I is always already with others and it is "only on the basis of Being-with" that empathy becomes possible (162). On this account, hostility, indifference, "passing one another by, not 'mattering' to one another" are modes of "being-with-one-another" that, however deficient, characterize "everyday" sociality and are the condition for the possibility, or "motivation," for richer forms of knowledge and solicitude (*Fursorge*) (158, 161–162).

The complexity of the phenomenal fact of intimacy in romanticism involves the demurral, disappointment, and frustration of the mutual identification and recognition that eighteenth-century theories of sympathy presupposed and that Kantian respect compels. Romantic renderings of intimacy arise from proximity but do not seek to extract a coherent and symmetrical structure of recognition from the destabilizing flux of relational experiences in which feelings might be shared but not reciprocated, in which others might be misunderstood or unheeded but not, thereby, altogether unknown. Does this mean that romantic-era writing surrenders ethical expectations and yearnings to phenomenological dynamism and particularity? The drive toward an identificatory equality is thwarted; the expectation of reciprocity is suspended; the horizon of mutual respect recedes. But in the clearing, indeterminate and undetermined modes of attention and appreciation come to account. The humbling of sympathetic presumptions and aspirations for respectful recognition allows for acknowledgments of dependence that seek no rectification or vindication in reciprocity or equality.

1

FEELING FOR PHILOSOPHY

The Limits of Sentimental Certainty

We often feel the Pain of Compassion; but were our sole ultimate Intention or Desire the *freeing ourselves* from this Pain, would the Deity offer to us wholly to blot out all Memory of the person in Distress, to take away this Connection, so that we should be easy during the Misery of our friend . . . [or] would relieve him from his Misery, we should be as ready to choose the former way as the latter; since either of them would free us from *our Pain*, which upon this Scheme is the *sole End* proposed by the compassionate Person—Don't we find in ourselves that our desire does not terminate upon the Removal of our Pain? Were this our sole Intention, we would run away, shut our Eyes, or divert our Thoughts from the miserable Object, as the readiest way of removing our pain: This we seldom do, nay, we crowd about such Objects, and voluntarily expose ourselves to this Pain.

Francis Hutcheson, *An Inquiry into the Original of Our Ideas of Beauty and Virtue*

The "ethical turn" in literary studies has been broadly characterized by a preoccupation with an emergent poststructuralist ethics where the dynamics of recognition is central and where the miscarriage of recognition is virtually unavoidable. The Levinasian face evinces an infinite responsibility that a fortiori confounds and shames mundane modes of attention and solicitude. Giorgio Agamben's *homo sacer* appears as the figure for an exclusion that vexes all forms of communal participation.[1] If ethics has returned to literature by means of these theoretical approaches, then so has philosophy as a mode of cultural analysis that is not reducible to strictly ideological or psychoanalytic diagnoses of the dynamics of objectification. Nevertheless, renewed attention to ethics has only rarely extended to the written corpus of moral philosophy and to the long intellectual history within which the problem of recognition repeatedly arises.[2] To bring ethical writing to the foreground of literary critical work on ethics is not to displace contemporary theoretical approaches but to recover some part of the history of our current sense of the impossible-yet-imperative dynamics of mutual recognition. This chapter offers an account of the rich contradictions between claims of knowledge and assertions of feeling in eighteenth-century ethics. This recurrent and vexing tension is crucial to an understanding of how responsiveness to and identification with others manifests itself as a specifically moral (rather than epistemological) challenge in the period. Indeed, the ethical aspirations and imperatives that emerge from undiminished and unsatisfied epistemic longings constitute a climactic fulfillment of a certain line of Enlightenment inquiry—a fragile victory wrought from failures and misgivings that are not overcome but left unresolved.

WE DO NOT FEEL THEIR SENSATIONS: LOVING OUR LIKE WITHOUT KNOWING OUR LIKENESS

In a late twentieth-century lecture hall, the philosopher Derek Parfit invited a show of hands in agreement with the proposition that individuals are fundamentally driven to avoid pain and pursue their own pleasure. Faced with a clear majority of students willing to concede that conviction, Parfit (characteristically) proposed a thought experiment designed to confound, and stretch to the point of absurdity, the very meanings of pleasure, pain, and the self subject to those sensations. Suppose yourself a parent magically transported to the heavenly halls of the omnipotent deity. You are seated before two levers. One ensures you a lifetime of contentment, free from all concern for the child you see thriving and bound for all good things, but upon your death that same child will suffer untold misfortunes and misery. The other lever dooms you to a lifetime of anxiety, weighed down with care for the child you see bound for trouble and pain, but upon your death that same child will come to enjoy great good fortune and fulfillment. You have a choice to make in this instant, about your life and the life of your child—a choice that will be permanently forgotten as soon as it is made. The same preponderance of students who moments before had pledged their belief in basically self-interested motivations now readily "chose" years of suffering and placed the welfare of their child over their own well-being. More remarkable than the result of this thought experiment was the obduracy with which many strove to reconcile this un-self-serving choice with the theory of fundamental self-interest, stretching and extending the boundaries of the self so as to encompass the child and to count the child's pleasures and pains as, in some sense, one's own—even, indeed, especially (given the terms of the experiment) after one's own death.[3] The ensuing debate reproduced, in virtually the same terms, eighteenth-century defenses of self-interest derided by philosophers who insisted on the motivational force of sympathy in social experience. Here, for example, is Francis Hutcheson's exposure of the specious expansion of "self" necessary to turn love of others into a derivative of self-love:

An honest Farmer will tell you that he studies about the *Preservation* and *Happiness* of his Children, and loves them without any Design of Good to himself. But say some of our *Philosophers*, "The Happiness of their Children gives Parents Pleasure, and their Misery gives them Pain; and therefore to obtain the *former*, and to avoid the *latter*, they study, from Self-Love, the Good of their Children." . . . Do the Child's *Sensations* give Pleasure or Pain to the Parent? Is the Parent *hungry, thirsty, sick*, when his Children are so? No; but he [is] . . . affected with Joy or Sorrow from their Pleasures and Pains. . . . "No," say others, "Children are *parts* of ourselves, and in loving them, we but love *ourselves* in them." A very good Answer! Let us carry it as far as it will go. How are they *Parts* of ourselves? Not as a *Leg* or an *Arm*: we are not conscious of their Sensations. "But *their* Bodies were formed from Parts of *ours*." So is a *Fly*, or a *Maggot*, which may breed in any discharg'd Blood or Humour—Very dear Insects surely! there must be something else then which makes Children *Parts* of ourselves. . . . Love makes them *Parts* of ourselves. . . .

Another Author thinks all this easily deducible from Self-Love. "Children are not only made of our Bodies but *resemble* us in Body and Mind; they are rational Agents as we are, and we only love our own Likeness in them." Very good all this. What is *Likeness*? . . . There is Likeness between us and other Mens' Children, thus any Man is like any other. . . . Is there then a natural Disposition in every Man to *love his Like*, to wish well not only to his individual Self, but to any other like rational or sensitive Being? . . . If all this is called by the Name Self-Love; be it so: The highest Mystic needs no more disinterested Principle; 'tis not confined to the Individual, but . . . may extend to all, since each one some way resembles each other. Nothing can be better than this Self-Love, nothing more generous. (*Inquiry*, 160–162; original emphasis)

Here, as in Parfit's thought experiment, questions of intention and desire become inextricably entangled with questions of identity, identification, and the sensory and affective boundaries of the self. Hutcheson clearly insists on the irreducible difference, at the elemental level of sensation, between one person's pains and pleasures and another's: "Is the parent hungry, thirsty, sick, when his children are so?"; "we are not conscious of their sensations." At the same time, and in spite of this absolute difference between two separately embodied beings, Hutcheson proposes that love brings others into the ambit of the self's concerns. "Children are parts of ourselves," not because they are flesh of our flesh like the microbial creatures we unknowingly nurture on our bodies. In the somewhat macabre literalization of his imaginary interlocutor's claim, Hutcheson effectively exposes the fact of biological kinship to be, in this context, a metaphor for some other, ineffable ground of identification between one and another, concern of one for another. What is this ground if not a recognition of likeness, as another imaginary disputant proposes? If "we love our own likeness" in our children, and thereby love ourselves in loving them, then how many others must be comprehended in the circle of the self that loves those akin to it? The empire of self-interest, in Hutcheson's rendering, is really more a kingdom of ends where each "wish[es] well not only to his individual self, but to any other like rational or sensitive being."

As the context out of which, and against which, idealism and utilitarianism arose, eighteenth-century debates about sympathy and fellow feeling present an opportunity to reconsider the shared history of what came to be opposed views of ethical motivation and deliberation. Philosophers of moral sentiment—principally Shaftesbury, Hutcheson, Joseph Butler, David Hume, and Adam Smith—arrayed themselves against the influential formulations of Thomas Hobbes, emphasizing what Hutcheson called the "bright side of humane nature" against the dark view of men as "all injurious, proud, selfish, treacherous."[4] Insofar as their works collectively constitute a powerful counter-tradition to Hobbesian views of human individuals as fundamentally self-interested creatures, the arguments of the sentimentalists might be seen as the necessary background for the constitutively moral recognition of others implicit in Kantian notions of dignity and respect. (Recall Hutcheson's demonstration that efforts to reduce all motivation to "self-love" amount to arguments for a radically "disinterested principle" of concern for all others.) More commonly, the sentimentalists' naturalistic approach to moral psychology, with its emphasis on the motivating role of emotions and affective attachments, has been viewed as a historically discarded alternative to the austere rationalism of Kant's ethics, but one ready for revival. (Recall Hutcheson's evocation of the "honest farmer's" uncomplicated love for his children.)[5] Important as these revisionary interpretations are, philosophical study of eighteenth-century sentimentalism remains embedded within the context of contemporary Anglo-American ethical debates, too removed from the characteristic tensions and challenges specific to the era in which it arose and certainly more liable to be mined for the current relevance of its arguments than arrested by its rhetorical complexities.[6]

Particularly unaccounted for in contemporary philosophical engagement with moral sentimentalism are the epistemological implications of its arguments, especially its vital and vexed struggle with proliferating and troubling analyses of knowledge in the eighteenth century. Consider, for example, Hutcheson's conclusion in the previous passage that what we mistakenly call "self love . . . may extend to all, since each one some way resembles each other." The easily asserted resemblance of "one" and "each other" takes for granted a certainty about the grounds of identification that the passage's earlier insistence on the absolute separation and individuation of bodies countermands. Insofar as "we don't feel [the] sensations" of others, how can we know the degree and depth of our likeness? And if we don't feel the sensations of others, then precisely how are we affected in the presence of others? The scene described in the opening epigraph to this chapter presents—albeit inadvertently—the same difficulty. I am afflicted by the "Pain of Compassion" in proximity to a "person in Distress," presumably because I cannot fail to see the evidence of the other's misery. This pain of compassion is unquestionably mine in Hutcheson's rendering; it is not a vicarious experience of the other's distress; I do not feel the other's sensation. I could seek relief by fleeing this sensational occasion, running away, shutting my eyes, diverting my thoughts, but instead I stand transfixed before the "miserable Object," willingly suffering the pain. Hutcheson's argument here, as in his discussion of the parent's love for her child, is that our desires and intentions include concern for others and that this concern cannot be reduced to the narrowly selfish pursuit of pleasure and avoidance of pain. Were that the case, we would easily free ourselves from the "pain of compassion" by turning away from the person who arouses it. Whether or not we accede to the agreement presupposed by Hutcheson's rhetorical question ("Don't we find in ourselves that our desire does not terminate upon the Removal of our Pain?"), it would be a mistake to imagine that the feeling of and for the other that Hutcheson describes here involves a perception of resemblance or experience of identification that amounts to a (re)cognition of the other. Hutcheson's rhetoric seems to drift in altogether the opposite direction, turning the "person in Distress" into a "miserable Object" and, finally, into an undifferentiated example of many "such objects."

The strange cleavage between sympathetic feeling for others and recognition of others is a pervasive and recurrent problem in British eighteenth-century writing about the moral sentiments. It is perhaps nowhere more pronounced than in the writing of Adam Smith, whose *Theory of Moral Sentiments* (1759) has become the most common touchstone in literary scholarship on sympathy and sensibility in the period.[7] In fact, among the sentimentalists, Smith is uncharacteristically explicit in articulating the contradictory presuppositions of empirical and moral psychology. The first paragraph of *Moral Sentiments* takes it "as a matter of fact too obvious to require any instances to prove it" that we "derive sorrow from the sorrow of others"; the second paragraph places this fact alongside the equally obvious truth that "we have no immediate experience of what other men feel," that "our senses . . . never did, and never can, carry us beyond our person."[8] As is well known, Smith will allow the imagination to do for us what the senses cannot, to "form some idea of [the other's] sensations" (11). Far from transporting us "beyond our own person," however, Smith's imagination transposes the feelings of one onto the other. "By changing places in fancy with the sufferer," the sympathetic "spectator" (in Smith's terms) considers only "what he himself would feel if he were reduced to the same unhappy situation," and, quite crucially, the feelings that arise by virtue of this projection might not and need not "be the reflection of any sentiment of the sufferer" (15). In being both explicit and explicitly untroubled about the radical limitations of our knowledge of others, Smith develops a theory of sympathy that is often more emphatic and eloquent in its articulation of emotional distance than emotional proximity between subjects. The affective disjunction between persons is poignantly articulated when Smith writes of the limits of our sympathy for even those friends and intimates with whom we feel some "correspondence of sentiments" (26). Even in such ideal cases, "the secret consciousness . . . from which the sympathetic sentiment arises, is but imaginary" (27) so that even as "we sit down by them . . . [and] listen with gravity and attention," we cannot, as it were, reach our close companions because we cannot "keep" (or, let us say, share) time with them ("how far are the languid emotions of our hearts from keeping time to the transports of theirs"?) (52). Not surprisingly, in such moments, a friend might be "confounded by my violence and passion" while I grow "enraged at [her] cold insensibility and want of feeling" (26). Subsequent chapters will explore how romantic literature reshapes these epistemic and affective disjunctions as forms of intimacy that can neither be assimilated nor subordinated to a predetermined concept of fellow feeling. For the moment, it is simply worth noting that even though Smith is typically found at the core of arguments critiquing the factitious, self-absorbed, even narcissistic qualities of sympathy, it would be a mistake to read *The Theory of Moral Sentiments* as the definitive eighteenth-century text on the subject. The paradox with which Smith begins—the fact of compassion alongside the fact that we cannot know what others feel—is symptomatic, but his apparent comfort with the implications of that latter fact is exceptional. Indeed, the intellectual history and conceptual fate of sympathy in the period cannot be fully understood without an appreciation of just how troublesome it is to concede that "we have no immediate experience of what other men feel."

The richest theories of moral sentiment advanced during the eighteenth century entail assumptions about intersubjective knowledge that run counter to the prevailing empiricist epistemologies with which they are contemporary. In his authoritative history of the philosophy of the period, J. B. Schneewind emphasizes that eighteenth-century philosophers' "insistence that everyone can just see what morality requires bears on both moral and epistemological concerns"—specifically insofar as that insistence is "epistemologically . . . directed against moral skepticism."[9] I argue that the moral and the epistemological are mutually implicated in the bold assertions of intersubjective access put forward by the sentimentalists, in spite of explicit efforts to wrest a realm of certainty (affective, moral) from the encroachments of (epistemic) doubt and uncertainty. Francis Hutcheson's claim that "moralists after Mr. Hobbs [*sic*] . . . never talk of any kind instincts . . . of natural affections, of compassion, of love of company, a sense of gratitude . . . which yet all may be observed to prevail exceedingly in humane life" may be taken as typical of the insistence Schneewind observes.[10] Hutcheson's confidence in human benevolence aggressively counters moral skepticism, but it requires and rests upon a rejection of uncertainty about human knowledge of the world, particularly the knowledge of other persons. It would be a mistake to read this rejection as mere neglect or indifference to questions about the reach of human knowledge. In an age when epistemology, ethics, and politics were intertwined in philosophical discourse generally (nowhere more clearly than in the works of central figures such as Locke, Hume, and Rousseau), Hutcheson's use of the term "observed" in the previous passage is daring in its apparent complacence. The seemingly innocuous phrasing—"yet all may be observed"—provocatively forecloses questions of perception, or rather conceals that foreclosure under the insistence that compassion, love, and gratitude "prevail exceedingly" in human life. We are swiftly struck by a ready certainty in the *prevalence* of affections for others that is itself so novel that we fail to wonder how, and especially whether, such affections are *observed*.

The disturbing implications of the fact that "we do not feel their sensations," even in texts insisting, as Schneewind puts it, that "everyone can just see what morality requires," suggests the close relation of apparently opposed intellectual spheres and a dynamic, if not quite dialectical, entwining of ethics and epistemology. Whether moral sense is presented as a perception of resemblance and identification not at all inconsistent with empirical psychology (as in Hutcheson) or whether it is presented as a feeling that theories of knowledge fail to credit (as in Shaftesbury), it is in the effort to explain, or avoid explaining, what I make of others—when, if, or given that I do not feel their sensations—that eighteenth-century sentimentalism attempts, but does not quite succeed, in banishing anxieties about the fragility of the intimacies, friendships, and familial and social engagements that are the constitutive contexts of ethical experience.

Shaftesbury's work is a particularly significant case for the study of sentimentalism, not only because it is among the earliest and most vigorous affirmations of the irresistible self-evidence of moral feeling but also because its deliberate eschewal of systematic argumentation sets distinctive challenges for later eighteenth-century theorists of sympathy who sought to integrate his insights and their own work within the dominant philosophical current of empiricism. Shaftesbury's confident avowals of fellow feeling evidently belong to an intellectual history that extends from Hutcheson to Adam Smith. Less evident are the unsuccessfully resolved anxieties about intersubjective correspondence and affective constancy that Shaftesbury's work bequeaths to Hume, Rousseau, and Kant.

SENTIMENTAL SELF-EVIDENCE

The central thesis of the *Inquiry concerning Virtue or Merit* and *The Moralists*— virtue is based in and derived from "affections" that are natural to the species—is tirelessly and exclusively advanced by appeals to what we cannot deny, cannot fail to see, cannot choose but feel. Shaftesbury's remarkable claim that a "sense of right and wrong ... [is] as natural to us as natural affection itself" rests on a number of related, often circular, assertions about nature, affection, and the "good" of individuals, the species, and the universe as a whole.[11] The anti-empiricist (specifically anti-Lockean) core of the argument lies in its insistence on a "first principle in our constitution and make," a foundation of "original and pure nature," something "inborn," "innate," or "instinct" (defined as "that which nature teaches, exclusive of art, culture or discipline").[12] Shaftesbury deduces both the existence of impulses "so strong ... that it would be absurdity not to think [them] natural" (*M*, 325) and the specific moral and emotional content of those impulses, from the observation that social life is natural to human beings. The term "natural" is made to work in two philosophical registers at once. The undeniable fact of human sociality is effectively invoked against hypothetical "states of nature" (especially the Hobbesian) that derive principles of human nature from a view of individuals as isolated antagonists. But then the banal self-evidence of sociality is also taken to affirm the existence of innate ideas ("nature's teaching"), thus countering, without directly addressing, Locke's influential theory of the constitutive, determining force of experience ("art, culture, discipline") on the individual mind. In other words, Shaftesbury's emphasis frequently shifts from what might be called the ethological to the psychological or cognitive—from quasi-anthropological observations about the species to claims about the motivations, pleasures, and aims of individuals.

In the context of Enlightenment genealogies of society, Shaftesbury's insistence on basic human sociality constitutes a substantive reproach to the speculative denial of the obvious typical of "state of nature" theories. Thus, where Hobbes begins by overturning what he calls the mere "supposition" that "man is a creature born fit for society," Shaftesbury repeatedly appeals to the "apparent," "plain" evidence of what he calls "natural history," rejecting altogether the distinction between "the state of nature and that of society" (*M*, 288, 284).[13] The "imagination" or "supposal" of individuals living "unassociated, unacquainted" entails a radically untenable metamorphosis of the human constitution:

That it was their natural state to live thus separately can never without absurdity be allowed. For sooner may you divest the creature of any other feeling or affection than that towards society and his likeness . . . would you transform him thus and call him still a man? . . . The bug which breeds with the butterfly is more properly a fly, though without wings, than this imaginary creature is a man. For, though his outward shape were human, his passions, appetites and organs must be wholly different. His whole inward make must be reversed to fit him for such a recluse economy and separate subsistence. (*M*, 285)

Against this "imaginary creature" self-sufficiently inhabiting the "pretended state of nature," Shaftesbury presents the readily observable realities of human infancy.

A human infant is of all [other animals] the most helpless, weak, infirm. And wherefore should it not have been thus ordered? . . . Does not this defect engage him the more strongly to society and force him to own that he is purposely, and not by accident, made rational and sociable and can no otherwise increase or subsist than in that social intercourse and community which is his natural state? (*M*, 283)

From the facts of infantile weakness and human sociality, Shaftesbury introduces a series of complex emotions and associations as equally self-evident: "Is not both conjugal affection and natural affection to parents, duty to magistrates, love of a common city, community or country, with the other duties and social parts of life, *deduced from hence and founded in* these very wants [i.e., the weakness and infirmity of the infant]?" (*M*, 283, emphasis added).

The very terms "love" and "duty" signal a perspectival shift away from reflection on the human being as a particular kind of animal, one unfit from birth for "separate subsistence," to consideration of the human as an ethical subject, one moved by affection, able to love, constrained by duty. The sociability Shaftesbury urges us to accept as an undeniable implication of infant needs and parental nurture becomes the foundation from which he "deduces" the naturalness of the "principles of fair, just and honest" and their force in "conscience" (*M*, 325). "Innate ideas" in this exposition are synonymous with the "natural affections" and constitute no less than an irresistible "foreknowledge" of right and wrong (*M*, 325). A weak anti-Lockean argument reviving innate ideas is embedded within a powerful anti-Hobbesian argument challenging the state of nature, thereby allowing the claim that a "sense of right and wrong . . . [is] as natural to us as natural affection itself" (*IVM*, 179). It is precisely at those junctures where anthropological observation is transmuted into moral psychology that Shaftesbury's writing betrays an evasion and displacement of questions about love and duty that are as much epistemological as ethical.

In fact, the two most important eighteenth-century responses to Shaftesbury leave his premise of natural sociability undisputed while challenging the moral and affective "senses" he deduces therefrom. Bernard Mandeville, certainly his most acute critic, admits the "sociableness" of the species and the existence of "natural affections" while scorning their facile conflation with virtue.[14] Pity, for example, is "neither good nor bad," Mandeville explains, but an amoral "impulse of nature" (49–50). "Natural affection prompts all mothers to take care of the offspring they dare own," but this "natural drift and inclination" belong to the "vilest of women" as well as the most virtuous (200, 60). At stake in these distinctions is an austere sense of virtue as a difficult human endeavor, an "arduous rugged path" (150) demanding an exertion of the will in addition to, and occasionally against, the "drift" of affectionate impulse.[15] Hume, who openly professes his admiration for Shaftesbury, largely adopts his predecessor's evocation of infantile weakness in his earliest sustained writing on morals.[16] Arguing that "the very first state and situation [of human beings] may justly be esteem'd social," Hume goes so far as to posit a psychic evolution from instinct-driven union (the "natural appetite betwixt the sexes") to affection-based association ("a new tie takes place in their concern for their common offspring") and even to find, in this love of immediate relations, "our first and most natural sentiment of morals" (*T*, 312–317). However, where Shaftesbury presumes a necessary evolution from love of "father, child, or brother" to "love of mankind" in general (*M*, 256), Hume is careful to distinguish the affections "evidently implanted in human nature" (especially the love of near relations) from "love of mankind, merely as such," for which he finds "no proof" (*T*, 309).

Although it is couched in empirical terms, the contrast Hume draws between our evident (interpersonal forms of) love and an unproven love of mankind becomes the core of a moral psychology that sets nature and culture, love and duty, against one another. The inevitable conflicts between natural, preferential, "partial" affections and a "public" or "common" good compel Hume to introduce an important distinction between sentimentally driven benevolence and the humanitarian demands of justice.[17] From a Humean perspective, Shaftesbury misrepresents the very substance of moral experience when he asserts that "partial affection, or social love in part, without regard to a complete society or whole, is in itself an inconsistency and implies an absolute contradiction" (*IVM*, 205). It is precisely in the persistent pressure of that contradiction between love for proximate others (our "partiality" for family, friends, neighbors, countrymen) and a just regard for the social whole that Hume locates the challenge of moral life. Thus, even as Hume espouses the benign view of human nature typical of sentimentalism, his moral psychology—especially as it is developed in the *Enquiry concerning the Principles of Morals*—ever more explicitly acknowledges the conflicting emotions and affective complexity that make the "love of mankind, merely as such" a vital cultural and individual endeavor rather than a natural endowment.

Focusing on the same simplification underlying Shaftesbury's conflation of natural affections and more complex forms of love and duty, Mandeville's criticism cuts more deeply into the heart of sentimental psychology, complicating even the affectionate partiality Hume takes for granted. Shaftesbury proposes that the "natural affection which is between the sexes . . . [and] towards the consequent offspring" necessarily leads to affection "between the offspring themselves" and thus to the formation of "clan or tribe" and, ultimately, inevitably, to the "good correspondency and union" of a broad "public."[18] Where Hume questions this evolution and finds the affective complexity of ethical experience in the discontinuity between natural affection and attachment to a social whole, Mandeville questions the simplicity of the natural affections themselves, finding contrary tendencies, mixed feelings, and disturbing ambivalence within Shaftesbury's prototypically untroubled relationship.

Natural affection would prompt a wild man to love and cherish his child; it would make him provide food and other necessaries for his son. . . . But this affection is not the only passion he has to gratify; if his son provokes him by stubbornness or doing otherwise than he would have done, this love is suspended; and if his displeasure be strong enough to raise his anger, which is as natural to him as any other passion, it is ten to one but he will knock him down. If he hurts him very much and the condition he has put his son in moves his pity, his anger will cease; and, natural affection returning, he will fondle him again, and be sorry for what he has done. (209–210)

Thus, Mandeville concludes, "the savage child would learn to love and fear his father": Hobbesian and Shaftesburian emotions are at work in Mandeville's representation of nurture (as well as the contradictions that will come to inform psychoanalytic constructions of early childhood). Where Shaftesbury projects the future development of broad communal attachments from an originary moment of simple conjugal and filial affection, Mandeville offers a narrative dilation of that original moment whereby the foundational relationship is complicated from the outset by alarming affective vicissitudes. Suspended by anger, resentment, aggression; restored by pity, contrition, remorse—the love between parent and child is inconstant, discontinuous. They appear bound to one another through a flux of passions, hostilities, regrets, and conciliations.

Mandeville's narrative evokes an instability in the lived experience of emotional engagement with others that Shaftesbury does not simply ignore. Rather, where ambivalence and inconstancy appear in his account, they are represented as pathological manifestations of natural affection. Love and kindness are, or ought to be, consistent and generously extensive. Conflicting feelings—whether arising from a preferential attachment to family and friends against larger associations or from affective volatility within a specific relationship—are symptomatic of malign disorder. Love of just one other or of a few intimates ("partial affection") is "the most dissociable and destructive of the enjoyments of society," not because it conflicts with regard for society as a whole (as in Hume) but because it is "capricious," "easily removable," ever "subject to alteration" (*IVM*, 205). "The variableness of such sort of passion which . . . undergoes the frequent succession of alternate hatred and love, aversion and inclination," writes Shaftesbury, "must of necessity create continual disturbance and disgust, give an allay to what is immediately enjoyed in the way of friendship and society, and, in the end, extinguish in a manner the very inclination towards friendship and human commerce" (*IVM*, 205). It is tempting to suggest that Mandeville is more optimistic about sentimental attachments than Shaftesbury insofar as the suspensions and alterations of love he imagines entail cycles of estrangement and reconciliation rather than an unswerving trajectory away from social attachment.

"Variableness" appears to strain the sense of affection itself in Shaftesbury, posing so great a threat to the "enjoyments of society," the "very inclination towards friendship," as to compel a sustained rhetorical effort to exclude inconstancy from the very definition of affection. Essentially different from "capricious," "partial" love is what Shaftesbury terms "entire affection"—a love that is "irrefragable, solid and durable" (*IVM*, 205). This true love suffers no vicissitudes and so sustains the continuity and consistency Shaftesbury wants to establish between affection toward others and a sure "sense of right and wrong." After all, a moral sense based in the affections can be only as reliable as the affections from which it arises. Shaftesbury clearly recognizes the implications for moral sense of the "precarious and uncertain" affections he calls "partial": "What trust can there be to a mere casual inclination or capricious liking? Who can depend on such a friendship?" (*IVM*, 206). By direct and necessary contrast, "entire affection (from whence integrity has its name)" precludes these corrosive questions.

MISANTHROPIC SUSPICION

In its vulnerability to destabilizing insecurity, trust—so integral to love, so implicitly fundamental to the affective stability Shaftesbury presumes—is also precisely the point at which epistemological and moral inquiry intersect, precisely the point at which epistemological mysteries and moral challenges are confounded. Having excluded troubling inconstancy from his definition of "entire affection," Shaftesbury nevertheless seems driven to a deeper exploration of its implications. The final pages of the *Inquiry concerning Virtue or Merit* are surprisingly and disproportionately dominated by the imagination of a creature "void of natural affection and wholly destitute of a communicative or social principle" (*IVM*, 194). This solitary figure, existing in a kind of conceptual quarantine from benevolent mankind, comes to embody, represent, and contain all those emotional disruptions of love (hostility, enmity, anger, gloom, suspicion) that Mandeville admits into the flow of relational experience and that Shaftesbury finds so destructive of the "very inclination towards friendship."

How wretched must it be . . . for man, of all other creatures, to lose that sense and feeling which is proper to him as a man . . . ? How unfortunate must it be for a creature whose dependence on society is greater than any others to lose that natural affection by which he is prompted to the good and interest of his species and community? Such, indeed, is man's natural share of this affection, that he, of all other creatures, is plainly the least able to bear solitude. (*IVM*, 215)

Shaftesbury introduces this unfortunate creature as innately damaged ("imperfect from birth, by having suffered violence within in their earliest form and inmost matrix"), his disaffection and estrangement from others a tragic accident of nature rather than the result of tragic experience among others (*IVM*, 215). His misanthropy is etiological in origin; the sociability "proper to him as man" in the ethological sense is defective. But, as we have already seen, Shaftesbury's discussion tends to shift from the quasi-anthropological to the psychological, from instinctual tendencies (such as the reproductive drive) to more complex pleasures and aims (love and duty). Similarly, his discussion of the misanthrope slides from the diagnostic classification of monstrosity to elaborate conjectures about his mental and emotional state.

How thorough and deep must be that melancholy which, being once moved, has nothing soft or pleasing from the side of friendship to allay or divert it? Wherever such a creature turns himself, whichever way he casts his eye, everything must appear ghastly and horrid, everything hostile and, as it were, bent against a private and single being, who is thus divided from everything and at defiance and war with the rest of nature. . . . Now if banishment from one's country, removal to a foreign place or anything which looks like solitude and desertion, be so heavy to endure, what must it be to feel this inward banishment, this real estrangement from human commerce, and to be after this manner in a desert and in the horridest of solitudes, even when in the midst of society? (*IVM*, 228–229)

It is not clear whether the solitary's feeling of "inward banishment" and "estrangement" shapes his perception, ensuring that wherever he "casts his eye" he sees enemies rather than friends, or whether it is the mistaken but irresistible perception ("everything must appear ghastly") that determines the feeling of being "in the horridest of solitudes, even when in the midst of society." What is important and unusual about this passage in Shaftesbury is the articulated distinction between seeing and feeling, one generally elided in his insistence that the passions and affections of others are "most of them as soon discerned as felt." Misanthropic interiority is shot through with misgivings and doubts that appear inextricably bound up with epistemic uncertainty. The "consciousness of such a nature," writes Shaftesbury, "must overcloud the mind with dark suspicion and jealousy, alarm it with fears and horrors" (*IVM*, 194). Evidently the suspicion cannot be allayed, nor the alarm dispelled, because casting his eye about him, the misanthrope sees no reliable other. The dangerous questions raised in Shaftesbury's discussion of inconstant, capricious affections ("what trust can there be?" "who can depend on . . . friendship?") resound in the "consciousness" of the misanthrope, who embodies an intersubjective form of skepticism that seems to take shape in the psychic space between perceiving and feeling for others.

The estranging dread, anxiety, and suspicion symptomatic of misanthropic consciousness in Shaftesbury are precisely the affective inflections of skepticism memorably expressed in the notorious conclusion to Hume's book "Of the Understanding" in the *Treatise of Human Nature.*

I am at first affrighted and confounded with that forelorn solitude, in which I am plac'd in my philosophy, and fancy myself some strange uncouth monster, who not being able to mingle and unite in society, has been expell'd [from] all human commerce, and left utterly abandon'd and disconsolate. Fain wou'd I run into the crowd for shelter and warmth; but cannot prevail with myself to mix with such deformity. (*T*, 172)

Having found that the "manifold contradictions and imperfections in human reason" leave him "ready to reject all belief and reasoning," the philosopher is driven to pose a set of desperate questions that suggest a compelling entwining of existential uncertainty and anxiety about relational experience:

Who am I, or what? From what causes do I derive my existence, and to what condition shall I return? Whose favour shall I court, and whose anger must I dread? What beings surround me? and on whom have I any influence, or who have any influence on me? I am confounded with all these questions, and begin to imagine myself in the most deplorable condition imaginable, inviron'd with the deepest darkness. (*T*, 175)

The character of Shaftesbury's misanthrope is easily recognizable in Hume's melodramatic representation of epistemological despair, but the first-person voice ("I fancy myself some strange uncouth monster") clarifies something rather puzzling in the earlier philosopher's representation. Shaftesbury's descriptions are strangely sympathetic to the misanthrope, dwelling on the misery of his estrangement rather than censuring the moral failing of his malignant suspicion or elaborating on its pathological origins. The imaginative access to a "consciousness" Shaftesbury defines as essentially "unnatural" and monstrously defective tends to undermine his own explicit efforts to separate the misanthrope from the healthy portion of mankind whose inclinations toward friendship and human commerce are unimpeded by dark suspicion and alarm. How is that we (including Shaftesbury) can apprehend the feelings of such a monster? Hume's avowed sense of alienation in the *Treatise*, his "fancying" himself monstrously separate from and unlike all others, internalizes the mood Shaftesbury tries hard to expel from healthy consciousness in the personification of a "monster ... misshapen or distorted in an inward part" (*IVM*, 215). The different types of persons Shaftesbury describes as "natural" and "unnatural" are, in Hume, different orientations toward the world that he calls "natural" and "philosophical." These orientations, attitudes really, might succeed one another, alternate, fluctuate, but they inhere within the same person.

In the solitary "closet" of philosophy, "skeptical doubt arises naturally from profound and intense reflection," obstructing the "instinct or natural impulse" that ordinarily determines what Hume calls our "belief" in the stability and constancy of the world of persons and things around us (*T*, 142–144). The dissipation of the skeptical mood in the conclusion to "Of the Understanding" famously occurs in the movement from the isolated closet to the crowded drawing room ("I dine, I play a game of backgammon, I converse, and am merry with my friends" [*T*, 175]), a turn that also determines the movement of the *Treatise* toward the remarkably reassuring arguments of the books on passions and morals. In those later books, Hume's figures for the mind (the mirror, the responsive strings of musical instruments) stress intersubjective accessibility and attunement, the prevalence of a "consciousness" always sure of whose favor to court and whose anger to dread. The very condition of being among others seems to make the "melancholy and delirium" of the skeptical mood appear "cold, strain'd and ridiculous" in Hume (*T*, 175), and the *feeling* of being "expell'd [from] all human commerce" is thus both indulged, acknowledged to "arise naturally," and also safely confined to a space of seclusion we willingly enter (at times) and from which we can easily withdraw. Thus, by specifying the conditions in which the skeptical mood of estrangement arises, Hume is also able to imagine its alleviation, if not its definitive resolution.

Shaftesbury's misanthrope does not so much inhabit as embody seclusion; a change in his mood, a clearing of his doubts, suspicions, and alarm, would entail a change in the very structure of his consciousness. The problem is that the structure of this consciousness turns out to be not so very different, after all, from that of the unestranged lover of mankind. In the end it is only his mood, not his mind, that distinguishes him. Earlier I suggested that the anti-empiricist core of Shaftesbury's argument in *Characteristics* lies in the hypothesis of a moral instinct derived from and based upon natural affections intrinsic to all human beings as essentially social creatures. While Shaftesbury's emphasis on sociality reverses the counterintuitive independence posited as the original human condition in Hobbes and challenges the moral implications derived from that assumption (natural hostility, suspicion, enmity, selfishness), the idea that individuals are existentially isolated from one another proves an intransigent epistemic assumption, simultaneously shaping and eroding the grounds of Shaftesbury's sentimental certainty that "human affections and passions" are "as soon discerned as felt." I now want to draw attention to how his descriptions of the workings of moral sense within the individual consciousness implicitly rely on empiricist assumptions of the mind as a secluded interior space separated from the external world—rely, in other words, on an image of the mind as permanently contained within that space Hume calls the philosophical closet.

FEELING FOR UNKNOWABLE OTHERS

As Shaftesbury develops his thesis that a sense of right and wrong necessarily accompanies perception itself, the idiom of empiricism is unmistakable:

It is impossible to suppose, a mere sensible creature . . . so ill-constituted . . . as that, from the moment he comes to be tried by sensible objects, he should have no one good passion towards his kind. . . . It is full as impossible to conceive that a rational creature, coming first to be tried by rational objects and receiving into his mind the images or representations of justice, generosity, gratitude or other virtues, should have no liking of these or dislike of their contraries. (*IVM*, 178)

The structures of cognition evoked here are entirely of a piece with Locke. The mind is "tried" by objects (including other persons) external to it, "receives" impressions of those objects, and shapes them into internal "images or representations." Moral feeling (the "liking" of virtue and "good passion" toward others) seems to entail a rather complex process of discernment. If we bear this context in mind, the climactic claim of the philosophical dialogue staged in *The Moralists*—"happiness is from within, not from without" (*M*, 336)—is surprisingly consistent with the empiricist psychology Shaftesbury openly derides as a "specious" distraction from the study of "human affairs" (*IVM*, 134).

"Within" in Shaftesbury's formulation signifies a space of self-determination: "that original, native liberty, which . . . gives us the privilege of ourselves and makes us our own and independent" (*M*, 260). The condition for the possibility of this independence is an irreducible, ontological individuation that stands in unresolved contradiction with the important implications Shaftesbury draws from natural sociability. Indeed, psychic individuation, or independence, exerts such a constitutive force on perception that it throws into doubt the very possibility of communicable, let alone shared, sentiments. Theocles, philosophical hero of *The Moralists*, relentless exponent of Shaftesbury's convictions about natural benevolence, teaches that there might be radical individual differences in the experience of even the most basic sensations: "What is grievous to one is not so much as troublesome to another. . . . What is pain to one is pleasure to another, and so, alternately, we very well know, since men vary in their apprehension of these sensations" (*M*, 253). Or as Locke puts it in *An Essay concerning Human Understanding*, "Because one Man's Mind could not pass into another Man's Body, to perceive, what Appearances were produced by [his] Organs," we cannot assume that any two minds share the same ideas about the same object.[19] Or again, as Hutcheson puts it, "We are not conscious of their sensations." If there is no (knowable) correspondence between individual experience of sensations as elemental as pleasure and pain, then surely that natural "sense of right and wrong" must also be radically variable. Theocles concedes that "all is opinion. It is opinion which makes beauty and unmakes it. The graceful or ungraceful in things . . . the amiable and unamiable, vice, virtue, honor, shame, all this is founded in opinion only" (*M*, 328); but he veers away from the corrosive implications of this conclusion. Instead of contending with the evident potential for conflicting, ever-shifting opinions of vice and virtue, Theocles offers a reassuring reinstatement of universality in the mere propensity to form "opinions." "As long as I find men either angry or revengeful, proud or ashamed, I am safe," reasons Theocles, "for they conceive an honourable and dishonourable, a foul and fair as well as I. No matter where they place it or how they are mistaken in it, this hinders not my being satisfied that the thing is, and is universally acknowledged" (*M*, 329).

Remarkably, Shaftesbury's confident insistence that the "sense of right and wrong is as natural as the natural affections" entails no shared sense of right and wrong; it is no more than a formal drive to make (and unmake) the distinction between right and wrong. The "original, native liberty" Theocles claims, the freedom to determine one's own good, arises precisely from the absence of commonly held concepts of right and wrong: "Whom shall we follow, then? . . . Whose judgment or opinion shall we take concerning what is good, what contrary?" (*M*, 332). Far from being cause for despair, recognition of extreme variation in moral discernment calls for a kind of bold complacence in one's own judgment: "All . . . go different ways" in pursuit of the good, Theocles argues; "All censure one another and are despicable in one another's eyes. . . . What is it, then, I should be concerned for? Whose censure do I fear or by whom, after all, shall I be guided?" (*M*, 333). The striking resonance of these questions in Hume ("Whose favour shall I court, and whose anger must I dread? On whom have I any influence, and who ha[s] any influence on me? [*T*, 175]), where they issue from skeptical despair, suggests that Shaftesbury's man of moral feeling stands on the same existential ground as Hume's alienated man of reason. The radically individualizing premises of Shaftesbury's psychology are ultimately more decisively formative of the ethical subject in his writing than are the sympathetic bonds of affection he derives from the anthropological premise of natural human sociability.

The despairing mood in which Hume echoes the questions Theocles poses so complacently ("On whom have I any influence, and who ha[s] any influence on me?") arises from an epistemological investigation that has come to grief but also expresses longing for the common meanings that Hume holds to be constitutive of ethical community. The "very notion of morals," he argues in *An Enquiry concerning the Principles of Morals*, "implies some sentiment common to all mankind, which recommends the same object to general approbation."[20] To fear censure or to seek guidance is to concede dependence on others—a benign condition in Hume's moral theory (and clearly at odds with the independent judgment Theocles advocates). "We find it necessary to prop our tottering judgment on the correspondent approbation of mankind," Hume writes in the *Enquiry*, where to be propped up is not to submit to alien, imposed values but to find support on the solid ground of shared values ensured by the "correspondence of human souls."[21] The "liberty" of independent judgment that Theocles embraces in *The Moralists* is as much a refusal to reckon with the intersubjective uncertainty consequent to the admission that no "sentiment common to mankind . . . recommends the *same object* to general approbation" as it is a bold affirmation of the imperative to determine one's own good. That very imperative ("everyone, of necessity, must reason . . . what his good is and what his ill" [*M*, 338]), and its reassuring corollary ("happiness is from within, not without" [336]), seems to concede the possibility of intersubjective correspondence altogether and to relinquish with it a dependence upon others that can only be imagined as "unhappy" (*M*, 334).

Although Shaftesbury avoids explicit engagement with theories of knowledge, the inner happiness enjoyed by the philanthropic Theocles seems to issue from a deeply subjectivist view of perception and judgment that is not only vulnerable to the kind of skeptical impasse Hume dramatizes in the *Treatise* but also indistinguishable from the epistemic limitations associated with misanthropic misery.[22] Theocles's teaching in *The Moralists* unfolds in a lengthy dialogue presented by his interlocutor, the young Philocles, who introduces his recollections by crediting Theocles for "curing" his "skepticism" (*M*, 246). Philocles is inspired to share "the memoirs" of his "two philosophical days" at Theocles's estate with Palemon, whose bitter complaints about "man, that wretched mortal, ill to himself and cause of ill to all" (*M*, 236) fill the first pages of the dialogue. Theocles's inner contentment, cause and consequence of a resolute conviction in human benevolence, is certainly meant to repudiate Palemon's pessimism. But the "self-enjoyment" of sentimental fellowship represented by Theocles and the misanthropic "aversion" represented by Palemon are opposed affective attitudes to the *same* intersubjective limits.[23]

Theocles promises "constant security, tranquility, equanimity" through enjoyment of the "good things we can bestow upon ourselves" and detachment from "uncertain" objects that can be "taken from us," objects "variable and inconstant," objects that "by being ardently beloved or sought" render us vulnerable to "solicitude, cares, and anxiety" (*M*, 334–335). But this autonomy removes Shaftesbury's "benign and good nature[d]" philosophical enthusiast from affective engagement with others as surely as dread and suspicion drive his misanthrope from community with others. The kinship between these figures becomes all the more evident if we recall the framing occasion for the dialogue Theocles comes to dominate. *The Moralists* begins with the young Palemon's passionate complaints about social life, giving voice to the convictions of a "complete Timon or man-hater." "What treacheries! What disorders! How corrupt is all!": thus begins a lengthy declamation on the topic of dissimulation:

What charms there are in public companies! . . . How pleased is every face! How courteous and humane the general carriage and behaviour!—What creature capable of reflection, if he thus saw mankind and saw no more, would not believe our earth a very heaven? What foreigner—the inhabitant, suppose, of some near planet—when he had traveled hither and surveyed this outward face of things, would think of what lay hid beneath the mask? . . . Allow him leisure till he has gained a nearer view and, following our dissolved assemblies to their particular recesses, he has the power of seeing them in this new aspect.—Here he may behold those . . . who not an hour ago in public appeared such friends, now plotting craftily each other's ruin. (*M*, 238)

The governing insight here—appearances can be deceptive—necessarily assumes an inner realm of thought, intention, and feeling that can be only mediately, unreliably, and imperfectly known to others. Palemon's interlocutor attributes these dark insights to romantic disappointment ("I concluded you in love and so unhappily engaged as to have reason to complain of infidelity" [*M*, 238]), but insofar as his estrangement also evinces his attachment ("unhappily engaged"), it involves him with the same inscrutability of other minds and unpredictable variability of others' affections that compels Theocles to seek the "constant security" of detached happiness "from within." The fundamental suspicion that every face is an "outward face," a "mask" of concealment, is never challenged in *The Moralists* because the "universal friendship" (*M*, 256) Theocles professes is sustained independent of, and in spite of, the intersubjective failures and disappointments that are bound to arise when the very basis for sympathetic apprehension of others is indeterminate. Given that "what is pain to one is pleasure to another," it is no wonder that Shaftesbury imagines that we can only be (misanthropically) bent to regard others with anxious suspicion or (philanthropically) resolved to befriend all mankind. To the extent that the affections of each have no necessary bearing on how real others stand to them, or with them, both the misanthrope and the philanthropist seek shelter from the challenging uncertainties of intersubjective experience in the certainty of sentiment. Thus, "whichever way he casts his eye," regardless of what he sees, "everything" and everyone "must appear hostile" to the misanthrope who feels "real estrangement from human commerce" (*IVM*, 228–229). With the same resolve, a "good nature" will "fram[e] in itself an equal, just and universal friendship" (*M*, 256) by turning in and away from the "solicitude, cares and anxiety" of "unhappy dependence" upon others (334).

. . .

The "sense of right and wrong . . . is as natural as natural affection itself" (*IVM*, 179), but "everyone, of necessity, must reason . . . what his good is and what his ill" (*M*, 338). The uneasy alliance of sentimentalism and individualism in Shaftesbury's writing maintains the certainty and simplicity of ethical discernment—"everyone can just see what morality requires" (in Schneewind's characterization)—but does so by setting aside anxieties about the possibility of seeing *together* what morality requires. It is not so much the autonomous standpoint articulated in *The Moralists* that would trouble moral philosophers after Shaftesbury as it is the manner in which that autonomy seems to arise, or be wrested from, epistemological premises that surrender the aspiration to intersubjective understanding. The feeling for others he names "natural affection" remains troublingly dissociated from the perception of others. In emphasizing the immediacy and certitude of the emotions, and then deriving moral sense from that certainty, Shaftesbury endeavors to elude the corrosive uncertainties generated by epistemological analysis, but even so bold a statement as that with which he concludes the *Inquiry concerning Virtue or Merit* demands to be reconsidered.

Let us carry skepticism ever so far, let us doubt, if we can, of everything around us, we cannot doubt what passes within ourselves. Our affections and passions are known to us. They are certain, whatever the objects may be on which they are employed. Nor is it of any concern to our argument how these exterior objects stand—whether they are realities or mere illusions, whether we wake or dream. For ill dreams will be equally disturbing, and a good dream, if life be nothing else, will be easily and happily passed. (*IVM*, 229)

This characteristically confident affirmation of the *Inquiry*'s findings needs to be understood as an affirmation made in the aftermath of a capitulation. A realm of certainty is claimed—"what passes within ourselves"—but that inner certainty is the only concern of the argument because we can indeed doubt "everything around us." The natural affections we cannot doubt appear to have no clear, sure correspondence to any objects.[24] If it does not matter whether "exterior objects"—including, especially, other persons—are real or illusory, then *for whom* does the Shaftesburian subject feel?

If it is of no concern whether the love and pain of another "are realities or mere illusions," then sympathy itself is merely, incoherently, a feeling that "passes within," unaffected by and detached from apprehension of others. This difficulty metastasizes in Smith, where the force of imagination engenders sympathetic emotions that need not and often "cannot be the reflection of any sentiment" of the other (15). Thus, notoriously, "we sympathize even with the dead," feeling it "miserable . . . to be deprived of the light of the sun; to be shut out from life and conversation; to be laid in the cold grave" (16). Evidently these sorrows are real, are certain, and just as evidently are they unrelated to the reality of the object that has roused them, for in the "profound security of their repose," the dead feel no pain. What Smith describes as a "lodging . . . [of] our own living souls in . . . inanimate bodies" (16) is by no means an exceptional form of sympathetic emotion in *The Theory of Moral Sentiments*; it is, rather, representative of that incapacity to reach others that makes fellow feeling, paradoxically, a register of existential distance between persons.[25] "I judge your sight by my sight . . . of your reason by my reason . . . of your love by my love," writes Smith; "I neither have, nor can have, any other way of judging of them" (23).

Like the concession to skepticism—we *can* doubt everything around us—which compromises the ethical bearing of Shaftesbury's confidence in the feelings that "pass within ourselves," the sensory limitations that make it impossible for Smith's "spectator" to apprehend how another sees, reasons, and loves threatens the coherence of the term "sympathy" itself. The very possibility of feeling-together appears to be foreclosed. This is the very difficulty Hume would address in the *Treatise* by explicitly distinguishing between equally "natural" epistemological moods or attitudes—the philosophical reflection that irresistibly engenders isolating doubt ("What beings surround me?")—and the sentimental inclinations that prevail when "we live, and talk, and act like other people in the common affairs of life" (*T*, 144, 175). To be "in that forlorn solitude in which I am plac'd in my philosophy" is to feel "expell'd [from] all human commerce" (*T*, 172); to be among others is "to receive," irresistibly, "their inclinations and sentiments," to be always vulnerable to that contagion of the affections Hume calls sympathy (206, 368). In Rousseau, so inescapable is the threat of illusion in intersubjective experience that nothing less than an emptying out of interiority in perpetual disclosure is required in order to secure the transparency he understands as the necessary condition of love and trust. In Kant, the contingency of emotional response to others, and with it the uncertain correspondence between the affections and their objects, is rigorously divided from the invariable recognition of the other's dignity as a rational being that is alone constitutive of the moral community he calls the "kingdom of ends."

Humean sympathy, Rousseauvian transparency, Kantian respect: while each of these is an effort to conceptualize a similitude between subjects essential to moral experience, it is also true that each leaves intact the dangers of intersubjective attachment that Shaftesbury seeks to avert by doing away with our concern for the real objects of our affections. Shaftesbury warns that the "love of one single person," the particularity and partiality of affection for one among all others, leaves us vulnerable to "the frequent successions of alternate hatred and love, aversion and inclination" (*IVM*, 205): "Who can depend on such a friendship as is . . . fantastically assigned to some single person?" (206). Shaftesbury's lonely certainty in "what passes within," his settlement for a "good dream" of relational life, avoids the perilous dependence with which Hume, Rousseau, and even Kant grapple. None of these later thinkers deny that the "unhappy dependency" of love exposes us to "solicitude, cares and anxiety," but from that epistemic risk they wrest distinctively ethical challenges. In each of these writers, how we "ought" to know others emerges as a question distinct from, but never separable from, ineluctable misgivings about how and what we know of others.

2

KNOWING BEFORE LOVING
Rousseau and the Ethics of Exposure

If I could change the nature of my being and become a living eye, I would gladly make that exchange.

Julie, or La Nouvelle Héloïse

Not a single movement takes place in his soul which his mouth or eyes do not reveal, and often the sentiments he experiences are known sooner to me than to him.

Emile, or On Education

A child stumbles, loses his footing, and falls into the deep waters of Lake Geneva. His mother flies after him without a moment's hesitation, plunges into the lake and, in saving him, contracts a fever from which she will not recover. This over-determined accident is the immediate cause of Julie's death in Rousseau's *La Nouvelle Héloïse* (1761), affirming the heroine's status as a model materfamilias in an act of self-sacrifice perfectly exemplifying the "natural sympathy" philosophers of moral sentiment such as Shaftesbury and Hume identify as the foundation of the "social virtues of humanity and benevolence." The "parent fly[ing] to the relief of his child, transported by that natural sympathy which actuates him," writes Hume, is irresistibly driven by "beneficent affections" that have the force of instinct.[1] It is not the child alone who occupies Julie's heart and mind in her final hours, however. The last words ascribed to her in the novel suggest that it is also her own life she imagines having saved with her fatal plunge, specifically her life as a wife whose conscience is untroubled: "virtue remains to me without spot, and love has remained to me without remorse."[2] The fall into the icy waters spares "the most virtuous of wives" (406) from the more destructive vertiginous fall she has feared. "Who knows whether seeing myself so near the abyss, I would not have been drawn into it?" she asks in a final letter to the erstwhile lover whom her husband has welcomed into the family as a friend and prospective tutor to their children. The potential calamity of their permanent reunion in her household can be averted, it seems, only by the absolute, and in this case, reassuring prospect of death: "I dare pride myself in the past, but who could have answered to me for the future? One day more, perhaps, and I was a criminal! How about a whole life spent with you? What dangers I have run unawares!" (609).

Julie's distrust of her own sentiments directly controverts the irrefutable emotional self-certainty Shaftesbury claims when he writes that we may "doubt . . . everything around us [but] we cannot doubt what passes within ourselves. Our affections and passions are known to us. They are certain." As I argued in Chapter 1, this very certainty allows no corresponding confidence in the relationship between emotions and their objects. Shaftesburian love for others is constant because and in spite of the fact that it does not matter "how these exterior objects [of the passions, especially other persons] stand to us—whether they are realities or mere illusions."[3] In destabilizing the grounds of this sentimental certainty from within, so to speak, by presenting us with a heroine who suffers corrosive uncertainty about her own affections, Rousseau concedes possibilities of emotional vicissitude, ambivalence, and conflicting, changeable feelings for others that had been effectively foreclosed in theories such as Shaftesbury's propounding the irresistible, reliable, self-evident force of affections in social experience.

The remarkable series of utopian writings Rousseau produces in the middle phase of his career—including the *Letter to d'Alembert* (1758), *La Nouvelle Héloïse, Emile* (1762), and the *Social Contract* (1762)—both expose and seek to redress the skeptical implications of sentimentalism. Fidelity, trust, constancy—virtues associated with and often derived from the moral sentiments in general and sympathy in particular—require, as the condition for their possibility, a confidence in the knowability of others, a mutual and reliable transparency. In the context of eighteenth-century moral psychology, Rousseau's preoccupation with "seeing through" others imports empiricist concerns with the limitations of the senses into the realm of relations between persons and thereby imagines ethical aspirations as consistent with and contingent upon epistemological possibilities. Whether expressed as nostalgia for a lost period of human or personal history (as in the mythic time "before art had fashioned our manners" in the early *Discourse on the Arts or Sciences* or in the blissful childhood conviction that his guardians were "Gods who could read our hearts" in *The Confessions*), or as utopian yearning for inescapably public forms of life (as in the civic festivals celebrated in the *Letter to d'Alembert* and in the concluding chapter of the *Social Contract*), or as indulgent surrender to imaginative visions of harmonious beautiful souls (as in the disappointment-driven fantasies of the *Reveries of a Solitary Walker*), the ideal of transparency in Rousseau's work can be understood as displacing the primacy of sympathy.[4]

Even though the affective intimacy engendered by sympathy, fellow feeling, and compassion remains at the theoretical heart of civic, interpersonal, and moral relations in Rousseau, its self-evidence and constancy are always in question. Rousseauvian transparency may therefore be understood as an implicit acknowledgment of, and an anxious effort to overcome, the epistemic insecurity of moral sentimentalism—to turn irresistible feelings for others into indubitable facts about others. The ethical implications of sympathy (including trust, fidelity, constancy, benevolence) are secured by, but also thereby contingent on, epistemological access to the thoughts and feelings of others—an access Rousseau imagines in terms of a constant mutual exposure that effectively hollows out interiority. This chapter explores the specificity and pervasiveness of Rousseau's efforts to retain the ethical orientation toward others entailed in sympathy (where feeling for others involves a respect and responsiveness based on the identification of kinship and likeness) by resolving anxieties about the epistemic basis of sympathetic recognition left unaddressed in sentimentalism. Understanding Rousseau's utopian works as a complex response to the contradictions of moral sentimentalism will, in turn, make it possible to ask why these conceptual and imaginative experiments abruptly collapse in Rousseau's romantic narratives.

POST-SENTIMENTAL FAMILY ROMANCE

Filial attachment—the instinctual love of parents for their children—is repeatedly invoked in sentimentalist philosophy as the foundation of natural affections and the origin of more complex emotional and social bonds. In Shaftesbury, Hutcheson, Hume, and others, sympathy, fellow feeling, and even benevolence are all ultimately derived from an imagination of the irresistible feelings engendered by the fact and through the experience of sexual partnership and parenting. Shaftesbury, for example, argues that because the "long and helpless infancy" of human creatures ensures that "union and strict society is required between the sexes to preserve and nurse their growing offspring," affective attachment is equally ensured: the sexes "pair and live in love and fellowship."[5] Similarly Hume locates our "first and most natural sentiment of morals" in the "concern for offspring" that "unites" the two sexes.[6] Given the tradition on which he might have drawn, it is notable that, for Rousseau, the notion that "the most natural of all societies and the only natural one, is that of the family" has no necessary implications for moral psychology.[7]

Rousseau's insistence on the conceptual factitiousness of "nature" necessarily complicates our understanding of claims based on that category both in his own work and those of his immediate predecessors. Family might be the "most natural" of all societies, but no form of social life is natural in the sense of given, or inevitable, for Rousseau.[8] His argument that there is no obvious relation between sexual intercourse, pregnancy, and prolonged union between the sexes exposes the epistemological presuppositions at work in the arguments of his philosophical interlocutors. In the state of nature, "once the sexual appetite is satisfied, the man no longer needs the woman, nor the woman [the] man" because neither has the "least idea of the consequences of [his or her] action. One goes off in one direction, and the other in that, and there is no likelihood that at the end of nine months they will remember ever having known each other."[9] Even though "conjugal love and paternal love" eventually become the "sweetest sentiments known to man," they arise from the acquired "habit of living together" that comes about only through a "concatenation of extraordinary circumstances," not inevitable, natural evolution (*DOI*, 164, 159).[10] The "first developments of the heart" originate within the family and are the basis for wider forms of social association, but Rousseau does not attribute these feelings to nature. To do so would be to evade the critical work of providing a conceptual foundation for that which is necessary but not given: affectionate attachment and reliable association. The opening assertion about the familial origins of communal life in the *Social Contract* is no sooner ventured than qualified: the prolonged union of persons we call a family is not "natural, but voluntar[y], and the family maintains itself only by means of convention" (*SC*, 142). Yet no more and no less than the constitution of civil, political, and moral life rests on that convention. Not natural, yet essential: it is a troubling but characteristically Rousseauvian paradox.

Sentimentalist writing typically transforms the anthropological fact of kinship into a powerful metaphor for an irresistible operative sympathy that could be assumed, without explanation, without need for foundation. Insofar as these arguments arise in response to Hobbes's view of natural egotism, they assume a benign form of interdependence that Hobbes does not grant even to the relationship between mother and child. Reasoning that "it cannot be understood that any man hath . . . afforded life to another, that he might both get strength by his years, and at once become an enemy," Hobbes concludes that "every woman that bears children [in the state of nature] becomes both a mother and a lord" because a mother will "breed up" her child only "on the condition that he obey her when full-grown."[11] Neither love nor instinct moves a woman to the benevolent caretaking of mothering. The earlier philosopher's imagination of an implicit, mutually self-interested contract between parent and offspring is a reminder both of the basic disagreement over natural inclinations that is always in the background of eighteenth-century discussions of sympathy and of the weakness of examples intended to preclude explanation in moral philosophy of the period. The fact that a mother nourishes her child does not necessarily correspond to an emotional or sentimental fact about human experience in Hobbes. Mother and child are related, but what they feel for one another or what they ought to be to one another remains undetermined.

Assuming neither a natural egotism in need of constraint nor an innate sympathy, Rousseau imagines that filial love itself requires a kind of cultivation, that the affections sentimentalism attributes to nature arise from the experience of nurture. "The child ought to love his mother before knowing that he ought to," writes Rousseau in *Emile*, but "if the voice of blood is not strengthened by habit and care, it is extinguished in the first years, and the heart dies, so to speak, before being born."[12] The insinuation of the "ought" in this formulation, and the reciprocity implied by the interdependence of the child's love with the mother's care, places this relationship squarely in the domain of an ethics that concedes the possibility of failure of a kind unimaginable in sentimentalism. ("No mother, no child," Rousseau stipulates; "between them the duties are reciprocal, and if they are ill fulfilled on one side, they will be neglected on the other" [*Emile*, 46].) To say that the "heart" might die before being born is to suggest not so much a stillbirth of the affections as it is to figure the affections as still to be born, always in gestation, vulnerable to miscarriage, and bound to involve labor. Rousseau's complaint at the beginning of *Emile* is telling: "There are no longer fathers, mothers, children, brothers, or sisters. They all hardly know each other. How could they love each other?" (*Emile*, 46). "No longer," like the death of the still unborn heart, suggests not so much (or at least not only) a loss or demise but also a disappointment at unfulfilled possibilities. What Rousseau promises the devoted mother—"solid and constant attachment on the part of their husbands, a truly filial tenderness on the part of their children"—is the *cultivation* of the very sentiments and loyalties that earlier theorists had assumed to naturally link members of a family. The "natural sentiments" to be awakened arise from rather than underlie cultural practices and convention. "Let women once again become mothers," Rousseau urges; "men will soon become fathers and husbands again" rather than being solitary cohabitants who "all hardly know each other" (*Emile*, 46).

It is by no means clear in what sense the members of a family can be said to be unknown to one another, but the implications of Rousseau's lament are intriguing. Loving in this formulation is contingent upon knowing: "They all hardly know each other. How could they love each other?" The conjunction between knowing, loving, and being related or affiliated is not only critical to Rousseau's imagination of stable social relations but also marks a significant divergence from the moral psychology of his immediate predecessors.

When, in *Julie*, *Emile*, and *The Letter to d'Alembert*, Rousseau writes of marriage rather than family as the "root of all social order," the association he elects to treat as foundational is one in which neither love nor trust can be taken for granted. In the context of sentimentalist claims for the moral feelings engendered by familial ties, Rousseau's emphasis on marriage, the two-person union that is, after all, the necessary condition for the formation of family, is not so much an explicit rejection of the idea of natural affections as it is a methodological return to the work of establishing a secure foundation for the interpersonal, social, and political possibilities that might be derived from the affections. If, in sentimentalist writing, the attachment of parent and child evinces the immediacy and givenness of an emotional responsiveness to others that is also at work among friends and within civic communities (and for Shaftesbury at least extends to humanity at large), then, in Rousseau, the fragility of the association between husband and wife evinces an instability endemic to those other relational forms. The conjugal relation is an especially appropriate site for the incursion of epistemological anxieties within the heart, as it were, of sentimental certainty about the natural affections—precisely the anxieties that hypotheses of natural sympathy fail to dispel.

The turn from sentimental assurance to anxious uncertainty is perhaps nowhere more apparent than in the recurrent evocations of sexual betrayal and illegitimacy that arise in Rousseau's discussions of marriage. Although ignorance of the relationship between intercourse and birth is among the reasons that the independent male and female described in the second *Discourse* reproduce but form no families, the question "why will he help her raise a child that he does not know belongs to him alone?" remains both pressing and unanswerable outside the state of nature, after the "habit" of living together has been established. Rousseau's formulation in the first draft of the *Social Contract* is straightforward on this point: "It is important to [the husband] that the children he is forced to recognize do not belong to anyone other than himself."[13] It is no accident that Rousseau's most important, prescriptive work in political theory is written during the same period as the works on culture and education in which he proposes an ideal of female conduct designed to ensure that men live free from doubt about their paternity. "All the austere duties of the woman [are] derived from the single fact that a child ought to have a father," explains Rousseau in the *Letter to d'Alembert*.[14] Although generally treated as part of Rousseau's elaboration of the "moral difference" between the sexes, the specter of sexual betrayal is not simply or only a justification for turning female "virtues" of chastity, modesty, and obedience into severe "duties." The obsessive concern with infidelity is also continuous with, and derivative of, anxieties that Rousseau finds endemic to all forms of relational life. The "unhappy father" who "wonders, in embracing his child, whether he is embracing another's" (*Emile*, 361) suffers the same insecurity as the weak member of a society ungoverned by a social contract who "finally perishes as a victim of the deceptive union [*union trompeuse*] from which he expected happiness" ("Geneva," 77). In stressing this implication, I do not mean to deny that Rousseau's concern with adultery provides a rationale for the sexual inequality he so emphatically espouses in his social theory. Rather, the melodramatic implications of infidelity as Rousseau imagines them are symptomatic of an underlying existential problem that is exemplified, but by no means limited to, the relation between the sexes.[15] The unfaithful woman creates a "society of secret enemies" condemned to dwell with one another in a state of unrelieved suspicion precisely because the "sweetest sentiments of [the] heart" rest on a confidence in the other that love cannot secure and for which trust seems insufficient.

Rousseau's effort to secure female fidelity appears as something deeper and more urgent than a patriarchal sexual contract when seen in the broader context of sentimental assurance about natural feeling. "Who will give a father confidence in the sentiment of nature when he embraces his own child?" (*Julie*, 297): The question explicitly conjures up uncertainty where Shaftesbury would find untroubled necessity, making a sentiment as "natural" as parental love conditional upon a confidence that can easily be shaken. But in assuming that a father cannot help feeling stirrings of sentiment, Rousseau also evokes a longing for attachment and intimacy that does not trouble Hobbesian reasoning about filial relations. Rousseau's man is vulnerable precisely because he is inclined to love his wife and her child, but that love for the child is bound up with and entirely dependent upon confidence in his wife. What painful upheavals would follow from loss of confidence? There is no more "frightful condition in the world," Rousseau writes in *Emile*, than "that of the unhappy father who, lacking confidence [*confiance*] in his wife, does not dare yield to the sweetest sentiments of his heart" (*Emile*, 361). Insofar as it represents an anxious recognition that the feelings that bind persons in relation to one another both require and lack epistemological grounding, the doubt about paternity, with all its troublesome implications for the natural affections of conjugal and filial love, may be seen as a distillation of Rousseau's fundamental insight and revisionary contribution to eighteenth-century sentimentalism: we must know the other before being obliged to love the other.

ROUSSEAU'S UNHAPPY ENDINGS

When set in the context of the particular threats to social unity envisioned in the *Social Contract, Letter to d'Alembert, Julie,* and *Emile,* Rousseau's repeated insistence that "the first and holiest of all the bonds of Society is marriage" is best understood as an anxiously prescriptive statement of necessary conditions for political and communal harmony rather than a confident description of a given state of affairs. Julie's avowal that "nothing can subsist in the legitimate order of human things" without the "public and sacred faith of marriage" is phrased as a conclusive discovery, but it comes at that awkward moment in the novel when the promise of fidelity made to Wolmar is most clearly also the breaking of a promise to St. Preux. Indeed, Julie's turn from resolutely resisting paternal command to willingly embracing the duties of daughter and wife is presented with deliberate abruptness. The tersely delivered pronouncement that St. Preux's "lover is no more . . . Julie is married" (279) is followed by a long letter tracing a series of events and realizations that might have been allowed to unfold gradually, the outcome left uncertain, instead of being presented as a fait accompli. The suddenness of the announcement hastily dispels the drama of Julie's conflict, or, rather, narrative suspense is surrendered while philosophical tension is heightened by the emphatic coincidence of rupture and commitment at this point in the novel.

Julie's conversion is meant to be irreversible, her revelations of conjugal virtue deepened and confirmed by her experiences and achievements as Madame de Wolmar. But the idea that one marries "in order to fulfill conjointly the duties of civil life," however definitively asserted, remains as liable to revision as the idea it so suddenly displaces, that a "union of hearts" is the "freest" of engagements "subject neither to sovereign power nor to paternal authority" (158–159). "I am weary of serving an illusory virtue at the expense of justice," writes Julie in her last letter to St. Preux as an unmarried woman (275), placing justice and duty on the side of the commitment she has made to her lover in private exchanges and intimate acts above and against their misleading manifestations in the social order represented by her father's promise and his power to command her obedience. Her next letter reverses this understanding, identifying the illusions of virtue with cherishing love instead of the "chaste and sublime duties" she now recognizes in her marriage (291). "I will be faithful because that is the first duty which binds the family and all of society. I will be chaste because that is the first virtue which nurtures all the others" (294): thus, Julie vows "obedience and absolute fidelity" to Wolmar, assuring St. Preux (and the readers of their correspondence) that "my mouth and my heart made the promise" (292). But Julie's sincerity cannot itself make self-evident the principles she espouses upon marrying, nor does her apparent resolution make the vows she utters more binding than her promises to St. Preux. The burden of all that depends on her marriage vows (the binding up of "the family and all of society") appears radically precarious given that it is taken up in the middle of a letter that reinterprets and overturns prior sincere and impassioned vows of faithful attachment. The deliberate juxtaposition anticipates doubts about the endurance of attachment that become the heroine's singular preoccupation and can be seen, more broadly, to both motivate and undermine the ameliorative political and cultural projects of Rousseau's utopian works.

If this moment of wholehearted commitment is ultimately no more secure than any other, why is it supposed or felt to be different, no more and no less than a "revolution" in Julie's being? First among Julie's explanations is one that deepens rather than dispels the mystery of her conversion given the romantic love plot to which the entire novel has been devoted up to this point. Questioning and revaluating her commitment to St. Preux, Julie differentiates between the attachment of lovers and the bond of spouses, attributing the fragility of the former, paradoxically enough, to the power of the passions aroused, and the solidity of the latter to the relative absence of intense feeling: "Honesty, virtue, certain conformities . . . of character and humor suffice between husband and wife; that does not prevent a very tender attachment from emerging from this union which, without exactly being love, is nonetheless sweet and for that only the more lasting. Love is accompanied by a continual anxiety [*inquiétude continuelle*] of jealousy or deprivation, ill-suited to marriage" (306). The key distinction here, for Rousseau if not for Julie, is not between the agitation of love and the tranquil sweetness of conjugal compatibility but between the presence and absence of anxiety about the authenticity and continuity of emotional attachment. In *Emile*, where the same distinction between the "sweet habit" of marital affection and passion is drawn, the lover's anxiety is defined in terms of epistemic vulnerability: "Unbridled ardor . . . intoxicates him with the chimerical attractions of an object which he no longer sees as it really is [*il ne voit plus tel qu'il est*]" (*Emile*, 430). Conversely, Julie boasts of her union with Wolmar that "we see each other as we are [*nous nous voyons tels que nous sommes*]" even though, or perhaps precisely because, the "sentiment that joins us is not the blind transport of passionate hearts" (307). Passion does not itself blind the lover, however, but rather makes him liable to feel as strongly both extremes—either utter confidence or deep suspicion. Passion is "credulous," "easy to persuade," and thus "love is anxious [*inquiet*]" (*Emile*, 430–431).

In *Letter to d'Alembert*, Rousseau proposes that poets "teach the young to distrust the illusions of love, to flee the error of a blind penchant . . . and to be afraid of confiding a virtuous heart to an object that is sometimes unworthy," but it would be a mistake to see impassioned romantics as alone in a vulnerability that they only demonstrate more vividly (*LA*, 292). Rousseau finds the same misgivings and insecurities inherent in all social life. The illusion and error distorting the lover's perception of his object threaten friendships, partnerships, and civic associations as well. "Everything you tell me about the advantages of the social law would be fine, if while I were scrupulously observing it toward others, I were sure that all of them would observe it toward me," objects an imaginary interlocutor in the "Geneva manuscript," interrupting the reasonings of the social contract theorist, "but what assurance [*sureté*] of this can you give me?" ("Geneva," 79). As suggested previously, in *La Nouvelle Héloïse*, Julie's sense of this vulnerability is self-reflexive, originating in and directed at herself: "What assurance [*sureté*] had I of loving you alone in the world," she asks St. Preux, "except for an inner sentiment all lovers think they have, when they pledge everlasting constancy to each other?" (293).

Like the corrosive self-doubt that will afflict her throughout her marriage, Julie's alarm about the certainty of her own "inner sentiments" is an introjection of disquiet that more properly belongs to those who count on her constancy.

The "inner sentiment all lovers think they have" is no more and no less than the feeling of being in love ("loving you alone in the world"); one does not generally need further assurance of one's own feeling (any more than one needs assurance of other inner states: pain, for example, or curiosity or fear). To pledge "everlasting constancy" in the grip of that passion is, perhaps, simply another way of saying "I love you alone," so Julie's doubt confuses a familiar sense of wonder about love (the banal "is this really love?") with a troubling question about the security of commitment that might equally be asked of the companionate marriage. "Inner sentiment," be it love or mere tenderness, is in fact irrelevant to the *sureté* of a pledged attachment, so while Julie claims that unreliable passions are insufficient guarantee of future constancy, it is not yet clear what provides that assurance for her union with Wolmar.

To read Julie's demise as a surrender to fatally ineradicable self-doubt is to say that *La Nouvelle Héloïse* undoes the narrative of the heroine's definitive conversion at the altar quite as effectively as that conversion undoes the romance of the first half of the novel. Julie's concern for the perilous fragility of her own virtue (especially after St. Preux is welcomed into the community of Clarens) is throughout belied by her evident fulfillment in and of the role of devoted wife and mother. Her cousin and confidante Claire would seem to be entirely justified in asserting that "the circumspection that you base on your past faults is insulting to your present state" (412). "The only failing I find in you is your inability to regain the confidence [*confiance*] you owe yourself," her husband, Wolmar, observes, adding that "it is not enough for me that [my wife] keep her faith; I am offended that she doubts it" (406, 408). Julie herself acknowledges what her loved ones know: "The more I try to sound my soul's present state, the more I find in it to reassure me" (409). But such introspection gives her no relief. After all, her anxieties are prospective rather than retrospective (only an "excess of confidence [*excès de confiance*] . . . makes us gauge the future by the present," she reasons) so that the self-certainty of the present, as she explains to St. Preux, must always involve the incipience of doubt: "We think of ourselves as being always the same, and we change every day. Who knows whether we shall love what we now love, whether we shall want what we now want, whether we shall be what we now are?" (553). Recognizing the irresolvable form of Julie's worries, St. Preux dismisses them as the "scruples of a timorous soul that considers it a duty to take fright, and believes one must fear everything so as to protect oneself from everything" (560). He warns that "extreme timidity has its danger just as an excessive confidence [*confiance excessive*] does. By constantly pointing out monsters to us where there are none, it exhausts us in tilting against phantasms" (560). But the doubts that plague Julie are self-perpetuating precisely to the degree that they seem inexorably rational. "Is it enough for my heart to reassure me, when reason should alarm me?" she asks. "Who can promise me that my confidence [*confiance*] is not again an illusion of vice? How can I trust [*me fier*] sentiments that have so many times deluded me?" (409).

Julie's unease is clearly a self-inflicted and powerful introjection of an uncertainty that ought, properly, to torment her husband, and while it is intriguing that Rousseau effects this transference of anxiety onto the wife he typically tasks with the duty of assuaging it, the most remarkable feature of this *self*-doubt may well be how little it seems to differ from doubts about the constancy of persons or even objects in the external world that we associate with the skeptical implications of empiricist psychology. Julie's despairing inability to "trust anything I see or feel [*me fier à rien de ce que je vois ni de ce que je sens*]" (410) itself suggests a strange similitude between destabilizing doubt of her (inner) sentiments and more familiar doubts cast on the (outer) world of persons and things. The "objects" Julie fears she "confuses and disfigures" are affective and relational rather than material, but her compulsion to doubt is consonant with Descartes's resolution "never to trust wholly in [the senses] which have once deceived us."[16] Rousseau's later autobiographical works are permeated with intersubjective versions of Cartesian doubt, their narratives shaped by estrangements and betrayals involving untrustworthy objects and unreliable sentiments, indicting both but invariably identifying the former as cause of the latter; others are disappointing, deceptive, perfidious, and therefore feelings for them are vulnerable to doubt. Specific to Julie, however, is the internalization binding her affections to their objects so indissolubly that all doubt or misgiving or anxiety about her ties with others can resound only within the self. The comfort she ultimately takes in the notion that death will safeguard her virtue hardly mitigates the bare fact that her marriage, and all it represents in the novel, is retrospectively dissolved by her final conviction that she has all along "deluded" herself (*je me suis longtemps fait illusion*) about the inclinations of her own heart (608).

The emotional inconstancy internalized in Julie corresponds, at a conceptual level, with the melodramatic collapse of the only other marriage Rousseau imagines as a model of secure invulnerable union. The unfinished narrative sequel to *Emile* begins abruptly with the revelation that Sophie—conceived in the earlier book as a woman who "will be chaste and decent until her last breath" (397)—has irredeemably violated her marriage: "Another has defiled your bed," she confesses; "I am with child—our persons shall never be united [*je suis enceinte; vous ne me toucherez de ma vie*]."[17] The elaborately contrived education designed to ensure that this wife provide "evidence of her virtue to the eyes of others as well as to her own conscience" and thereby give her husband "the confidence to call [her children] his own" (*Emile*, 360–361) fails under sketchily described circumstances of estrangement that do not, in any case, prepare Emile for Sophie's confession. He is struck "motionless," "benumbed," "annihilated" by a shockingly unanticipated betrayal. In formal terms, the novel emphasizes this sudden reversal of fate, opening with the revelation that "all is vanished like a dream. . . . I have lost all that was dear to me—wife—children—friends, everything, in short, even the intercourse of men [*commerce de mes semblables*]" (*ES*, 7), an unexpected and alarming reintroduction to a character Rousseau had left happily married and on the brink of fatherhood in *Emile*. The preceptor had introduced Sophie to his pupil as one whose "expression gives promise of a soul and does not lie," a certainty Emile directly overturns in the sequel: "My friend you think you knew this enchanting girl. O how you have been mistaken!" (*ES*, 11). Emile does not cease loving the woman he finds he does not "know," but he loses forever that "confidence [*confiance*] without which regret, disgust and despair are the inseparable attendants of the marriage state" (*ES*, 42). Emile's despair radiates inexorably outward from the collapse of his marriage, leading him to the conviction that "every tie [is] broken . . . every relation altered" (*ES*, 36). If this seems a gratuitous and undermotivated ending to the romance contrived in *Emile*, at a conceptual level it also represents the exhaustion of an effort to imagine secure epistemic grounds for love. This betrayal is especially remarkable because in Sophie, Rousseau attempts to construct for Emile an exemption from uncertainties endemic to social experience.[18]

I take the collapse of the exceptional marriages Rousseau contrives in *Julie* and *Emile*—unions formed under conditions meant to ensure that appearances can indeed be counted on as "evidence of virtue"—to be symptomatic of tensions between affect, cognition, and ethics that Rousseau's utopian works attempt to resolve by giving primacy to knowledge. Certainty displaces love as the ground of attachment, but his novelistic construction of worlds in which each sees the other as he "really is" disintegrates in endings that revive the very kinds of doubts they were designed to eradicate.

In preparing him to meet the woman whom he will never have cause to doubt, Emile's preceptor had warned that the lover's difficulty of seeing the other as she "really is" is compounded by corrupt social forms that "have made women so dissembling . . . that one can hardly count on their most proved attachment" (*Emile*, 430), a complaint that returns to the opening protest of Rousseau's earliest social criticism: "One never really knows with whom one is dealing" because hatred, fear, offense, and betrayal are all always "hidden under a uniform and deceitful veil of politeness."[19] This insidious possibility is by no means redressed by Rousseau's insistence in *Emile* and elsewhere that the duties of a married woman must include maintaining the "appearance" of fidelity and chastity:

It is important, then, not only that a woman be faithful, but that she be judged to be faithful by her husband, by those near her, by everyone . . . that she give evidence of her virtue to the eyes of others as well as to her own conscience [*qu'elle porte aux yeux d'Autrui le témoignage de sa vertu*]. If it is important that a father love his children, it is important that he esteem [*estime*] their mother. These are the reasons which put even appearances among the duties of women, and make honor and reputation no less indispensable to them than chastity. (*Emile*, 361)

The same point is made by Julie on the occasion of Claire's marriage, which she marks as an entry into "a new order of things": "It is not enough that [a wife] be honest, she must also be honored . . . were she innocent, she is in the wrong the moment she is suspected; for appearances themselves are counted among her duties" (211). In the critique of *Emile* that takes up a central portion of the *Vindication of the Rights of Woman*, Mary Wollstonecraft cuttingly repudiates this prescription by cautioning husbands to "beware of trusting too implicitly to . . . servile appearance" and warning that "winning sweetness" might itself be "preparation for adultery."[20] Effectively turning the appearance of fidelity into grounds for suspicion rather than reassurance, Wollstonecraft revives doubts that Rousseau hopes to dispel but also points to dangers that Rousseau himself recognizes even as he issues these strictures on female conduct. The need to secure reliable "evidence" for the other's faithful attachment is occasionally confounded with and discussed in the same context as the problem of masks, inscrutability, and other forms of deliberate, conventional concealment but is not, ultimately, reducible to that problem.

In the disappointment of Rousseau's utopian aspirations, the collapse of relationships constructed on the most secure foundations the philosopher-turned-novelist could conceive, the problem of assuring correspondence between being and appearance—the unifying, recurrent preoccupation in all of Rousseau's works—manifests itself in unexpectedly disruptive and unpredictable ways. Let us look more closely at the broader social structures within which Rousseau imagines that external appearances could be counted upon as "evidence of virtue." Certainly a world in which the duty of appearing faithful reliably coheres with fidelity is one in which possibilities for the kind of concealment that cleaves "inner sentiment" from outward bearing have been eliminated. How is this possible?

DISPASSIONATE SUBJECTS
AND UNPREDICTABLE OBJECTS

For Rousseau, perceptual constraints are, literally and metaphorically, insurmountable obstructions to the knowledge of others. The body conceals the mind and heart; the face masks thought and feeling; the spoken word secretes undisclosed ideas and intentions. These are the familiar implications of a radically individualized empirical psychology that Rousseau understands to be symptomatic of forms of social life that engender divisive particularity. The privacy and inwardness that are existential features of the mind in Locke, for example, are effects rather than explanations of the cultural and political ills Rousseau describes in the first and second *Discourses*. Consequently, his imagination of a social world in which each can be sure that she sees the other as he really is entails neither a transcendence of empirical bounds (an insightful, telepathic gaze) nor a supplemental sense or instinct such as sympathy. Rather, Rousseauvian transparency seems to involve something far stranger than penetrating access to the other. What is imagined is an emptying out of interiority itself. Rousseau in effect approaches the problem of knowing others from the inside out. Instead of positing a special capacity for feeling or judging or perceiving the thoughts and feelings "hidden" inside another mind or heart (as in Shaftesbury's "inward eye" or Hume's "remarkable propensity to sympathize"), Rousseau describes conditions under which there is neither cause nor opportunity for the cultivation of privacy.

Where Shaftesbury implicitly concedes to empiricism an unknowable and potentially radical difference in the most elemental sensations ("what is pain to one is pleasure to another"), Rousseau envisages an effortless recognition of likeness among identical beings. Among the earliest articulations of this possibility is the mythic prehistory evoked in the first *Discourse*: "How sweet it would be to live among us if the outward countenance were always the image of the heart's dispositions," for then "men found their security in how easily they saw through one another [*se pénétrer reciproquement*]."[21] Reliable disclosure of the heart makes life among others safe; what makes such a life sweet, however, is the unarticulated assumption that the "heart's dispositions" will accord not only with the "outward countenance" but also with the disposition of all other hearts (so that pain to one is always also pain to another). Rousseauvian transparency entails an affective harmony that is not the condition for the identification upon which sympathy depends but a likeness so thoroughgoing as to make identification itself seem a mediated form of knowledge. The conjectural past of the first *Discourse* is the fantastic other world Rousseau recollects in the *Confessions* as his inspiration for *La Nouvelle Héloïse*:

The impossibility of attaining the real persons precipitated me into the land of chimeras; and seeing nothing that existed worthy of my exalted feelings, I fostered them in an ideal world which my creative imagination soon peopled with beings after my own heart. . . . Altogether ignoring the human race, I created for myself societies of perfect creatures celestial in their virtue and beauty, and of reliable, tender and faithful friends such as I had never found here below.[22]

"Reliable, tender and faithful friends" prove impossible to find "here below" because the social world Rousseau describes and laments is one in which individual survival involves a set of adaptive traits designed to exploit the inherent limits of intersubjective perception. The evolution and pursuit of private interests, desires, and motives, the advantages of suspicion, deliberate misrepresentation: such cultivation of inner depth makes use of a reciprocal opacity and thus engenders differences that destroy the basis of sympathetic recognition. The powerful social criticism of Rousseau's earliest writings is succeeded by a series of works unified by the task of imagining conditions under which human beings would be shaped by altogether different adaptations to the inherent insecurity of intersubjective knowledge. Commitment to shared interests and a common good, participation in public surveillance and spectacle, uninhibited candor: the social relations described in *Letter to d'Alembert*, *La Nouvelle Héloïse*, *Emile*, and the *Social Contract* offer no space for the cultivation of privacy and thus foster and sustain similarity and equality. Individuals are liberated from suspicion and anxiety because they can be confident of dwelling among "beings after my own heart." Sympathetic recognition, based on utter transparency, is ensured because there are no unknowable depths to the other, no hidden difference between my self and the other's.

From the intimacy of romance to the civic space of the polity, Rousseau's middle works indulge a fantasy about expunging the unknowable in others by imagining them to be self-evidently the same, absolutely exposed, and therefore fully predictable. In *Emile*, this aspiration is articulated as a longing to give human relations the same "inflexibility" as laws of nature so that "dependence on men would then become dependence on things" (*Emile*, 85). The preceptor thus shapes Emile into a wholly knowable object: "He ought not to take a step without your having foreseen it" and "ought not to open his mouth without your knowing what he is going to say" (*Emile*, 120). His virtue is bound to this knowability. He "does not think of dissembling" because "not a single movement takes place in his soul which his mouth or his eyes do not reveal" (*Emile*, 319). Julie's children are raised on the same model with the same effect: "They know not how to lie, nor to hide, and in everything they say . . . they allow to be seen without constraint whatever they have in the depth of their souls" (478). This reliable transparency is consonant with the law of constant disclosure that governs Clarens: "A single precept of morality can do for all the others," Julie explains; "never do or say anything that thou dost not wish everyone to see and hear" (349).

Tensions between coerciveness and freedom, oppression and fulfillment, constraint and virtue unavoidably arise in Rousseau's "societies of perfect creatures." Transparency is achieved but under conditions that so restrict the unpredictable play of passions and personalities as to make one wonder whether the epistemic limits that make our commitments so vulnerable are not, somehow, constitutive of ethical life rather than the underlying cause of moral failing.

Describing the elaborately rigid divisions of labor, space, and time at Clarens, St. Preux observes that the "ordering of a house must begin" with the inclusion of "only honest folk who do not bring in the secret desire to upset that order," adding, crucially, that "to have them one must not look for them, but make them" (384). The "making" of "honest folk" (or of what Rousseau calls a "people" in the *Social Contract*) involves a radical reconstruction of persons that effectively eliminates the pernicious individuation of interiority. In a small and peaceable world where "several men together consider themselves to be a single body" with "but a single will," neither distance nor difference separates minds and hearts, and "the common good is clearly apparent [*se montre*] everywhere, demanding only good sense in order to be perceived [*être aperçu*]." To speak in such a world is "merely [to] say what everybody has already felt" (*SC*, 203–204). "The whole charm of the relationship that prevailed among us," explains

Julie, "lies in the openness of the heart that places all sentiments, all thoughts in common, and makes it so that each one, feeling he is what he ought to be, reveals himself to all such as he is" (566). This effortless self-revelation only affirms that all thoughts and feelings are public in the sense of shared, held in common. To say that the charm of this openness would be destroyed by concealment ("Imagine for a moment some secret intrigue, some liaison that had to be hid, some reason for reserve and secrecy: instantly the whole pleasure of being together [*de se voir*] vanishes" [566]) is simply to reason in a circle unless it is understood that secrecy implies the presence of the not-shared, the uncommon, the different.

"Good social institutions are those that best know how to denature man," writes Rousseau in *Emile*, a reformation that "transport[s] the I into the common unity . . . with the result that the individual . . . no longer feels except with the whole" (*Emile*, 40). The eradication of privacy and cultivation of conformity in the utopian works are designed to re-create human beings as fully knowable objects and so to secure human association on the firm basis of an identificatory unity. These communities engender beings who behave with the dependable consistency of objects and can therefore certainly be counted on to keep their mutual commitments. Consider the courtship balls described in both *La Nouvelle Héloïse* and *Letter to d'Alembert*. These "occasions for gathering in order to form unions and for arranging the establishment of families" make a public matter of the couplings upon which the order and continuity of the larger civic association depend: "from the bosom of joy and pleasures would be born preservation, the concord, and the prosperity of the Republic" (*LA*, 347–348). Regular dances allow marriageable men and women "to get a taste for one another and to see one another" in a space where "the eyes of the public are constantly open and upon them." Rousseau identifies the superlative advantage of these "entertainments" as the achievement of clear and certain knowledge of the other: "Can a more decent way of not deceiving one another . . . be imagined?" he asks, or a better way of "show[ing] themselves off . . . to the people whose interest it is to know them well before being obliged to love them?" (*LA*, 345).[23] Knowledge as the precondition of love: It is tempting to suggest that the epistemological ideal of grounding relations upon a secure basis of knowledge underlies or precedes the moral aspiration of commitment to a decent way of not deceiving others. But knowledge effectively substitutes for and displaces love in these worlds of publicly formed beings.

It is particularly telling that the denaturing alteration of the human constitution Rousseau describes can be achieved only through the intercession of figures who are not themselves subject to the specific human vulnerability they will remedy. In the *Social Contract*, the lawgiver who "discover[s] the rules of society" is one who "beholds all the passions of men without feeling any of them" (*SC*, 162). This "superior intelligence" is not merely dispassionate and disinterested but omniscient by virtue of that very lack of human passions and interests: he has "no affinity with our nature, yet knows it through and through" (*SC*, 162–163). In *La Nouvelle Héloïse*, Wolmar describes himself as "a tranquil soul with a cold heart," and it is precisely this curious freedom from feeling that he credits for an unerring ability to "read what is in men's hearts" (402–403). The emotions that neither distort nor inform Wolmar's observations are precisely those of moral sentiment: "interest and humanity," "pity," "pain." Julie reports that he is ungoverned by passion and that his attachment to her is an even-tempered, rational form of love. This dispassion makes him "superior to all us people of sentiment," according to Julie, because he is invulnerable to deception: "the heart deceives us in a thousand ways and acts only on a principle that is always suspect; but reason has no end save what is good" (304). Wolmar is not only a proto-Kantian figure of disinterested judgment but also a figure for transpersonal omniscience whose invulnerability to deceit is inextricably bound up with an absence of emotions. While Julie appears to aspire to this state of dispassionate, knowing guardianship over others, she (and the novel) also appropriately, ultimately, identify this condition with death. A soul separated from the body might dwell "near those it cherished," she conjectures in her final hours, "to learn for itself what we are thinking and feeling, through a direct communication, comparable to that by which God reads our thoughts" (597).

The establishment of a "people" in the *Social Contract* requires a lawgiver who will "alter [*altérer*] man's constitution in order to strengthen it" (*SC*, 163). But this is a well-known revision of the earlier, bolder formulation the philosopher sets down in the "Geneva manuscript": "He must, in a sense, mutilate [*mutile*] man's constitution" ("Geneva," 101). The revision is emblematic of arresting contradictions in Rousseau's imagination of societies of perfect creatures—between amelioration and deformation of human "nature," liberation and constraint, manipulation and guardianship, carefree disinhibition and oppressive surveillance. Nevertheless, the apparent ambivalence of Rousseau's presentation of this project keeps open the possibility that unknowability might be intrinsic to valuation of others, that the very idea of knowing others before being obliged to love them entails loss of precisely that which makes others desirous to love and receptive to loving.

. . .

I have argued that the anxious effort to secure marital union in Rousseau's utopian works involves questions of transparency and emotional constancy that are not only deeply connected to his works of social criticism and political theory but also point directly to unresolved epistemological tensions within eighteenth-century moral sentimentalism. To stake the possibility of broader forms of social association on conjugal union is, at one and the same time, to reject the notion that feelings of attachment are the natural foundation for social bonds while still maintaining the centrality of those feelings and the relationships they engender to a social world Rousseau envisions as ideally one of shared pleasures, projects, and concerns. His imagined communities of mutually transparent, like-minded, openhearted persons make possible an epistemic security that results in ethical achievements such as honesty, fidelity, and esteem. Sympathetic correspondence and identificatory unity are ensured among beings who appear just as they are and who are all deeply similar. Whether the utter unity and conformity Rousseau imagines ought to be understood as anticipating Kant in the vision of individuals participating in a kingdom of ends, or as an unrealistically oppressive eradication of individual experience, remains an open question. It is nevertheless clear that Rousseauvian transparency entails a radical alteration of the human constitution aimed at the formation of individuals who behave toward one another with reliable predictability.

In this context, Julie's fatal anxieties about her own "inner sentiments" represent the eruption of troubling inconsistency in a place that has hypothetically been eradicated by the structures and rules governing Clarens. The heroine's self-doubt *internalizes* the kind of inscrutability that typically obtains between persons in a world where all thoughts, all sentiments, are emphatically and evidently not held in common. At Clarens, however, Julie is fated and constrained by uncertainty about herself rather than others. Her fear that she will not be tomorrow the faithful wife she is today transforms anticipation about the unknowable affective vicissitudes of the future into an anxiety that impinges upon the present. Haunted by the thought that she is (and will one day show herself to be) other than what she appears to be, Julie becomes opaque to herself. The self-doubt she suffers is a vestige, or residue, of a form of privacy ostensibly eliminated in the ideal community of Clarens, where "each one, feeling he is what he ought to be, reveals himself to all such as he is" (566). Rousseau's utopian structure ensures that each one is always knowable by others, but the epistemic insecurity thus resolved nevertheless erupts again *within* his heroine rather than between her and those with whom she dwells. "How can I know what I [will] feel?" is at once a transposition and introjection of the more familiar "How can I know what you feel?"—with equally disruptive consequences for the sentimental and ethical possibilities Rousseau ties to epistemic certainty.

The tragic and unanticipated endings he contrives for the ideal marriages he constructs in *Emile* and *La Nouvelle Héloïse* are flagrant reassertions not only of the unpredictable and unknowable but also of psychic interiority itself. The relentless self-doubt rejected by all who know Julie, her own insistence on the "triumph of virtue" in transforming illicit love into honorable friendship (546), her final avowal to Wolmar that "I die as I have lived, worthy of being your spouse" (590)—all these assurances of conjugal devotion and fidelity make the posthumous professions of emotional conflict and renascent love for St. Preux as abrupt and shocking as was the sudden, wholehearted renunciation of St. Preux and commitment to married life that divide and redirect the plot of the novel. Certainly the unforeseen disintegrations of carefully conceived and idealized unions suggest an exhaustion of the idea that knowledge could secure love or constancy, and perhaps also of the effort to align knowledge of others with feeling for others. But in so doing, the possibility that vulnerability and emotional vicissitude itself might be what binds us anxiously together verges on articulation.

3 SENTIMENTAL JUSTICE
Hume, Wordsworth,
and the Ends of Sympathy

For let the impediment be what it may
His hands must clothe and nourish them, and there
From hour to hour so constantly he feels
An obligation pressing him with weight
Inevitable, that all offices
Which want this single tendency appear
Or trivial or redundant; hence remains
So little to be done which can assume
The appearance of a voluntary act,
That his affections in their very core
Are false, there is no freedom in his love.
      . . .

        What then can we hope
From one who is the worst of slaves, the slave
Of his own house? The light that shines abroad,
How can it lead him to an act of love?
Whom can he comfort? Will the afflicted turn
Their steps to him, or will the eye of grief
And sorrow seek him? Is the name of friend
Known to the poor man? Whence is he to hear
The sweet creative voice of gratitude?

     William Wordsworth, fragment (composed between 1798 and 1800)

In this fragmentary verse, Wordsworth imagines the inhibition of sympathy by the constraint of poverty, a psychic oppression bound to pressing material urgencies.[1] Anxiety and preoccupation with mere sustenance, the "weight / Inevitable" and "so constantly" felt, constrict the possibilities of affective experience. Conceptually condensed, almost telegraphic, and at the same time so precise in its appropriation of sentimental rhetoric, the fragment is no less than explosive in its exposure of the complacencies of theories of moral feeling. Wordsworth offers sympathetic observation of a person in need (the compulsively iterated case through which the moral sense theorist would have us affirm our responsiveness), but instead of a spectacle of need to which we might vicariously respond, we are placed in the strange position of sympathizing with—recognizing—one who cannot sympathize, for whom the name of friend is unknown. "The poor man" is not the sentimental stranger in distress but one too impoverished to meet the stranger in distress, one who is unsought by the "eye of grief / And sorrow." The important conceptual specification of love as free or voluntary at once distinguishes emotion from impulse or instinct and marks its vulnerability to inhibition. Love "is falsely deemed / A gift . . . / Of vulgar nature," Wordsworth writes in *The Prelude*, refusing to take as a given that which ought to be willfully given but also attending to the limited exercise of will when "labour in excess and poverty / From day to day pre-occupy the ground / Of the affections."[2] In the fragment, affective freedom and affective truth are implicitly aligned and conflated by the comma that apposes the observation (or is it a judgment?) that "his affections . . . / Are false, there is no freedom in his love." This is not the factitiousness of feigned affect—of insincerity or affectation—but a more existential falsehood, hinting of feelings that can only be simulations of feeling. When there is "so little to be done which can assume / The appearance of a voluntary act," love it would seem cannot even take on, or affect, this appearance of freedom.

Wordsworth by no means forsakes or discredits the value of the moral sentiments, of benevolent response to affliction, of broad philanthropy construed in the intimate terms of friendship. The privations here described depend on appreciation of their significance. Indeed, their import seems to ramify and intensify through imagination of their failure. The successive questions with which the fragment concludes—so absolutely the reverse of the consensus on the pleasures of benevolence that moral sentimentalism confidently presumes—invite us to see receptivity itself as a gift. Others must seek us, and we must be led "to an act of love": this would appear to be the condition of the possibility for "freedom in his love." Yet so many impediments may block the paths of approach and reception that Wordsworth provides no closure to the imaginative projection he elicits here, leaves open questions of just how poor the poor man is, of just how far his poverty is shared, of just how true or false the affections are. To ask "is the name of friend / Known to the poor man?" is to raise questions of identity and identification (Is he known as a friend? Can he make himself known as a friend? Does he know himself as a friend? Would he answer to the name friend? Is he called on as a friend? Dare I presume to name him friend?). Wordsworth's poor man does not invite sympathy but instead compels reflection on the conditions, the obstructions, and the blessings of responsive attention to others.

. . .

The unsettling shifting of the grounds of preromantic conceptions of sympathy in Wordsworth's poetry—his refusal to take love as a "gift of vulgar nature" and his unwillingness to cede sentimentalist aspirations altogether—needs to be understood as a complex response to the unresolved tensions between ethics and epistemology in eighteenth-century accounts of moral sense. In Chapter 1, we traced the underlying conflict between confident claims of fellow feeling and uncertain grounds of knowledge in moral sentimentalism to the disturbing implication that sympathy may be altogether dissociated from its ostensible object (our "passions are known to us," Shaftesbury concludes, moving us whether or not those who rouse them "are realities or mere illusions"). In Chapter 2, we followed Rousseau's unsuccessful efforts to bring knowledge of others into predictable and reliable alignment with feeling for others so that the ethical orientation toward others entailed by sympathetic recognition might rest on solid epistemic grounds. In moving toward romantic-era writing in which the tensions between epistemology and ethics are not so much overcome as suspended, I argue that the terms of eighteenth-century sentimentalism are retained while its paradigmatic structures are challenged and reshaped by phenomenologically complex and dynamic accounts of intimate engagement with others. The force of this romantic turn in Wordsworth's sustained investigations of the possibilities and failures of intimacy between strangers emerges with particular clarity when set against and in relation to David Hume's effort to define the relationship between passions, morals, and the possibility of a sentimental justice so universal as to extend to friend and stranger alike. Hume offers perhaps the most complex eighteenth-century account of sympathy as the basis for moral recognition, but at the same time, in severing the immediacy of encounter from the occasion of ethical response, he clears the space for distinctively romantic configurations of sentimentalist aspirations.

HUME'S SYMPATHIES: THE JUSTICE OF FEELING

Hume's analysis of cognition in *The Treatise of Human Nature* (1739–1740) famously culminates in the melodramatic skeptical impasse that concludes Book 1, but the analysis of passions and morals in the succeeding books proceeds upon (and never corrodes) the proposition that human beings stand in a special epistemological relationship with one another—that of "sympathy"—which is at once a feeling, a faculty (a way of knowing), and an irresistible receptivity to others. The "nature and force of sympathy" are educed through a trope of affective harmony that would be variably and repeatedly adopted in romantic-era writing:

The minds of all men are similar in their feelings and operations; nor can any one be actuated by any affection, of which all others are not . . . susceptible. As in strings equally wound up, the motion of one communicates itself to the rest; so all the affections readily pass from one person to another, and beget correspondent movements in every human creature.[3]

It bears emphasis that however much such a passage sounds like the "responsive sympathy" Wollstonecraft describes ("the harmonized soul sinks into melancholy or rises to extasy, just as the chords are touched, like the Aeolian harp agitated by the changing wind"), or Coleridge's more famous evocation of the soul as an "organic harp . . . trembl[ing] into thought" in response to wind and breeze, it would be a mistake to read Hume's emotional concord as an anticipation of these related figures.[4] Its claims exclusively involve the constant, mutual passage of feeling between persons, and it is precisely in Wordsworth's resistance to the assumptions and implications of this intersubjective susceptibility that the romantic inheritance and transformation of eighteenth-century sentimental ethics can be brought to account. And these assumptions and implications need, in their turn, to be understood within the context of the eighteenth-century theories of sympathy to which Hume offers perhaps the most complex and challenging contribution.

Affective correspondence, in the passage just cited, circumvents the individualism of an empiricist psychology that Shaftesbury's sentimentalism retains and that Rousseauvian transparency attempts to negate. Sympathetic feeling is itself taken as evidence for a similarity of sensory experience that empiricist psychology never presumed.

'Tis obvious that nature has preserv'd a great resemblance among all human creatures, and that we never remark any passion or principle in others, of which, in some degree or other, we may not find a parallel in ourselves. The case is the same with the fabric of the mind, as with that of the body. However the parts may differ, their structure and composition are in general the same. There is a very remarkable resemblance, which preserves itself amidst all their variety; and this resemblance must very much contribute to make us enter into the sentiments of others, and embrace them with facility and pleasure. (*T*, 207)

The idea that mutual resemblance makes it virtually impossible to avoid knowing the thoughts and feelings of others is, as Hume recognizes, a necessary presupposition for any moral psychology that takes human sociality as its starting point. (The relevant contrast here would be Adam Smith, whose *Theory of Moral Sentiments* begins with the empiricist presupposition that "we have no immediate experience of what other men feel.") The epistemic access to others assured by the corporeal and intellectual likeness of minds and hearts provides a kind of missing theoretical link between Shaftesbury's inborn or instinctive associative affections and the more complex forms of fellowship that he attempts (unsuccessfully) to derive from those innate drives. In Hume, the self-evident "nature and force of sympathy" refute the hypostatized individualism of empirical psychology.[5]

If in Shaftesbury sentimental affinity coexists uneasily (indeed, untenably) with an implicit acceptance of the notion that there may be radical individual variation in the simplest of sensations—the fabric of my mind and body may so differ from yours as to make my sweet your bitter, my displeasure your delight— then Hume offers not so much a resolution of this problem as a perspectival choice. His analysis of the understanding in Book 1 insists upon both the irreconcilability and the need to strictly distinguish between philosophical reflection and natural belief;[6] his treatment of the passions begins and remains resolutely within the realm of natural, untroubled belief. In the drawing room, where "I dine . . . I converse, and am merry with my friends," compelling radical doubts recede as the philosopher finds himself "absolutely and necessarily determin'd to live, and talk, and act like other people in the common affairs of life" (*T*, 175). Sympathy is explicitly situated in that untroubled space: "A good-natur'd man finds himself in an instant of the same humour with his company" (*T*, 206). The company of a "rational and thinking being like ourselves, who communicates to us all the actions of his mind [and] makes us privy to his inmost sentiments and affections" is literally vitalizing: "The blood flows with a new tide: The heart is elevated: And the whole man acquires a vigour, which he cannot command in his solitary and calm moments" (*T*, 228). Intersubjective knowledge never undergoes the same corrosive analytic scrutiny that Hume applies to our common sense of cause and effect, say, or to the constancy of material objects.[7] Nor is the appeal to common experience in his account of sympathy qualified by acknowledgment of all the mundane and grievous failures of mutual understanding that are surely also common to our experience in the company of beings like ourselves (the very failures that haunt Rousseau as ever-present threats to sociality, and that Jane Austen would exploit to create dynamic narratives out of adventureless plots). The "remarkable . . . propensity we have to sympathize with others, and to receive by communication their inclinations and sentiments" (*T*, 206) has an ethical rather than an epistemological limit in Hume's writing.

Remarkably, Hume's sympathy—the ease with which we "enter into the sentiments of others," the ready passage of "affections . . . from one person to another"—is not necessarily a *moral* phenomenon. In the *Enquiry concerning the Principles of Morals* (1751), he is careful to distinguish habitual, irresistible sympathetic feelings from impulses and acts of good will: "There is no human creature to whom the appearance of happiness . . . does not give pleasure, that of misery uneasiness. This seems inseparable from our make and constitution. But they are only the most generous minds, that are thence prompted to seek zealously the good of others, and to have a real passion for their welfare."[8] That human beings perceive one another's pain or joy is a quasi-anthropological epistemic fact in Hume's account ("inseparable from our make and constitution"), but sympathy in itself engenders no wish to do well by the other. The severance of sympathetic insight from ethical engagement is the crucial, distinctive feature of Hume's sentimentalism; the moral value of sympathetic feeling is retained, but at the same time detached and distinguished from the irresistible immediacy of sympathetic perception.

As pervasive, as common, as "inseparable from our make and constitution" as sympathy may be for Hume, and in spite of being presented as an originary moral sentiment, its limitations as a mode of ethical judgment are repeatedly foregrounded. In Shaftesbury, a universal love of humankind evolves naturally from instinctual attachment to kin. In Hume, by contrast, sympathy is naturally partial, aroused by, but also restricted to, family, friends, and immediate neighbors. On the one hand, "our first and most natural sentiment of morals" has its foundation in the love of near relations; on the other hand, by "giv[ing] the preference to ourselves and friends above strangers," such love is potentially in conflict with "universal affection to mankind" (*T*, 315, 309).[9] Hume does not resolve this conflict in the *Treatise*; he instead offers a genealogical account of "justice" as an "artificial" virtue, "an extensive sympathy" with the "interests of society" that draws on but also alters the "natural" passion we feel for those to whom we are closely related (*T*, 368, 316).[10] But insofar as Hume's account depends upon the distinction between natural, partial sympathy and the extensive concern for others he calls justice, it also distinguishes between affective susceptibility and concern for others and ethical regard for others, introducing an important and troubling incommensurability between different forms of recognition and response.

Between the instinctive partiality of sympathetic feeling and the "extensive sympathy" of justice Hume insinuates the imperative to adopt what he calls a "general point of view" (*T*, 372). The important appendix to the *Enquiry* devoted to justice contains Hume's most concise explication of this difference. The "social virtues of humanity and benevolence exert their influence immediately, by a direct tendency or instinct," writes Hume. Examples of such automatic, irresistible response include "a parent fly[ing] to the relief of his child, transported by that natural sympathy which actuates him," and a "generous man cheerfully embracing the opportunity of serving his friend, because he then feels himself under the dominion of beneficent affections" (*E*, 93). Unlike Mandeville before him, or Kant and Wollstonecraft after him, Hume credits the "benign influence" of these powerful sentimental motives with moral value, but one that is relative and subordinate to the demands of justice.[11] The impassioned acts of "natural sympathy" always "have in view a single individual object, and pursue the safety and happiness alone of the person loved and esteemed" and therefore have to be distinguished from the "social virtues of justice and fidelity," which have in view the entirely abstract, immaterial, collective object of "mankind" (*E*, 94). Hume is hereby taken to advocate a kind of impartial humanitarian regard—an overlooking of the narrow bounds and prejudices of filial, regional, national, and even historical attachment, and in this sense his moral sentimentalism is almost proto-Kantian in its insistence on the possibility that human beings can and ought to "choose some common point of view, from which they might survey their object, and which might cause it to appear the same to all of them" (*T*, 377).[12]

However legible this opposition between affective partiality and the necessary impartiality of ethical regard may be when assimilated to lines of moral philosophy that have hardened since the nineteenth century, its articulation depends on perceptual terms (looking and overlooking, viewing, imagining, seeing) that confound the forms of sympathy Hume aims to differentiate. It is important to bear in mind, for example, that the "single individual object" of "natural" sympathy might not be a "person loved or esteemed" but might be a stranger in evident need. As a mere perception or apprehension of another, sympathy has everything to do with proximity, with near exposure to particular others at particular moments. "*All* human creatures [as "rational and thinking beings"] are related to us by resemblance," according to Hume, and it is the irresistible, indubitable perception of that resemblance that makes us as "privy to [the] inmost sentiments and affections" of a stranger as of a loved one. Phenomenologically, the intimacy of cohabitation or coexistence in the same space at the same moment is the minimal but sufficient condition for sympathetic recognition.[13]

In the immediate presence of another, sympathy makes no distinction between the beloved and the stranger. However, Hume argues that in the case of strangers we must at times overlook what we cannot help seeing and attend to something other than the "single individual object" whose misery is so immediately apparent. "Giving alms to beggars is naturally praised," Hume explains in the *Enquiry*, "because it seems to carry relief to the distressed and indigent; but when we observe the encouragement thence arising to idleness and debauchery, we regard that species of charity rather as a weakness than as a virtue" (*E*, 19). Presumably we regard the sympathetic perception and generous will prompting the charitable act as a weakness from the point of view of "justice," which sees through and beyond the distressed and indigent beggar to the "well-being of mankind." The presumed collectivity of the "we," the way in which "regard" inflects perception with appraisal, the temporal distance "thence" introduces between the present occasion of charity and its imagined causes and effects: these details distract and abstract from the simple immediacy of that single individual object whose distress elicits recognition and response. But more troubling and more surprising is the apparent disarticulation of ethical regard from intersubjective encounter. Consider, for example, Hume's account of the particular form of sympathy he calls "pity" and associates quite specifically with concern for "strangers, and such as are perfectly indifferent to us":

Pity depends, in great measure on the contiguity, and even sight of the object; which is proof that 'tis derived from the imagination. Not to mention that women and children are most subject to pity, as being most guided by that faculty. The same infirmity that makes them faint at the sight of a naked sword, tho' in the hands of their best friend, makes them pity extremely those whom they find in any grief or affliction. (*T*, 238–239)

Imagination here is not so much opposed to the real as it is an affective introjection of the real, the "vivacity" of which depends entirely on contiguity.[14] Thus, Hume's derision of pity has more to do with the intensity and appropriateness of what is felt for a proximate other than it does with a failure to distinguish actual and apparent occasions of concern, though his examples confuse the issue. The child who fears the "naked sword" imagines the wound the weapon might inflict instead of seeing the threatening object in the harmless hands of a friend. Fear is the prevailing passion in this case because he is struck by and taken in by only one element of the scene. But the woman who pities a stranger she finds in "grief or affliction" cannot be said to have missed something in the same way. Pity is the prevailing passion in this case because her sight, her attention, her imagination enliven the object before her. And if she acts on her pity, she would be moved by none other than the "social virtues of humanity" and generosity Hume elsewhere praises. The problem with pity, in the case of the stranger, has less to do with female frailty, childish gullibility, or imaginative distortion than with the unresolved tensions between sympathetic perception and justice in Hume's account. Pity is a weakness (like alms giving) only if proximity—the bare intimacy of being and remaining contiguous to another—is somehow transcended, the imaginative and affective recognition of the person immediately present circumvented and displaced by regard for a remote object.

What is most troubling here is Hume's effort to retain the affective insight and impulse of responsiveness while sweeping its immediate object out of sight. The sympathy engendered by proximity, by the urgency of encounter, is effectively transferred onto the ostensible object of justice ("society," "mankind"). "When I relieve persons in distress, my natural humanity is my motive," Hume explains, "and so far as my succour extends, so far have I promoted the happiness of my fellow creatures" (*T*, 370). But such a coincidence of sympathetically inspired charity and the aims of justice is merely fortuitous because "if we examine all the questions that come before any tribunal of justice, we shall find that, considering each case apart, it wou'd as often be an instance of humanity to decide contrary to the laws of justice as conformable to them" (*T*, 370).

As Hume imagines it, the potential conflict between humanity and justice almost always entails revulsion at inequalities of wealth.[15] "Judges take from a poor man and give to a rich," Hume concedes; "they bestow on the dissolute the labor of the industrious"; in so doing they apparently look at neither the poor man nor the rich man, or rather they have an "eye to the whole plan or system" that supports civil society and in which distinctions and inequalities are both neutralized and sustained (*T*, 370; *E*, 95). The eye of justice is impartial (it disregards "the characters, situations, and connexions of the persons concerned" [*E*, 94]), but it is not unfeeling: "The whole scheme . . . of law and justice is advantageous to the society and to every individual. . . . After it is once establish'd . . . it is *naturally* attended with a strong sentiment of morals; which can proceed from nothing but our sympathy with the interests of society" (*T*, 370, original emphasis). The paradox here is not the potential conflict between natural sympathy and the demands of justice but that justice itself is sentimental—not merely attended by but proceeding from an altered or reformed or redirected but still-powerfully moving sympathetic feeling. "The public good" in itself "is indifferent to us," Hume writes in his conclusion to the *Treatise*, "except so far as sympathy interests us in it" (*T*, 394). On the one hand, sympathy binds individuals to one another because proximity ensures the ready passage of affections from one person to another (*T*, 368); on the other hand, sympathy with "public good" seems to vindicate what is, after all, a relatively habitual inclination to turn away from distress and affliction "brought near to us" in the intimacy of encounter.

Hume's sympathy is epistemically secure but ethically unstable: Our capacity to enter into the thoughts and feelings of others is not in question; it is a "fact of our nature" that we do. Affective (re)cognition of an other is only coincidentally bound up with a just response to that recognition. "When the misery of a beggar appears very great . . . we sympathize with him in his afflictions, and feel in our heart evident touches of pity and benevolence" (*T*, 249), but if I am affected by this encounter, I am not necessarily moved to respond—by giving alms, offering assistance, or, perhaps, agitating for public relief. I cannot help perceiving another's grief or affliction; however, not only am I not thereby bound to relieve his distress (perhaps I am not so generous; perhaps I am not so weak) but sometimes I ought (in service to justice!) to disregard this distress in its very proximity and in its pressing particularity.

Unwilling, as Kant would be, to disarticulate emotional and ethical response, Hume seems to justify a complacence to the stranger in need, the beggar, the poor man by at once offering me reassurance of my sympathies in the moment ("there is no human . . . whose happiness or misery does not, in some measure, affect us, when brought near to us" [*T*, 309]) and by reimagining my indifference or disinterest at such moments as an "extensive sympathy"—a justness of feeling toward "society and every individual" rather than a lack of feeling for the one before me, with me, intimately akin to me at the moment of encounter. It is within the context of this paradoxical effort to sustain the association between sympathetic feeling and ethical regard while apparently dissociating sympathy—not simply from its object but from the intersubjective context in which it arises—that Wordsworth's radical revaluation of eighteenth-century moral sentimentalism becomes most readily legible. In his many poems of encounter, we find Wordsworth turning again and again to the phenomenological complexities of that bare proximity and contiguity to the other that, in Hume, is the necessary and sufficient condition for sympathetic insight. Offering neither celebration nor certitude of the propensity to sympathize, censuring sympathetic pretensions while at the same reluctant to renounce sympathetic inclinations and conjectures altogether, the poems trace the uneasy affective vicissitudes of giving and withholding, recognizing and responding.

SYMPATHETIC MISGIVING:
WORDSWORTH AND THE POETRY OF ENCOUNTER

Wordsworth's many poems of encounter with the poor have been, from the time of their publication, sites of critical attention and, oddly enough, of a recurrent disapprobation that seems disproportionate to the various failings (of sentimentality, objectification, moral complacence, quietism) for which they have been derided.[16] From the "hunger-bitten girl," Beaupuy's object lesson in revolutionary zeal in *The Prelude* (abstracted into a "that" against which "we are fighting"), to the exotic gypsy who becomes an object lesson in suspicious solicitation in "Beggars" ("Such woes, I knew, could never be; / And yet a boon I gave her"),[17] there is something undeniably troubling about these ostensibly edifying encounters with the poor, a something that is perhaps no more and no less than the apparent aim of edification itself. If, in their most generous reception, the poems may be said to advocate a Kantian principle of recognition—of seeing all others as ends in themselves—they must also, necessarily, use the particular other (that girl, this old man) as the means to that end. The objects of charity in these poems appear to be conjured up in the service of a revelation about moral perception that their very mode of representation undermines. So evident is this paradox, so condensed is it in the compulsively repeated structure of these poems, that the Wordsworthian encounter has itself become an object

lesson or paradigmatic symptom of the ethical and political failings of romantic aesthetic practice—the sympathetic fallacy of mistaking feeling for another
with recognition of another. While the ideological presuppositions of this interpretive indictment have been challenged on both historical and theoretical
grounds, the concatenation of aesthetics and ethics in Wordsworth's poems,
and specifically the ways in which affect shapes the relationship between these
categories, has only recently emerged with greater clarity as a problem for and
within romanticism.[18]

Insofar as a recognition of others that is potentially reciprocal and grounded
in the assertion of abstract equality or sentimental fellowship (as in "we have
all of us one human heart") is assumed to be the ethical standard Wordsworth's
poems fail to meet, so has it also necessarily been assumed that their end or aim
must coincide with an ideal they both consistently articulate and consistently
defeat. Without denying the ethical interest of these poems, it is worth asking
whether that interest might be hidden in plain view, so to speak, in the many
forms of engagement and responsiveness between persons that are neither reciprocal nor reciprocated but not, thereby, failures of recognition. In other words,
if in Wordsworth's poetry the ideal of sentiment and the sentimental ideal of
sympathetic exchange and identification appear in a stubbornly enigmatical
form—as at once the earnestly articulated and the jarringly reductive "morals"
of the stories of encounter—then that impasse suggests a convergence of aesthetics, ethics, and emotional experience rather than the collapse of the effort
to align them. Including, but at the same time suspending, the epistemic longing to know the other and the ethical drive to love the other, the poems hover
over possibilities of recognition and intimacy that cannot be settled on grounds
of mutuality, equality, or similitude. "So all the affections readily pass from one
person to another," Hume proposes, but not, for Wordsworth, with any harmonious affinities and certainly without any assurance of "correspondent movements" between one and another.

The representational procedures of the poems shape their apparently ethical and sentimental reflections in unexpected ways. The poem's narrators are
themselves, evidently, representations; the narrators' characteristic modes of
seeing and feeling—their idiom, which both does and does not coincide with
the idiom of a particular poem—are themselves objects of aesthetic scrutiny.[19]
What Wordsworth's speakers give us to see and hear and think about the strangers
they meet is the means by which the poems give us the other: not the poor man

or the beggar, as it turns out, but the one who encounters the poor man. This is not to confirm the now-familiar conclusion that the ostensible object of ethical attention is displaced by the aggrandizing self-reflexivity of the poet/narrator but rather to suggest that the poet/narrator himself is a subject for ethical attention in the poem—even when that narrator is Wordsworth himself (speaking as and also shaping the youth recollected in *The Prelude*). To approach the poems in this way allows the evident paradoxes and failings of these encounters to be understood, not as unintended implications but as integral to them as aesthetic investigations of the limitations of recognition as a form or model (ethical, narrative, political) for intersubjective experience.

Wordsworth places at the end of Book 4 of *The Prelude* an episode originally conceived as an independent poem under the title "The Discharged Soldier." "The face of every neighbor whom I met / Was as a volume to me" (59–60) is Wordsworth's bold epistemological claim in this book devoted to a time when he felt he could "read, without design, the opinions, thoughts / Of . . . plain-living people, in a sense / Of love and knowledge" (203–205), though it is curiously unsubstantiated by memories of any one of these neighbors. Instead of fond recollections of those the poet "read" with "love and knowledge," what lives in memory ("single[d] out" as a "remembrance" that is "not lifeless" [362–363]) is an encounter with a stranger in which no intimacy is achieved. That stranger appears unexpectedly at a "sudden turning" of a path the youth believes to be deserted, interrupting his indulgence in the sensory disorientations of solitude. "Thus did I steal along that silent road," Wordsworth recalls of this particular late-night walk,

> My body from the stillness drinking in
> A restoration like the calm of sleep,
> But sweeter far. Above, before, behind,
> Around me, all was peace and solitude;
> I looked not round, nor did the solitude
> Speak to my eye, but it was heard and felt,
> O happy state! what beauteous pictures now
> Rose in harmonious imagery; they rose
> As from some distant region of my soul
> And came along like dreams—
> (385–395)

The inwardness of this mood hardly needs more elaboration; it is, in any case, abruptly interrupted—I would almost say refuted—by the appearance of another man on the public path. Just as this sudden presence, merely by being present, belies the heard and felt sensuous certainty of solitude that the poet has just described, so too does the encounter as a whole—from the youth's initial withdrawal from view, through his hesitation to greet the stranger, through their awkward walk together and the stranger's parting admonition—cast a dubious shadow on the new "human heartedness" to his love that has been the central theme of Book 4.

> It chanced a sudden turning of the road
> Presented to my view an uncouth shape,
> So near that, slipping back into the shade,
> Of a thick hawthorn, I could mark him well,
> Myself unseen. He was of stature tall,
> A foot above man's common measure tall,
> Stiff in his form, and upright, lank and lean—
> A man more meager, as it seemed to me,
> Was never seen abroad by night or day.
> His arms were long, and bare his hands; his mouth
> Shewed ghastly in the moonlight; from behind,
> A milestone propped him, and his figure seemed
> Half-sitting, and half-standing.
> (401–413)

Initially the phenomenology of this encounter seems to shift between epistemological uncertainties and ethical urgings. But I think that there is no serious doubt that the "uncouth shape" who suddenly appears is a man (not a specter or phantom): the youth "slip[s] back into the shade" so as to "mark *him* well," not to ascertain what the shape really is. Perceptual ambiguities that blur the humanity and the aliveness of the figure excuse and justify the initial retreat, as if the poet's capacity for figuration and fantasy were itself the cover, or "shade," for a withholding of acknowledgment. The stranger seems a giant, "a foot above man's common measure tall," an exaggeration that nevertheless relies on common observation. The impression of great height is, after all, a trick emaciation can play on the eye—precisely the feature to which the poet next attends. "Upright, lank and lean— / A man more meager . . . / Was never seen abroad by night or day," the poet decides, turning the giant into a skeletal specter, whose "mouth / Shewed ghastly in the moonlight." Ironically, the point of greatest perceptual and poetic abstraction coincides with and inspires the youth's sense of kinship with the stranger and the shame-induced awareness that "marking" the man has been a way of avoiding the man. The gratuitously obvious observation that "he was alone," yields the highly conceptual impression of "a desolation, a simplicity / That seemed akin to solitude," which, at the same time, serves as the ground of his identification with the man (415, 418–419).

Being alone is what the youth most obviously shares with the stranger; they are "akin" in solitude. The solitude that was "above, before, behind, / Around me" has been literally personified. By means of this identificatory projection, the dreamlike self-absorption preceding the encounter is both recapitulated and transformed into poignant attention to another. Solitude, in the shape of this man, now "speaks to [the poet's] eye"—not only do his perceptions become inflected with affect (he now looks with a "mingled sense / Of fear and sorrow") but also affective interest motivates interpretive conjecture, a new way of marking the man. The speaker now hears "murmuring sounds, as if of pain / Or of uneasy thought" (420–421, 422–423)—not sounds of pain, but "as if" of pain. Surmise rather than mere perception, or rather perception shaped by surmise, a movement coinciding with, and indistinguishable from, the speaker's being moved by and toward the unknown man. The "stillness" of the surroundings from which the poet had been "drinking in restoration like the calm of sleep" is transferred onto and transformed into the disturbing immobility of this man whose shadow does not stir: "*still* his form / Kept the same steadiness" (423–424). "I wished to see him move" (429), the youth confesses, a wish only to be fulfilled if he allows himself to be moved by the solitary yet kindred stranger. "Without self-blame / I had not thus prolonged my watch," the poet admits; "and now / Subduing my heart's specious cowardice, / I left the shady nook . . . / And hailed him" (432–437). And as if in recompense for this small act of self-overcoming, the stranger "[rises] from his resting place," brought to life as it were by the greeting (437). (Recall Hume's genial description of the vitalizing effect of sympathy: When solitude is broken by the appearance of another, the mind "awakes, as it were, from a dream. . . . And the whole man acquires a vigour which he cannot command in his solitary and calm moments" [*T*, 228]).

Thus far, the episode would seem to be a fairly straightforward moral tale in which a minor act of ethical bad faith (cowardly withdrawal from the stranger) is overcome, the needs of the other addressed, and the indulgence in self-absorption rectified by recognition of kinship. But this greeting is just the beginning of what proves to be a curiously disappointing encounter in which sympathetic expectations are roundly frustrated. The youth has been moved from his solitude but does not, with so simple a gesture, come to know the stranger. "I ask'd his history," Wordsworth reports, and the soldier acquiesces but is "unmoved" (441, 442). Is it the youth's question that does not move him, or is it his own history, which he offers with an "air of mild indifference" (444)? In either case, to be "unmoved" in the rhetorical context of this episode is to remain "still," and so to frustrate the youth's "wish to see him move" even as the two have come together. "Indifference," moreover, mildly refutes the initial surmise—the "as if of pain"—at once obstructing and aggravating the poet's effort to mark the stranger.

The youth persists: "Nor while we journeyed thus could I forbear / To question him of what he had endured / From hardship, battle, or the pestilence" (469–471), seeking thus the story behind the very material detail that had roused his identification ("He was clad in military garb," the poet had noticed, and it is this "dress" that strikes him as "a desolation, a simplicity / That seemed akin to solitude" [414, 418–419]).[20] (Adam Smith, it is worth recalling, gives "curiosity" precedence over the "disposition to sympathize" with a stranger's grief or anguish. "The first question which we ask is, What has befallen you?" Smith observes in *The Theory of Moral Sentiments*, and "till this be answered, though we are uneasy . . . from the vague idea of his misfortune . . . our fellow-feeling is not very considerable.")[21] Wordsworth's stranger obliges the youth, though, crucially, what he says the poet withholds from us, thereby guiding our attention as readers away from the soldier and toward the expectations that the youth's disappointment betrays.

> Solemn and sublime
> He might have seemed, but that in all he said
> There was a strange half-absence, and a tone
> Of weakness and indifference, as of one
> Remembering the importance of his theme
> But feeling it no longer.
> (473–478)

For the youth who wishes to himself be moved (by solemnity, sublimity, strength of feeling), their conversation is clearly an anticlimax. The soldier maintains the distance the youth has been attempting to close, asks no questions of his own, invites no intimacy. In exposing the youth's longing to be stirred by the stranger, Wordsworth's narrative invites us to consider him as intruding on a privacy that the soldier does not surrender merely by appearing on the public path. The two advance together, but "discourse had ceased," we are told (480). "Together on we passed / In silence through the shades," a silence we must imagine to be acutely uncomfortable, heavy with inhibition and reserve (480–481).

On parting at the temporary lodging to which they have been heading, the youth recommends that "henceforth / He would not linger in the public ways / But ask for timely furtherance and help," and the soldier responds in those famous lines—the only words directly attributed to him—"my trust is in the God of Heaven / And in the eye of him that passes me" (489–491, 494–495). The homily is a curt reminder of all that ought to be sufficient for this or any other act of charity, as well as a reminder that charitable exchange is all that has transpired between the strangers. The youth is allowed nothing more than recognition of the soldier's need for food and shelter, and the soldier moves no further than acknowledgment of the help he has been offered.

The indulgence in solitude with which the episode begins is challenged by the sudden appearance of the stranger, but intimacy is avoided and distance maintained. Certain ambitions of the sympathetic imagination are thwarted here, even as trust in the ethical response entailed by recognition of the other is asserted. The strangers part with an exchange of blessings but become no more to one another than solitary men. "Solemn and sublime" the encounter might have been but for the discomfiting sense that to be drawn from solitude is not necessarily to enter into fellowship. And it is perhaps the vividness of this awkward disappointment that survives the encounter, singles it out among the "many wanderings that have left behind / Remembrances not lifeless" in *The Prelude*, its incongruity a fittingly paradoxical conclusion to a book about the dawning of a "human-heartedness to my love" (361–362, 225).[22]

At issue in the discharged-soldier episode is not the effort to recognize the humanity of the other but rather the frustrations of that effort in an encounter where response to the other is shaped and misshaped by the expectation of a sentimental perfectionism, an uncomplicated "love and knowledge." Of course, this expectation and its disappointment are themselves a response, roused by what Hume calls "proximity" and "contiguity" to another. But where Hume is certain that such intimacy engenders sympathy, and equally certain that such sympathy may not necessarily cohere with a "just" response to the other, Words-worth seems to suggest something almost exactly opposed. Proximity does not necessarily provoke sympathy, understood as an affective access to the other, but it does involve recognitions and acknowledgments that, however imperfect and disquieting, make the doing of justice sufficiently obvious. (This is not to say that the demand is met or that the soldier's trust means that assistance is forthcoming; rather, it leaves open a space where reluctance to approach, indif-ference, and even aversion to the other might come to account.)

While the intense attention to the intersubjective encounter in the discharged-soldier episode concedes the expectation, or demand, or desire for sympathy (the "wish to be moved"), it presupposes neither its achievement nor its affective content. If "reading" others "in a sense of love and knowledge" is the youth's confident version of his own habitual sympathetic engagement, then this encounter is unambiguously, retrospectively admonitory. At the same time, the very sense of failure and disappointment—even the thoughtfulness of a backward glance on the soldier—suggests the lingering of an aspiration rather than mere disillusionment. The feeling of being close to another falls short of the achieve-ment of love and knowledge without thereby negating the impact of the event. Humility, vexation, frustration arise in and from an encounter that has no deter-mined value (no definitive ethical or epistemic yield) but that has also indubitably taken place. Wordsworth's youth does not openly struggle with what Stanley Cavell calls "the limits of my answerability for or towards others"; he does not explicitly ask "how many times, and about just which matters, must I pity another, help another?," but the youth's initially reluctant and ultimately disappointed experi-ence with the soldier may be seen to dramatize such questions, to expose (rather than admonish) such a felt failure of love and knowledge as itself a form of in-timacy.[23] Even so, if the discharged soldier's "trust in God" and the "eye of him who passes me" to ensure his (re)cognition as a subject of attention articulates something like faith in what Kant would call the kingdom of ends, then the very meagerness of what the youth is thereby called on to provide suggests the con-strained reach of such an ethics. Sympathetic identification is not achieved, the other's immediate need is nonetheless recognized and met, but as both affective and ethical experience, the encounter is just that: a pause before each passes the other by, a moment of intimacy without consequence. How can such an experi-ence be valued, or rather what is the value of such experiences with and among others if they neither gratify the longing for love and knowledge nor permit the consoling thought of efficacious good will? What does Wordsworth imagine that the "eye of him who passes me" sees in and of another?

THE POVERTY OF CHARITY

Unlike Wordsworth's other encounter poems, "The Old Cumberland Beggar" has no narrative center, no focalizing incident of interest and reflection, no single occasion of exchange.[24] The title figure is first and throughout only "an aged beggar," "the old Man," "this old Mendicant," "this solitary man." He is given no name (as Michael or Ruth or Simon Lee is given); no tale of loss or illness or disappointed passion or war (as in "Salisbury Plain," "The Mad Mother," or "The Forsaken Indian Woman") teaches us how he comes to be a "helpless wanderer" in the village where he dwells. How then can the poem be read as "A Description" (as the subtitle indicates)? What does "The Old Cumberland Beggar" describe if not—instead of—the beggar himself, his history, the mere cipher of identity associated with a name?

My intuition is that what the poem repeatedly identifies as the old man's "solitude," in spite of his familiar, vagrant presence within a community, shapes itself around the absence of any intercourse with the poem's elusive speaker. "The Old Cumberland Beggar" is not a poem of encounter, nor even of missed encounter, but perhaps of the avoidance of encounter, an evasion so hidden to consciousness as to present itself in the form of concentrated attention. The "I" with whom the poem begins, who delivers, as a verbal still life, the sight of "an aged beggar" seated by the roadside, eating, with shaking hands, some meager scraps of bread, tells us also, "Him from my childhood have I known"—and then evanesces, appearing only once more to offer a series of moral convictions as what "I believe" ("man is dear to man"; "we have all of us one human heart"). "I saw" (1); "him . . . have I known" (22); "I believe" (125): a remarkably sparse articulation of what nevertheless must be understood as the poem's lyric subjectivity, the impersonated voice delivering these memories, reflections, and admonitions. Evidently this is not the lyric "I" of personal meditation and reverie (as in "Tintern Abbey"), nor is it the reflective "I" so conscious of, and conscientious in recording, its responsiveness, desires, and disappointments (as in the discharged-soldier episode or "Resolution and Independence"), nor is it the anecdotal "I" of a poem like "Simon Lee." The very impersonality of the speaker who names this sustained rumination "A Description" begs a question about who or what the poem purports to describe. In some sense, this narrator is as impersonated by his reticence as the narrator of "The Thorn" is by his volubility, no less implicated in the rendering of his subject and no less crafted an object of representation within the poem as the anonymous beggar himself.

The speaker's self-effacement directs, but also perhaps diverts, attention first to the beggar, then to the customs of charity and habits of sympathy that constitute his "service" to the community through which he daily travels but to which he somehow does not belong (being always "solitary," a "traveler," "wanderer"), and finally back to the beggar seated on the side of the highway. These movements correspond to explicit, abrupt shifts in address: the inaugural "I saw an aged beggar in my walk" followed by the reminiscences of "him from my childhood have I known," then interrupted by the sudden objection to a notion that is simultaneously introduced and negated: "But deem not this man useless" (67). The "argument" against this notion takes over the poem, proceeding from the thesis "'Tis nature's law / That none . . . / should exist / Divorced from good" (73–77) to anecdotal proof that "man is dear to man" (140), and finally, to the concluding, plaintive imperatives of the final verse paragraph ("Then let him pass, a blessing on his head!" [155]). This shift from description to expository illustration produces the disturbing ethical implications that trouble so many readers. Insofar as the speaker's efforts to demonstrate that the beggar is not useless lead away from conjured memories of the old man passing (by no means unregarded) among the villagers, to scenes and sentiments associated with his "service" (124) as an occasion for charity, the poem itself seems to pass away from evocations of the old man that might be understood to coincide with or enact moments of recognition (the initial, detailed sight of the old man is akin, let us say, to that "sidelong and half-reverted" [32] look that the horseman turns to the beggar).

The beggar recedes from view in the argument of the poem, appearing instead as "a record" of "past deeds and offices of charity" (89–90), as a "silent monitor" impressing on all appreciation of their own "peculiar boons" (123, 126). He becomes that which "compels / To acts of love" (99–100), offers the "sweet taste of pleasure unpursued" (103) to all those who "long for some moments . . . / When they know and feel that they have been / . . . the dealers out / Of some small blessings" (148–151). This is a perfect Humean moral universe, where the natural promptings of sympathy, the impulse to relieve distress where it touches us in proximity, harmonizes with a broadly conceived justice that includes and tolerates the presence of a "class of beggars" within the "whole system or scheme" of society. The speaker thus fulfills his aim of demonstrating that the old man is not useless, but in so doing he also abandons the initial aspiration of the poem as argument displaces description.

The implications of this shift from the mode of attention and recollection, *dwelling on* what is and has been, to exposition and polemic, *justifying* what is and has been, are obscured by its strikingly obvious consequence: the disappearance of the poem's ostensible object of representation, the beggar, under the immense burden of utility placed upon him. Even David Bromwich, cautioning against a perniciously simplified version of the poem's logic ("Charity is good; the beggar is a prompter of charity"), offers a reading that, while more complex, remains substantively consistent with a utilitarian valuation of the beggar as one who "sponsors the feeling of belonging to humanity that none of us would do without." (Whence is the poor man "to hear / The sweet creative voice of gratitude?" Upon the appearance of the beggar, it would seem.) He is above all "important to one class of persons, the 'poorest poor,'" argues Bromwich, allowing them a "power of giving . . . intimately connected with pleasure, with freedom, with self-respect."[25] Being "important" to another is, of course, not exactly always the same as being "useful" to another, and the speaker struggles in the effort to make this distinction legible (or rather to invest the useful with a value that is not merely instrumental), but how does this need arise? What drives the speaker to do more than, something other than, describe, attend to, dwell on the beggar whom "I saw" and "have known"?

I take the abrupt intrusion of the negated thought—"But deem not this man useless"—as a kind of prompting from the speaker's own recollections. "But" is, after all, an interruption, a qualifying hesitation in a train of thought ("*And* deem not this man useless" would mark explicit continuity with the preceding reflections; "Deem not this man useless" would at least imply continuity). The exclamation "Statesmen! ye / Who are so restless in your wisdom" (67–68) seems to conjure up an opponent after the fact.[26] The rejected idea ("this man [is] useless") is owned at the very instant it is disowned by the speaker, rejected yet articulated, intruding into the poem in response to an objection that—we can only assume—the speaker imagines might arise from the description he has thus far offered. So it is worth asking what, in the reminiscences following the speaker's declaration (or is it an admission, a confession?) that "him from my childhood I have known," might prompt a thought so untoward as to compel so urgent a refutation?

Through a remarkably concise temporal paradox, the narrator's acknowledged familiarity with the beggar introduces a question about what it might be
"to know" him that can have only the most unsettling of resolutions. The sense
that the beggar has not changed ("then / He was so old, he seems not older now"
[22–23]) need not, I think, betray the indifference of inattention but rather attest
to strange, yet utterly common, disjunctions between time and the perception of
age that are a typical effect of familiarity. To a child, for example, all adults are
old ("grown up"). Frequent contact with strangers and intimates alike can have
the gracious effect of arresting age, so it can seem as if close friends, colleagues,
neighborhood acquaintances look just the same as always despite the passage
of time (a twenty-year-old photograph of a familiar face, including our own,
will impress upon us the fact of change and age that habitual exposure softens
and effaces). "He seems not older now" captures this changeless face of familiarity and at the same time defines knowing the "solitary man" as a recognizing
of the familiar rather than, for example, an acquaintance with his history, with
the past that has made him a "solitary man," as the speaker of "Simon Lee" offers as the necessary context for his own incidental good deed, or as the Pedlar
provides in "The Ruined Cottage," inundating the scene of momentary repose
with memory of the life and death of its "last human tenant." By contrast, the
speaker of "The Old Cumberland Beggar" has no account of ineluctable change,
nothing apparently to tell of even the gentle decay of aging.

Consequently, and appropriately, what follows "him . . . have I known" is not
a story about the beggar but a rendering of a continuous familiar present—or, to
be grammatically precise—a story told in the present tense about the recurrent
appearances and encounters that have made the beggar such a well-known figure. The use of the present tense in this case is also an avoidance of the imperfect
past tense, which more appropriately captures habitual, repeated actions. The
horseman (typically) "throws not . . . his alms upon the ground, / But stops, —
that he may safely lodge the coin" in the beggar's hand (26–28); when she sees
him on the road, the toll-gate keeper (ordinarily) "quits her work, / And lifts
the latch for him" (35–36); the post-boy (usually) "turns with less noisy wheels
to the road-side" (41), altering his course to make room for the beggar on the
highway. These habitual occurrences are all instances of the routine pauses or
interruptions of activity occasioned by recognition of the beggar (the horseman would always stop; the gatekeeper would always quit turning her wheel;
the post-boy would always slow his progress), but in their very repetition and

predictability, they are also themselves part of a continuous past in which the beggar's "day to day" is a "for ever" of passing and being passed ("Thus, from day to day / Bowbent, his eyes for ever on the ground, / He plies his weary journey" [51–53]). Movement itself appears arrested by this temporality of repetition, so even as the man "plies his weary journey," he seems to go nowhere, "scarcely do his feet / Disturb the summer dust, he is so still / In look and motion" (59–61). This recurrent passing of and passing by the beggar is also a passing of time without movement, change, progress, rupture, or climax, and in this sense a shadow of futility is cast over the familiar and routine, as if futility were precisely the imperfection of habitude, the imperfection of the past. "But deem not this man useless" follows as a kind of defensive protest against the insight that the very form of these recollections has provoked—an almost existential futility of human actions over time, the uselessness of acts of humanity that effect no change. The old man is "now" what he was "then" in spite of all good turns.

The imperative pleadings "deem not this man useless . . . / deem him not / A burthen of the earth" (67, 72–73), ostensibly addressed to the proud statesmen who would sweep the beggar away with a "broom still ready in your hands" (69), introduce a theoretical and didactic version of the recurrent acts of attention and assistance instantiated by the horseman, the gatekeeper, and the post-boy. The speaker conjures up an opponent who would remove the beggar from the village where he daily "creeps" (79) and "takes his rounds" (90), but in broader terms, he conjures up the optimistic advocate for the possibility of a historical change that would effectively render the class of beggars "extinct"—the very possibility Wordsworth had himself articulated some years earlier when he wrote that the "sorrow I feel from the contemplation" of indigents "is not unconsoled by the comfortable hope that the class of wretches called mendicants will not much longer shock the feelings of humanity."[27] Shock is precisely what has been dulled by the familiarity of the beggar to speaker and those among whom he dwells, and its attenuation is vindicated by the speaker's chronicle of the community's habits of generosity. In so doing, however, the poem not only suggests the symbiotic relationship between the villagers and the beggar (he receives their "offices of charity" [90] and from him they "receive" the "precious" gift of "sympathy" [111, 112, 114]), and not only thereby offers a straightforward illustration of the beggar's usefulness in awakening and cultivating the moral sentiments. The usefulness of the moral sentiments is itself at issue, for the beggar's persistent familiarity as beggar, his changelessness, his very availability for description as one whom "from my childhood I have known" all attest to the futility of these cumulative "acts of love" (100) prompted by the "kindly mood in hearts" (92). And it is precisely this implication that the poem reinforces and deepens even as the speaker expounds the beggar's gift of disposing the soul to "virtue and true goodness" (105), for insofar as the "villagers in him / Behold a record which together binds / Past deeds and offices of charity / Else unremembered" (88–91), the record shows a man surviving by virtue of the alms that sympathy offers, but also a man *merely* surviving. The beggar seen "from day to day," taking "his rounds" of the village is no more and no less than the impersonation of an action that he is doomed to repeat precisely because no accretion of deeds over time obviates his need to beg. The poem is as much a description of this futility as it is of the beggar himself. Surely there can be no more unsentimental an account of kindness and charity than this record of how bare a human life they sustain.

This doubled movement of coincidence and disjunction between the speaker's discursive aims and the poem's implications creates an inexorable distance between the sympathetic feeling and charitable acts commemorated ("deeds . . . else unremembered") and the old man who can only ever be known as one who begs. Thus, the speaker's apparent continuation of an argument that has shifted from the value of the beggar to the value of the moral sentiments (the penultimate verse paragraph: "Yet further. —Many I believe, there are / Who live a life of virtuous decency" [133–134]) moves stridently toward its most expansive assertion of virtuous affect ("man is dear to man") even as the center of the poem's ethical attention has shifted away from the beggar, away from the dealers out of small blessings, and on to the obdurately unchanging space between his need and their generosity. In those the speaker describes as "not negligent, / . . . in any tenderness of heart / Or act of love to those with whom they dwell, / Their kindred and the children of their blood" (138–140), we recognize the partiality of that sympathy with others that Hume both connects to and disassociates from the "extensive sympathy" of justice. For Wordsworth's narrator, such partial affections are meager sustenance for "the human soul" (146) that longs to be kind to anyone in need "for this single cause, / That we have all of us one human heart" (152–153). The single cause is here both the source of an unconditional ethical yearning (even "the poorest poor" share and indulge in satisfaction of this longing) and its irresistibly motivating insight (the sympathetic identification of "one human heart" in "all of us," and hence the finding of "kindred" wherever "want and sorrow" are [115, 116]). Yet this powerful and concise articulation of moral sentimentalism culminates with a disheartening illustration of the limitations of sympathy and the poverty of charity—an act so small (a poor neighbor's gift of an "unsparing handful" [158] of meal for the beggar's scrip) and so disproportionately fulfilling for her who gives ("from her door / Returning with exhilarated heart" [159–160]) as to humble what we might (adopting the speaker's condemnation of the statesmen) term the "heart-swoln" "pride" (71) of those who hold the ethical value of feeling too dear. For what end does the single cause serve, what is its good, if the kind neighbor now "sits by her fire and builds her hope in heaven" (161) while the beggar travels on, shelterless, a solitary man?

The speaker honors, and the poem by no means condemns, this modest exchange between the poor woman and the poor man (her hope in heaven for his small meal). Insofar as Wordsworth's poems are filled with tales of dispossession, this woman's warm shelter on earth is itself a blessing not to be begrudged, nor should the pleasure taken in this small generosity be seen to compromise its virtue. Even Kant allows for this consonance between duty and moral feeling.[28] The excess of the neighbor's exhilaration attests to both the poignancy and the ambivalence of the discovery that the "passions of men . . . do immeasurably transcend their objects." If, in the "Letter to the Bishop of Llandaff" (1793), Wordsworth attests to the "sorrow I feel from the contemplation" of beggars, by the time he composes "The Convention of Cintra" (1809), that sorrow is no longer attached to a miserable object but rather to the disappointing untouchability of those we long to touch: "The true sorrow of humanity consists in this . . . that the course and demands of action and life so rarely correspond with the dignity and intensity of human desires."[29] "The Old Cumberland Beggar" leaves the "dignity and intensity" of the poor woman's desire intact but does not, thereby, attenuate discontent with the "world where want and sorrow are."

The kind neighbor is left at the fireside to "build her hope in heaven," and we follow the beggar beyond the confines of the village, urged there by the speaker's conclusion: "Then let him pass, a blessing on his head!" (162). The imperative commands by suggesting, proposing, wishing, and also by implicating others in what it wills. Although the command is (still) ostensibly addressed to the "statesmen," readers of the poem must find themselves included in the soft behest. To "let him pass" is also to accede to the succession of imperatives that follow as apparent consequences and that almost aggressively unfold its implications: "let him bear about / The good which the benignant law of heaven / Has hung around him" (166–168); "let him breathe / The freshness of the valleys" (172–173); "let his blood / Struggle with frosty air and winter snows" (173–174); "let the . . . wind . . . / Beat his grey locks against his withered face" (175–176); "Let him . . . / . . . have around him . . . / The pleasant melody of woodland birds" (183–185); "let him, *where* and *when* he will, sit down" (192, original emphasis); "and, finally, / . . . let him die" (195, 197). Let him pass: Do not impede him, do not incarcerate him ("never . . . / Make him captive" [179–180]), but also do not arrest him, do not stay his wanderings, do not alter the circular course of begging and giving and begging again, the perpetual rounds of his experience. The kind neighbor sits by her fireside, and we "let him, *where* and *when* he will, sit down," shelterless, through the seasons of grassiness and of frosty air and winter snow.

I noted at the outset that "The Old Cumberland Beggar" is not an encounter poem or a poem of failed or missed encounter. What it does enact is perhaps the avoidance of encounter— the avoidance not only of direct exchange with a man who "from my childhood I have known" but also of the humbling sense of the futility, the uselessness, of sympathetic feelings and acts of charity, "tender offices and pensive thoughts" (170). If, in Hume, justice seems both to subsume and displace the sympathies engendered by intimacy, familiarity, and mere proximity to others, then "The Old Cumberland Beggar" seems to tender sympathy in lieu of justice—if by justice is meant something like equal blessings—a sharing of the burden of "the good" in a world where "want and sorrow are." "Bear[ing] about / The good which the benignant law of heaven / Has hung around him" inverts and again refutes the censured thought—"deem him not / A burthen of the earth"—by amassing and compacting the accumulated significance ascribed to the beggar in the figure of weight, the weight of a weightiness that he alone bears.

Given the gravity of the implications of this "description," it is worth reconsidering just what has been avoided or averted in the rush not to judge this man a burden of the earth. Bearing in mind Wordsworthian idiom, where weight is almost always associated with awareness of the world as a place "where want and sorrow are," awareness moreover that is heavy and dark because un(en)lightened by any consoling feeling of "kindred" with that misery, to imagine the beggar bearing about "the good" as he passes and wanders and travels is precisely not to acknowledge the burden of his persistent dwelling in need among us.[30]

The speaker lets him pass (back) to "that vast solitude to which / The tide of things has led him" (163–164), ascribing to his condition a kind of fated passivity that has been belied by the entirety of this poem, which has so carefully elucidated how the habits of charity, the history of giving, the kindly mood of hearts, the disposition to virtue all make up the "tide of things" that carry the beggar always to the same spots ("Beneath the trees, or by the grassy bank / Of high-way side" [193–194]), unchanged and unchanging ("He was so old, he seems not older now"). "As . . . he has lived, / So . . . let him die" (196–197): Do these final lines command us to let him pass finally away? Do they express a wish to bring the imperfect past of repeated, barely sustaining acts of kindness to a close? Do they imagine death as the only possible change for this specimen of a "class" that will "soon be extinct"? How, or in what way, do the speaker and the poem conceive the inevitability of this particular passage from life to death? "As in the eye of Nature, he has lived, / So in the eye of Nature let him die": Just as the "tide of things" includes all the "deeds and offices of charity" of which this poem is a record, so too "the eye of Nature" also catches in its sight the "sidelong and half-reverted" looks turned upon the beggar as he passes on his rounds. Nature is not, after all, even in the terms of this poem, a nonhumanized, ethically neutral territory, but the space where "Nature's law" (73) dictates that there is "a spirit and pulse of good, / A life and soul to every mode of being / Inseparably linked" (77–79). The "eye of Nature" here implicitly includes the inevitable recognition that the discharged soldier ascribes to the "eye of him that passes me." For the speaker to will (and urge us to will) to let the beggar die as he has lived makes this poem a merciless acknowledgment of the limits of that recognition.

· · ·

To subsist alone ("He travels on, a solitary Man" into "vast solitude"), and then to pass away alone, is to suffer an inhuman(e) fate in Wordsworth's terms. "The wisest thing / That the earth owns shall never choose to die, / But some one must be near to count his groans / . . . all things but man, / All die in solitude": thus, Mortimer laments Herbert's "cruel death" by exposure to cold and hunger in *The Borderers* (1797).[31] Rivers is, of course, the villain and Mortimer his instrument, but accidents of nature, time, and place also play a role in the old man's fate, as does the impotence of charitable impulse. *The Borderers'* vision of its victim, "an aged man," "shelterless" against a beating storm, imposes itself upon the fate of "The Old Cumberland Beggar" insofar as the play also implicates the peasant whose benevolence is constrained by weakness, cowardice, and poverty. "My heart was willing" to carry him to shelter, the peasant explains, "but I am one / Whose good deeds will not stand by their own light; / And, though it smote me more than words can tell, I left him" (2050, 2051–2053). The eye of him who passes the "man lying stretched upon the ground" (1918) does not fail to recognize "the damps of death were upon him" (1960), does not fail to "shed tears" (1909), but neither such recognition nor such feeling touches its object. In *The Borderers*, this failure shocks, as the peasant's wife presses forsaken possibilities upon us— "Where is he? You were not / able to bring him *all* the way" (1922–1923); "But you prayed by him? You waited the hour /of his release?" (1948–1949)—before arriving at the conclusion she can only articulate as a question: "And you left him alive?" (1959). If, in urging us to let the beggar die as he has lived, the speaker of "The Old Cumberland Beggar" fails to shock or to be himself shocked at his own urging, the reason is not that the case he describes lacks urgency, not that the "damps of death" do not immediately threaten the beggar as they do the victim of Wordsworth's tragic melodrama. Passing away takes the place of encounter in the poem, implicating the familiarity the speaker has passed off as recognition in an experiential emptiness and existential futility wherein letting live and letting die are effectively indistinguishable.

4 RESPECTING EMOTION
Austen's Gratitude

Alas! the gratitude of men
Hath oftener left me mourning.

Wordsworth, "Simon Lee, the Old Huntsman"

The final lines of Wordsworth's "Simon Lee," in which the speaker confides his discomfort at receiving thanks so passionately disproportionate to the effort expended in his performance of a good deed, can seem both disproportionately grave and mocking of that disproportion.[1] Mourning suffuses thoughtfulness with a peculiar excess of affect. What or who is the object of bereavement? What is to be grieved in the "gratitude of men"? A general condition of need that accepts charity instead of calls for justice? The debilities of age, illness, accident? What does that idle, factitious "alas!" add to the solemnity of the lines it introduces—metrical symmetry for sure, but also, for the proponent of a poetic diction consistent with ordinary language, a caution about the sentiment that follows.[2] "Alas!" is the sigh of a questionable disappointment in Wordsworthian poetics. The aid proffered to Simon Lee—an effective "single blow" struck at the stubborn tangled roots of the tree with which the old man has been struggling—is an opportune act of fellowship: "One summer day I chanced to see / This old man doing all he could"—to no avail (73–74). Chancing to see opens up a possibility; the sympathetic glance is turned to an exertion of good will. The severance of the tree roots—that finite act of aid—elicits a return that seems boundless, without end: "thanks and praises seemed to run / So fast out of his heart, I thought / They never would have done" (90–92). Alas, the gush of responsive gratitude reinstates a distance that the act of sympathetic recognition might have been imagined to traverse. I want to suggest that the speaker here projects onto Simon Lee a purely pathological form of pride, such as Kant describes in his *Metaphysics of Morals*. We typically "fear that by showing gratitude [*Dankbarkeit*] we take the inferior position of a dependent in relation to his protector, which is contrary to real self-esteem"—an anxiety arising from the misunderstanding of "duty to oneself" as the "duty of not needing and asking for others' beneficence."[3] "All men will feel shame at being beholden to the other," Kant concedes, so that in "warding off poverty," we ward off a "great temptation" to vice, ingratitude being among the "meanest and basest" (*MM*, 520).[4] Yet the duty to preserve "moral integrity"—indirectly sustained by the health, strength, and prosperity a figure like Simon Lee lacks—is, as Kant well recognizes, terribly vulnerable to both "fortune" and the social "injustice" that create inequalities of wealth (*MM*, 573). If standing in need of another's beneficence does not, in itself, erode the grounds of dignity, then gratitude need not be taken as the pitiable virtue of the degraded—at best the overcoming of shame, at worst the distressing face of shamelessness. So "Alas!": thus the poem's speaker grieves the dignity compromised by gratitude, and thus the poem succinctly exposes such grief as a kind of affectation.

Averted in the speaker's mourning for the dignity lost in the outpouring of thanks is the onus of the other's gratitude. To accept or be honored by uninhibited thanks and praises is to be passively arrested at the moment when, and by the recognition that, there can be no *other* return for one's good will. In putting it this way, I mean to restore a distinction that recent meditations on giving and receiving have rather stridently elided. In construing the gift as an interruption of the logic of exchange, an event that defies the dynamics of reciprocity and symmetry, Jacques Derrida, for example, is driven to claim not only that the return of a favor annuls the gift of a good deed but also that gratitude itself returns the good turn. The one who receives "ought not owe," writes Derrida, but nor ought he to *own* anything, for to acknowledge a gift is to give it back.[5] This analytic "aporia of the gift" is useful, I think, insofar as it alerts us to the ways in which all responses to others can be seen as reciprocations and, correspondingly, how difficult it is to dwell on or in moments of intersubjective asymmetry. The isolated instance of thanks giving is merely a "lapse of time" masking what Pierre Bourdieu describes as the "contradiction between the experienced . . . truth of the gift as an . . . unrequited act" and another truth—presumably beyond and truer than experience—that makes the moment a "stage in a relationship of exchange."[6] "Interruption," "suspense," "lapse," "interval": all these terms divert attention away from the urgent immediacy and irrevocability of the moment when the other can do nothing but receive and has nothing to give but thanks. *There is no time like the present.* Occasions of gratitude are evidently disturbances in the ethical drive toward reciprocity, sundering recognition of another from respectful exchange, dispelling the illusion of mutuality as even a deferred prospect of giving in return.

THANKS AND NO THANKS

What would be the less grievous alternative to Simon Lee's tearful thanks and praises? Perhaps not ingratitude but begrudging thanks, as for a favor that has not been sought, or for something given that I (secretly) regard as my due, or for an aura of condescension in the act of giving (if I am the type to resent condescension). How readily, in such cases, does a perfunctory "thank you" find utterance, so habitual is the courtesy, so thoughtless is the civility—even when not heartfelt. We hardly notice the "thank you's" of everyday exchange, so readily and so automatically are the words offered, rarely burdened with the task of conveying warm appreciation. Bearing this in mind, I turn to an exceptional moment in *Pride and Prejudice* (1813) when Jane Austen asks us to imagine that the perfunctory thank you might be spontaneously withheld.

Elizabeth Bennet has been listening, with an "astonishment . . . beyond expression" and with rising indignation, to Darcy's unexpected declaration of love. At the first opportunity to respond, she says:

In such cases as this, it is, I believe, the established mode to express a sense of obligation for the sentiments avowed, however unequally they may be returned. It is natural that obligation should be felt, and if I could feel gratitude, I would now thank you. But I cannot—I have never desired your good opinion, and you have certainly bestowed it most unwillingly.[7]

What does Elizabeth say in not simply saying "thank you"? Her words insist on a vitalizing causal correspondence between "natural" feeling and "established modes"—a curious claim for this character. Although moments of discomposure have occasionally disrupted her fluent civility,[8] Elizabeth has been altogether too witty and too consistently engaged in sophisticated verbal play to hold so ingenuous a view of sincerity. If, on the occasion of this proposal, she would not have her thanks betoken a gratitude she does not feel, the reason is not that she holds a naïve conviction that words ought to correspond to genuine sentiments.

In proposing sincerity as a license for incivility, Elizabeth's words reciprocate the insulting candor of Darcy's address—the "honest confession of the scruples" and "struggles" that she finds so "offending and insulting" in his proposal—"Was not this some excuse for incivility?" she retorts in response to Darcy's wonder at "being rejected" with "so little *endeavour* at civility" (126–127). The piquancy of this symmetry between the protagonists at the height of their injurious mis-construal of one another and at the extremity of their affective divide might be taken for a subtle reassurance of the mutual likeness and suitability they will eventually discover—but only if we harbor the presupposition that the central love match of the novel must assume a symmetrical form and take this equal exchange of injury as a prelude to the equal exchange of affections toward which the plot aims. Can we can suspend memory of, and desire for, the familiar fe-licitous ending? To read this scene without anticipating its narrative resolution is to find that the protagonists share only an ungracious and reckless heedless-ness to the impact of undisguised feelings on the other—not the most promis-ing of relational affinities.

But just as Elizabeth's stated reasons for withholding thanks cannot plausi-bly be taken as a naïve insistence that "established modes" should correspond to real feelings (this would have Elizabeth speaking out of character), so too they cannot be convincingly taken as a cleverly fitting rebuke of Darcy's scrupulous but offensive honesty. To be sure, pauses in this dialogue are filled with affec-tive and reactive echoes that impress likeness upon the characters—common, if not shared, feelings of rage, astonishment, incredulity, contempt; similar, if not mutual, struggles for composure and uncontrolled heightenings of color. But these responsive resemblances, the symmetrical sensibility to insult and injury passing between the characters, belong to the *narration* of the scene and can be only awkwardly transposed onto the dialogue they punctuate. To read Elizabeth's withholding of thanks as a neatly appropriate return of Darcy's offensive sincer-ity is to credit the words with too much deliberation, to elide their peculiarity as dialogue. The words are spontaneously uttered—hurled one wants to say—in the heat of the moment, in the grip of "resentment," "anger," and "exasperation" (all Austen's words). Given such emotional urgency, it is remarkable that Austen would have Elizabeth balk at uttering the automatic, thoughtless "thank you" that would be swiftly undone by the scathing rejection sure to follow: "Thank you, *but* . . ." Elizabeth's reasons for being unable to say "thank you"—the reasons Austen gives her—cannot account for the strange implausibility of this speech. The words stand in the stead of a perfunctory thank you but do not explain the absence of what would be an entirely unremarkable preface to scornful refusal of the undesired compliment of Darcy's attention.

It is worth recalling that in Elizabeth's refusing Mr. Collins's equally undesired proposal, Austen has Elizabeth repeatedly hew to the "established mode": "Accept my thanks for the compliment you are paying me. I am very sensible of the honour of your proposals, but it is impossible for me to do otherwise than decline them" (73); "I thank you again and again for the honour of your proposals, but to accept them is absolutely impossible" (74). The habitual civility hardly attenuates the uninhabited candor of her decisive rejection in this case. Collins's obtuse construal of her refusal as "mere words of course" does beg the question of how we are to distinguish the earnest from the perfunctory. "I thank you again for the honor you have done me in your proposals"; these are "mere words of course"; "but to accept them is absolutely impossible"—sincere plain speech that can willfully but plausibly be taken as encouragement according to the "established custom" of first refusing the man one means to accept. Established modes of civility and established customs of converse between the sexes allow Collins to be perfectly heedless of Elizabeth's words, or rather to heed them only insofar as they correspond to what "young ladies," members of her "sex," and "elegant females" might be expected to say (73–74). Elizabeth cannot in fact "speak plainer" than she does to him, but "being believed sincere" is evidently neither in her power nor in the power of speeches whose jarring particularity can be so readily assimilated to familiar forms by the complacent, inattentive, or purely self-regarding auditor.

Respect—the elusive form of pride understood as a dignified consciousness of self-worth, secure from the petty injuries of amour propre—is clearly at issue and at risk in this scene, as it is throughout the novel, especially and almost didactically in the novel's efforts to define the substance of "all real affection" between the sexes as a compound of "respect, esteem, and confidence" (155). Elizabeth's specific complaint—that Collins fails to attend to her "as a rational creature speaking the truth from her heart"—pleads for a highly generic form of consideration. To be heard "as a rational creature" (75)—among Austen's most explicit allusions to Wollstonecraft's defense of the rights of woman—is only to supersede and substitute the category "elegant female" with an even more abstract category.[9] Insofar as Kant (and arguably Wollstonecraft) identifies reason as the intelligible, invariable core of personhood we are bound to reverence in one another, Elizabeth demands no less than that fundamental regard but also no more. The plea is for a form of respect that has been historically and philosophically allied to justice, a call for recognition of equal claims to respect. But this turns out *not* to be the form of respect Austen binds to affection and imagines as driving one into active, intimate engagement with another.

If the exchange between Elizabeth and Collins is a comically extreme rendering of how little "mere words of course" can do to command the other's respect, it is nevertheless also clear that the form of respect Austen fashions into romance entails an appreciation for the other that dialogue can neither establish nor adequately evince. There is, in other words, an unutterable and indecorous excess to the form of respect Austen imagines as quickening into love. The romance between Elizabeth and Darcy ostensibly traces a steady development and awareness of mutual respect, but the constitution of that respect is oddly ruminative, largely divorced from the dynamics of conversational exchange, cultivated at a remove from the other, detached from expectation, anticipation, or anxiety for return. And it transpires in moods of gratitude.

What Austen has Elizabeth so implausibly say in the stead of a mere "thank you" will I think come to make a queer kind of sense if we are willing to follow the question implicit in the conditional "*if* I could feel gratitude, I *would* now thank you" to its resolution in the moment when, desiring but not daring to hope for a new avowal, Elizabeth "can no longer help" offering thanks (238). It is in the space between the perfunctory thank you awkwardly withheld and the warm thanks repeatedly given that I propose to trace the unlikely, romantic affiliation of gratitude and respect in the novel.

A KANTIAN ROMANCE?

The punctuated phases of Elizabeth's change of heart and mind toward Darcy present disturbing challenges insofar as they seem to undermine, distort, and problematically qualify the titular proposition that Elizabeth's prejudice yields to fair judgment of Darcy's character. An abstract meritocratic logic determines and rewards the achievement of this enlightenment, softening the humiliating self-reproaches that attend the heroine's discovery of her "prepossession" and "ignorance." Elizabeth deserves Darcy's love when she recognizes that he deserves hers, and such recognition ostensibly involves the lucid, though mortifying realization of her misjudgment. (I will not address how we are invited to imagine Darcy as coming to deserve Elizabeth's love except to recall what the novel offers as counterweight to her ordeal: Darcy's attestation that he has been "properly humbled," his temperamental "pride and conceit" corrected in the effort "to please a woman worthy of being pleased" [241].) This conception of an intimate union of love, respect, and enlightened recognition of the other's worth is so thickly embedded in the social, cultural, and material details that compose Austen's "realism" that it is, frankly, astonishing that it continues to elicit critical refutation. To summarize what are now-familiar objections to the romance of mutual esteem: Elizabeth falls in love with a house ("to be mistress of Pemberley might be something!" [159]); her developing regard for Darcy is really a submission to the lure of property, wealth, and rank; she is ultimately as obliged to Darcy's benefaction (his largely monetary intercession in the affair of Lydia's elopement) as all those other subordinates "in his guardianship" at Pemberley (162). The equality and respect Elizabeth's father insists on as her necessary requisite for happiness in marriage are, as he also stipulates, paradoxically contingent on "look[ing] up" to her husband "as a superior" (246). Consequently, Elizabeth's triumphant resistance to Lady De Bourgh—her confident assertions of merit, equality, and autonomy of judgment—seems like a pyrrhic rhetorical victory ("mere words of course"), incidental to the compromising capitulations to established social hierarchies that coincide with, and perhaps constitute the very substance of, the heroine's developing love and esteem. In Claudia Johnson's generous estimation of the political possibilities the novel ventures, the "insolence of rank and power [is] chastised, but never radically enough to make us doubt their prestige." Thus, the "worldly advantages that have not been allowed to bully Elizabeth into respect" (in the confrontation with Lady Catherine) are precisely those that "exalt her in the end" (as mistress of Pemberley).[10]

Current critical consensus tends to credit Austen and the novel for sustaining tensions between allegiance to received social forms—realism, say—and transformative, hypothetical, alternative modes of value, judgment, and affiliation—romance, say, or perhaps romanticism.[11] The contending definitions of "pride" introduced early in the novel are symptomatic of such tensions. Elizabeth's "I could easily forgive *his* pride, if he had not mortified *mine*" (14, original emphasis), however lightly proffered, assertively places her on equal ground, existentially and perhaps quixotically, with the "very fine young man" who culturally, politically, economically ("family, fortune, every thing in his favor") has an indubitable "*right* to be proud" (14, original emphasis). Two points of view evidently underlie these two, equally intelligible uses of the term "proud" in this early chapter of the novel. One abstracts the individual from "family, fortune, every thing" and thus allows that everyone has a "right to be proud" and, hence, equally, a value vulnerable to denigration. The other irrevocably situates the individual in a thick web of social and material determinations, including gender, and thus accedes to the fact that particular persons "should think highly of [themselves]" and hence will think less of others. There can be no dialectical resolution between these two points of view, only perspectival shifts from one position to the other, such as Kant imagines when he describes two ways of regarding ourselves as moral agents. On one view, we are free from determination by everything empirical, bound to one another by mutual respect and recognition of a common dignity, equal members of a kingdom of ends. On the other view, we are constituted by character, fortune, material needs, and proclivities of desire, unequal means to one another's ends.[12]

I invoke Kant's two standpoints here to serve as a schematic rendering of an implicit critical presupposition about the impasse against which Austen's fiction strains: anything short of a symmetrical conjunction of her lovers in a relationship of equally realized attachment and mutual respect would represent a worldly abnegation of relational aspirations, an elision of ethical possibilities for community in pursuit of necessarily compromised forms of happiness. Whether one argues that in its relentless attention to material constraints and social distinctions, *Pride and Prejudice* exposes (deliberately or unwittingly) the impossibility of such ethical mutuality, or whether one ventures to suggest that the novel's formal and rhetorical complexities nevertheless allow for the insinuation of other possibilities—"missed opportunities," to use Galperin's phrase—Elizabeth and Darcy are bound to be seen as stock characters in a Kantian drama. Either the novel tries and fails to present its protagonists as "intelligences" tending toward that most "intimate union of love and respect" Kant could only call "friendship" (*MM*, 584) but that post-Kantians might also like to imagine as "marriage," or the novel cannot help representing its lovers as particular phenomena "belonging to the world of sense" (*GM*, 98), appearing to one another first and finally as a "man of rank and fortune" and a "young woman of inferior birth [and] no importance in the world" (231–232).

I intend to resist the imposition of reciprocity as an ethical standard against which the novel strains and focus instead on undisguised relational asymmetries—emotions of humility, shame, and especially gratitude—that can neither be reduced to mere psychological derivatives of a constraining sociocultural-sexual-material matrix of inequalities nor assimilated as affective precursors of enlightened mutual respect.[13] Far from being obstacles to intimacy in the novel, these uncomfortable feelings of being utterly, abjectly, unequal to the other seem to engender an intimacy that exceeds the bounds, and exposes the constraints, of mutuality.

The succession of reflections (about Darcy's character and past, her mistaken judgments, her own feelings) through which the novel records Elizabeth's growing attachment to Darcy entail mortifications and lacerations that overturn the very grounds of her first articulation of self-worth. The trajectory of the plot itself conspires to transform the assertive parallel "I could easily forgive his pride, if he had not mortified mine" (14) into the asymmetric parallel "she was humbled; but she was proud of him" (212)—an unavoidable recognition of Darcy's efforts to restore Lydia and rescue the Bennets from disgrace. Formally too, as D. A. Miller has observed, a shift is marked in the representation of her character, away from the conversational settings in which the heroine speaks for, and so defines, herself and toward psycho-narration of the heroine's meditations, at once informing us of states of mind and feeling that would never be spoken publicly (thus drawing us into intimate confidence with the heroine) and, with one important exception, displacing first-person utterances with third-person exposures that turn the actively opining, observing, remarking "I" into a "she" undergoing and being reshaped by visitations of feeling that seem to take possession of the self—discomposing it, agitating it, repeatedly throwing it into a "flutter of spirits" (212).[14] These emotions are largely described and situated in solitary meditations, though insofar as they involve and are roused by thorough absorption and preoccupation with Darcy, they evince the pressures of intersubjective experience on the intrapsychic realm of recollections, projections, regrets, fantasies, and fears. (Solitude in Austen is never quite being by oneself.) The question I want to ask is, How do these unuttered, discomposing, unshared emotions about the other reconfigure the ideal of respect that the novel insists on as constitutive of "real affection" by severing it from any expectation of, any sense of entitlement to, reciprocity and return?

DISOBLIGING GRATITUDE

"It is natural that obligation should be felt, and if I could feel gratitude, I would now thank you": the apposition of obligation and gratitude is easy to pass over here as an unremarkable echo of the virtually synonymous expressions—"much obliged," "thank you"—that it eschews. What I am interested in are the relational possibilities, or relational phenomena, obscured by this apposition and subsequently brought to light by the disarticulation of these terms in the novel's imagination of emotional flux. More precisely, in sundering the feeling of gratitude from any sense of obligation, the novel is also sundering apart and distinguishing between an ethical logic of intersubjective recognition and an affective orientation toward others that neither makes nor meets any demand for recognition. Gratitude becomes the recurrent emotional note struck in the novel's rendering of Elizabeth's evolving regard for Darcy, an emphatic precondition for her belated reciprocation of his profession of feeling. In other words, Elizabeth's emotional entanglement with Darcy occurs outside any potential area for a mutual exchange of feeling—not only in the private spaces of reflection but also during awkward meetings that can seem uncanny emanations or enactments of those private moods—whereby shame and humility are actualized in an inability to meet the other's gaze, to find words, to be composed.

Another way to imagine the disarticulation of gratitude and obligation, of affect and ethics, is as a change of feeling toward the other that is not reducible to a change of mind; emotion is not the cause or prelude or precondition for a new cognition but in itself a mode of judgment.[15] Thus, emotional disruption and intellectual deliberation are set in contention only to be utterly confounded in the form of insights indistinguishable from, and compelling only insofar as they appear to arise from, paroxysms of mortification that ought to arrest judgment altogether. Consider, for example, the evident juxtaposition of the quasi-Kantian demand for "attention" and "justice" Darcy makes in the written account of his actions and motives that he delivers to Elizabeth following her rejection of his suit, and the intense affective turmoil involved in the reception, reading, and rereading of his letter—the crucial turning point in the drama of revaluation that comes to occupy the last volume of the novel. "Pardon the freedom with which I demand your attention," Darcy begins; "your feelings, I know, will bestow it unwillingly, but I demand it of your justice" (129). In fact, "feelings" clamorously command that Elizabeth attend to the letter, pressing upon her in a breathless narrative exposition. The "contrariety of emotion[s] . . . excited" by initial perusal of the letter includes "curiosity," "eagerness," "amazement," "anger," "resentment," "alarm," "pain," "astonishment," "apprehension," "horror," and "mortification"—a tumultuous emotional perturbation that undermines cognition altogether: "She read with an eagerness which hardly left her power of comprehension," "from impatience of knowing what the next sentence might bring [she] was incapable of attending to the sense of the one before her eyes," "scarcely knowing anything of the last page or two [she] put it hastily away," walking on "with thoughts that could rest on nothing" (134–135). Nor is this perturbation settled when Elizabeth "commands" herself to read and reread "with the closest attention" and "with what she meant to be impartiality." She "deliberate[s] on the probability of each assertion," "examine[s] the meaning of every sentence"—intellectual efforts that come to resolution in "*feeling* [rather than knowing, thinking, or understanding] that she had been partial, prejudiced, absurd" (136–137, emphasis added). If Elizabeth comes to "credit" and concede the "justice" of the account that makes "every thing now appear" so differently (136–137), it is by virtue of an irresistible flow of feelings—hers to neither bestow nor withhold—rather than a willed impartiality or reasoned overcoming of prejudice.

The existential culmination of this climactic scene—Elizabeth's self-loathing exclamation, "Till this moment I never knew myself" (137)—has a seductive philosophical beauty, binding self-knowledge to knowledge of the other. But this insight escapes Elizabeth as a "cry," arises alongside, and is itself an articulation of shame and humiliation. How distinct is this new knowing from these new feelings? How distinct is the humiliating discovery occasioned by the letter from a discovery of humiliation? A self-mortifying shame appears to be the disconcerting emotional precondition for the attention Elizabeth lavishes on this letter she comes to "know by heart" (140). Though "she could not approve him, or feel the slightest inclination to see him again," and in spite of not "for a moment repent[ing] her refusal," these resolutions are affirmed in the grip of "anger," "vexation," "regret," and "depression" at the rejected other that is—or was—her self (140). In spite of her aversion to him, but in conjunction with the aggravation, or perhaps arousal, of displeasure and disapprobation toward herself, new feeling and regard for Darcy arise: "His attachment excited gratitude, his general character respect" (140). Almost and apparently capriciously—with no more logical an association than the weak grammatical conjunction allowed by a comma—gratitude and respect are conjoined in this mood.

If respect—the common translation of the German *Achtung*—is the constitutive affect of Kantian regard for others (*GM*, 56), then its disturbing Austenian variation lies in its intimate association with the self-debasing emotions that overwhelm her heroine. Kantian respect is the other-directed, outward-looking projection of a self-conscious intrinsic dignity, presupposing and requiring recognition of similitude. Austen's gratitude reimagines respect as an appreciation for the other steeped in brooding humiliation, requiring recognition of abject dissimilitude. Is this the emotive basis for that odd definition of esteem as "look[ing] up to the other" as a superior that Mr. Bennet proffers at the end of the novel?

Certainly subsequent episodes foregrounding Elizabeth's evolving regard for Darcy seem to fix the protagonists more firmly on unequal ground. Most famously, and most obviously, in the portrait gallery at Pemberley, Elizabeth gazes (up I imagine) at Darcy's likeness, her thoughts echoing the housekeeper's commendation of him as "the best landlord, and the best master" (161). Thus, Elizabeth is led to "consider how many people's happiness were in his guardianship!—How much of pleasure and pain it was in his power to bestow!—How much of good or evil must be done by him!" (162). This emphatic recognition of what we might call Darcy's will, his power as a moral agent (to do good or evil, to give pleasure or pain) is elicited by the overwhelming, surrounding evidence of his wealth and social eminence as well as by the introjection of "every idea that had been brought forward" by an "intelligent servant," so "favourable to his character" (162).

Given the familiarity of this scene, given the overdetermined preparations for the heroine's intimidation, the surprising and gratuitous intimacy Elizabeth assumes toward Darcy's portrait is easy to pass over. Her initial admiration of Darcy's grounds and estate ("of this place I might have been mistress!") remains a memorable exposure of disturbingly worldly aspirations, but it is only in "viewing them as a stranger" that the wistful possibility of "rejoic[ing] in them as my own" comes to be articulated (159). And it is precisely consideration of herself "as a stranger" that Elizabeth spontaneously forgets in seeking out "the only face whose features would be known to her" in the picture gallery (162). The "striking resemblance" that "arrest[s] her" shapes itself into a greeting ("with such a smile over the face, as she remembered to have sometimes seen, when he looked at her" [162]), the familiarity of past intimacy being simultaneously presumed, revised, and transposed onto a present that is not quite *the* present—a now that is also then, and a then reinvented now. "As she stood before the canvas, on which he was represented, and fixed his eyes upon herself, she thought of his regard with a deeper sentiment of gratitude than it had ever raised before; she remembered its warmth and softened its impropriety of expression" (162): The affective excess of this "deeper sense of gratitude" is most striking for its temporal dislocation. The "warmth" now remembered and the "impropriety" now softened alter and return to the past profession of Darcy's regard for her or, rather, alter her return of that regard by exciting the very gratitude that the Elizabeth who did not know herself could not feel and would not utter.

Austen is careful to observe symmetries that her heroine does not feel when she is suddenly thrust into the presence of the object of this belated gratitude. "Their eyes instantly met, and the cheeks of each were overspread with the deepest blush" in a mutuality of regard and response, but this attunement is unsustainable in the discomposing mood of gratitude (163). She "receive[s] his compliments with an embarrassment impossible to overcome," "scarcely dare[s] lift her eyes to his face," looking down and away, unequal to meeting his gaze (163). The discomfiture of the encounter leaves her "wholly engrossed in her own feelings," mired in "shame and vexation" (163), yet attenuating this fresh mortification is a subtly resurgent sense of power—implicit in her venturing to wonder "whether he had felt more of pain or of pleasure in seeing her" (164). The question arises from an agitated longing "to know what at that moment was passing in his mind; in what manner he thought of her, and whether, in defiance of everything, she was still dear to him" (164), but this imagination of herself as an object of his thought is also an imagination of herself as one, like Darcy, with a "power" of bringing "pleasure or pain" to another.

The degrading, self-abasing mood that binds gratitude to respect is by no means dispelled or overcome by this nascent sense of potential agency. Consider the dense concatenation of gratitude, respect, and consciousness of power in Elizabeth's reflections after the embarrassing encounter on Darcy's property:

The respect created by the conviction of his valuable qualities, though at first unwillingly admitted, had for some time ceased to be repugnant to her feelings. . . . But above all, above respect and esteem, there was a motive within her of good will which could not be overlooked. It was gratitude.—Gratitude, not merely for having once loved her, but for loving her still well enough, to forgive all the petulance and acrimony of her manner in rejecting him, and all the unjust accusations accompanying her rejection. (172)

What is this motive of good will called gratitude? At what does it aim? And in what sense is it "above"—beyond, better than, more moving than "respect and esteem"? The change Elizabeth attends to in Darcy's behavior, the outward signs of his forgiveness, consists in not avoiding her, seeming eager to renew their acquaintance, soliciting the good regard of her friends—a perfect civility that excites "not only astonishment but gratitude—for to love, ardent love, it must

be attributed" (172). To unpack this sequence of associations: Darcy's "love" (un-
declared but intimated as the only possible explanation for his graceful reception) excites good will toward him and thereby affirms and presumes the power
to make him her beneficiary—at precisely the moment when the extent of his
worldly preeminence is most apparent and impressive and in spite of her feeling
absolutely undeserving of his notice. This motive toward the other is what the
novel now names "gratitude" and begins to render as an imagined confluence
of desire and determination: "She respected, she esteemed, she was grateful to
him, she felt a real interest in his welfare; and she only wanted to know how far
she wished that welfare to depend upon herself, and how far it would be for the
happiness of both that she should employ the power, which her fancy told her
she still possessed, of bringing on the renewal of his addresses" (172).

I have suggested that in sundering the sense of obligation from the feeling
of gratitude, the novel explores affective asymmetries, relational experiences
that we are liable to misconstrue or discount as failures of mutual exchange
and reciprocity. The passages I have been bringing forward associate gratitude
with a form of respect that is unsettlingly self-abasing. In the mood of gratitude, respect for the other is bound to a kind of humility, an almost submissive
awe that precludes any presumption or expectation of return—yet it is at this
almost abject affective distance that a sense of agency in relation to the other
might arise. Thus, Elizabeth's respecting, esteeming, and being grateful to Darcy
shade into and seem to find another iteration in her "feel[ing] real interest in
his welfare" and allowing herself the knowledge that this welfare might "depend
upon herself," fall within the ambit of her wishes, her power, her good will. Far
from recognizing an obligation, gratitude seems to involve realizing a freedom.
Gratitude names an occasion for willing that does not arise spontaneously within
the subject (as a self-determined inclination or choice) but as an implication of
appreciation for an other.

Insofar as wanting to know "how far she wished" his happiness to depend
on herself involves the discovery of a *power* to make another happy, and insofar
as that discovery follows from the "motive within her of good will," or gratitude,
the novel constructs an interdependence between self-regard and recognition
of the other too complex and too affectively unstable to be imagined as linear
or circular reciprocation. For if Elizabeth's abasing gratitude toward Darcy is
aroused by renewed conviction of his "ardent love," so too is an elevating sense of
her power to will—though it is a power entirely contingent on opportunities the

other presents. "Ardent love" by implication is being imagined as the provision of just such opportunities, a willed vulnerability that simultaneously bestows and concedes the other's power to give pleasure or pain. In avowing his attachment to me, the other gives me a possibility. I will feel gratitude if I take that power as a gift, as something I could not obtain by or for myself, as something I have always wanted but could not find, or something I have only discovered wanting now, in the other's giving. Respect can be returned, esteem can be mutual, but how can this peculiar gift of a motive for good will be reciprocated?

GIVING THANKS

In addressing the uncharacteristic incivility of Elizabeth's initial rejection of Darcy, I argued that she cannot be taken to mean, sincerely, that saying thank you must always coincide with feeling gratitude. Nor at the end of the novel can she be taken to mean, with unintended irony, that expressing gratitude is a kind of untoward indulgence of feeling. Seizing the opportunity to acknowledge Darcy's intercession in averting the disgraceful consequences of Lydia's elopement with Wickham, Elizabeth declares: "I am a very selfish creature, and for the sake of giving relief to my own feelings, care not how much I may be wounding yours" (238). This coy preface to her thanks, affecting heedless indifference to the other, is not only the charming obverse of the appreciation she will go on to express but it also (perhaps unwittingly) recalls the mutually offensive honest professions of feeling that each has inflicted on the other. "I can no longer help thanking you for your unexampled kindness to my poor sister," Elizabeth continues. "Ever since I have known it, I have been most anxious to acknowledge to you how gratefully I feel it" (238). In thus delivering herself, Elizabeth is described as desperately resolved, bold, and courageous, as if the offering of these thanks were a daring assertion of self rather than a difficult admission of the "painful, exceedingly painful" sense of being "under obligations to a person who could never receive a return" (as she puts it to herself earlier) (212). If Elizabeth ultimately brings herself to speak boldly, it is with something like the audacity of humility, giving thanks "in the name of all my family," willingly admitting her implication in their disgrace (238).

Darcy will not accept these thanks, however.

In responding by asking Elizabeth to thank him only on her own account—to acknowledge "the wish of giving happiness to you," having "thought only of *you*" (239, original emphasis)—Darcy articulates the thought that Elizabeth's vanity has been insufficient to admit, her own heart's whisper that "he had done it for her" (212). "If you *will* thank me," Darcy stipulates, "let it be for yourself alone" (239, original emphasis). These grounds expose a rather different object for thanks giving than the material "kindness" and generosity to a "poor sister" that places the whole family "under obligations." "Your *family* owe me nothing," Darcy asserts, because "I thought only of *you*" (239). This is not quite to say that *you* owe me something for thinking only of you; in the terms that we have been exploring, the implicit question is whether Elizabeth can feel gratitude for such a thought. "If you *will* thank me": an appeal, a stipulation, a concession to her agency. If she wills to thank him, then it must be precisely for "the wish of giving happiness" to her. Perhaps in romance, as in the unconscious, there is no time. At the cusp of its resolution, the novel turns back to the initial occasion of thanks withheld. Hence the precise appeal that follows: "If your feelings are still what they were last April, tell me so at once" (239), that is, if your feelings are still of the kind that exclude gratitude, are still averse to the reception of my "wish of giving happiness to you."

It is typical of Austen, but also appropriate here, that this climactic dialogue is described rather than reported, and not only by way of contrast to the earlier scenes of rejected proposals where the dialogic tensions of verbal exchange evince and intensify sharp affective disjunctions between the interlocutors. In lieu of conversation, in lieu of making reciprocity of affection explicit, the novel evokes a mood of receptivity in which feeling is given rather than returned. Elizabeth "gave him to understand" that her sentiments had changed rather than made him understand. The change is such "as to make her receive with gratitude and pleasure" the assurance that his own "affections and wishes are unchanged" (239). Eyes do not meet in this scene. The posture of receptivity is that of the lowered gaze, attending to the other in a way that face-to-face encounter apparently precludes: "Though she could not look, she could listen, and he told her of feelings" that give her to understand "of what importance she was to him" (239). "His affections [become] every moment more valuable" not as a recognition of her value but insofar as they bind such recognition to a wish that can be fulfilled—or perhaps gratified—only by her willingness to receive. Perhaps we can never know how equally sentiments avowed are returned; perhaps it is, as Kant suspects, virtually impossible "to bring love and respect subjectively into equal balance" (*MM*, 585); but perhaps there are moments when the preoccupying prospect of equality gracefully recedes. Gratitude is the motive of good will toward another that, in surrendering the anxious urge to reciprocate, respects the other's wish to give. Mutuality is suspended in the moment of gratitude: *There is no time but the present.*

The novel invites a reading that would belatedly, and perfunctorily, impose a logic of reciprocity and mutual indebtedness upon the affective possibilities of reception that allow for thanks giving. Darcy's self-incriminating condemnation of his "pride and conceit" credits Elizabeth for a reformation akin to that ostensibly achieved by the mortification of her own vanity and ignorance: "What do I not owe you! . . . By you, I was properly humbled. I came to you without a doubt of my reception. You shewed me how insufficient were all my pretensions to please a woman worthy of being pleased" (241). It is, of course, possible to understand Darcy's trajectory as the discovery of a conscious will to please or a consciousness of his will to please this woman—rather than having been "bewitched" (35), "attracted . . . more than he liked" (41), or succumbing to an "attachment . . . he had found impossible to conquer" (125) (as he initially imagines), "drawn in" against all reason and "made [to] forget what he owes to himself" (231) (as Lady de Bourgh puts it). But it is important to bear in mind that this hypothetical trajectory (whereby Darcy comes to own his willing and wishing to please) does not ever coincide with, or even run parallel to, the affective experiences of the heroine that dominate the latter half of the novel. The proper subject of humbling in the narrative has been Elizabeth, which is not to say that she has been humbled but that she has been repeatedly represented in the throes of humility and shame wherein self-reflection and preoccupation with another are insistently confounded. If we are now to take consolation in the thought that she has had a secret sharer in this affective drama, then I fear that we smooth the uneven ground upon which the novel has imagined the possibility of a resolution.

Darcy's affection is "every moment more valuable" to Elizabeth not because it affirms her worth but because it creates a space—call it an intersubjective space—for the experience of appreciation. Darcy's "what do I not owe you!"—an exclamation, an assertion, not a question—takes for granted and articulates the constitutive possibilities of gratitude that have formed the substance of the heroine's affective *Bildung*. In grateful reception of Darcy's affection, Elizabeth owes something very near to a constitution of her self. The dignified and imperturbable consciousness of self-worth that we might call pride forms no part of this self; rather, self involves a "motive of good will" toward the other that felicitously harmonizes with what one wishes, a power to "bestow pleasure or pain" on another that implies one's own subjection to the other's good will. "More than common awkwardness and anxiety" must accompany such occasions for gratitude (239), for who is ever ready to receive unrealized possibilities of will and desire from another?

5

ALONE TOGETHER
Romanticism, Psychoanalysis, and the Interpretation of Silence

One is free, or perhaps compelled, to speak because the other says almost nothing. If we are fortunate in our most intimate relations, the other's silence is rarely unintelligible. It might be a rebuke, waiting to be appeased by explanations or apologies; it might be an invitation, promising attentive forbearance. As often as anything, it is the frustratingly banal blankness of fatigue or preoccupation against which one gently hurls bits of banter. I take it that we recognize these moments of asymmetry as brief gaps or caesurae within ongoing conversation rather than as ruptures of communication. We abide, anticipating the resumption of dialogue, but also secure that the other is not altogether lost. Silences are gracious or strained, but they are tolerable punctuations of intercourse, to be borne or indulged because of a history of speaking with and to one another. To maintain silence as the other speaks, or so that the other will speak, is to draw on the very familiarity that gives one cause for anger at times, calls for consoling passivity at other times, occasionally permits withdrawal and distraction.

In his 1912 "Recommendations for Physicians on the Psychoanalytic Method of Treatment," Sigmund Freud admits that insofar as the entirely asymmetrical exchange sustained by the silent analyst and the speaking patient draws on the privileges of intimacy, the very efficacy of the treatment is also its point of greatest vulnerability to compromise and corruption. "One confidence [*Vertrauern*] repays another, and anyone demanding intimate revelations [*Intimität*] from another must be prepared to make them himself"; tempted by this logic, or even ethics, of reciprocal exchange, "one would expect it to be entirely permissible, and even desirable," for the physician to offer "intimate disclosures [*vertrauliche Mitteilungen*] from his own life."[1] The theoretical grounds upon which Freud rejects the appropriateness of this ordinary way of relating—insisting instead that "the psychoanalytic relationship is a thing apart"—need not be reviewed here in order to appreciate the paradox involved by his evocation of "situations in real life" when interpreting the challenge posed by patients who suddenly cease making intimate disclosures to their analysts.[2] Freud's bold surmise in "The Dynamics of the Transference" (1912) is that silence betrays a powerful transferential attachment to the physician, a love that the patient "refus[es] to speak": "An attitude of affectionate and devoted attachment can surmount any difficulty in confession; in analogous situations in real life we say 'I don't feel ashamed with you; I can tell you everything.' The transference to the physician might quite as well relieve the difficulties of confession, and we still do not understand why it aggravates them."[3]

Leaving aside the presupposition that love emboldens and disinhibits, it is nevertheless clear that the ground of Freud's famous interpretation of silence as resistance lies in this analogy to real-life expectations of intimacy, affection, and attachment. The "fundamental rules" of psychoanalytic exchange (the physician "has simply to listen" and the patient "to communicate everything that occurs to him") dictate entirely opposed orientations toward the "reality" of the relationship. For the patient, the intimacy of the analytic situation ought to be analogous to that in real life; the efficacy of the treatment, especially of the power of transference, depends on eliciting this affective authenticity. For the physician, on the contrary, the challenge seems to lie in resisting the pull of the real, disowning or setting aside the recognition that confidences are generally shared.

This is the kind of asymmetrical structure that succeeding generations have challenged—in theory, if not always in clinical practice—by insisting on the essential intersubjectivity of psychoanalytic experience. Scientistic models of analysis as an objective investigation of the patient's intrapsychic dynamics have given way to relational models that foreground conscious and unconscious exchange between the two individuals engaged in the analytic project. As Jessica Benjamin observes, psychoanalysis necessarily involves "two subjectivities, each with its own set of internal relations, [who] begin to create a new set of relations between them." Thus, "we now try to grasp the meaning of unconscious in terms of communication between ourselves and the other subject in the room."[4] From this perspective, the analytic silence Freud understands as a requisite professional withholding of the impulse to repay the patient's confidences is itself recognizable as a disclosure, a communication. "Looking [itself] can be either affectionate and empathic or hostile and rejective," notes Masud Khan, but "it cannot be neutral."[5]

It is a surprising but symptomatic paradox of both psychoanalytic and romantic interpretations of intimacy that they oscillate between affirmations of profound intersubjective attunement and emphatic assertions of a vital existential privacy that seem to obviate something it is hard not to think of as the ethical encumbrance of intimacy–the demand for and expectation of reciprocity. We have seen how Wordsworth and Austen—whose works are broadly representative of the related but distinct romantic preoccupations with humanitarian passion and passionate authenticity—forcefully move away from the assumptions and aims of sentimental ethics. If the ideals of mutual identification and reciprocal recognition persist within their works, they lie on a hazy aspirational horizon against which other forms of intimacy appear in sharp relief. Are ethical *imperatives* superseded by such attention to, and appreciation for, moments of engagement that do not involve the symmetries and affinities of sympathy and respect? Certainly the ethical *implications* of relational experience are reshaped to include (rather than discount, lament, or condemn) limitations, failures, and disappointments of fellow feeling among our modes of being with one another. Something similar may be said of psychoanalytic work insofar as it values and attends to the affective vicissitudes and instabilities of our involvement with others. The paradoxical senses of the term "intimacy"—most private, most shared—need not be fixed in opposition to one another but held together as coexisting inflections of time spent with one another. I explore this possibility and attempt to define its parameters by repeatedly moving from imaginations of intersubjective harmony and estrangement in romantic and psychoanalytic writing. And it will be helpful to begin by looking at the surprising reverence for solitude in some important post-Freudian interpretations of silence.

POST-FREUDIAN SILENCE

In a radical departure from Freud's interpretation of silence as a resistance symptomatic of a disturbance in the capacity for love, D. W. Winnicott attends to silent phases or sessions as a vital achievement of what he calls the "capacity to be alone." If Freud's silent patient is in love but refusing to avow attachment to the other, Winnicott's silent patient is boldly claiming the "right not to communicate." The 1963 essay in which Winnicott adumbrates this view of a "noncommunicating central self" makes surprisingly uncompromising claims for the animating and constitutive force of solitude, quietude, and stillness for the "true self."[6] More recently, Christopher Bollas has described this "generative silence" as a musing meditation, thoughtfulness, and tranquility in which the patient can receive "news of the self."[7] The patient who falls silent is enjoying, perhaps for the first time, Winnicott speculates, this "ability to be alone" that "belongs to being alive."[8] The conceptual alignment of authenticity with solitude, and of both those terms with vitality, is striking in its commitment to the existential value of privacy. The "incommunicado element" at the "center of each person" is "permanent," "sacred," and "most worthy of preservation," writes Winnicott, but a crucial qualification mitigates what he calls the "hard fact" that "each individual is an isolate, permanently non-communicating, permanently unknown."[9] "Awareness of the continued presence of a reliable other" is the condition for the possibility of this vitalizing solitude.[10] The capacity to be alone, no less than the capacity to love, necessarily involves another.

"The experience of being alone while someone else is present" appears to be the paradoxical apogee of intimacy in Winnicott's example of the pleasure of lovers after "satisfactory intercourse." Each "is alone and contented to be alone . . . able to enjoy being alone with another person . . . free from the property of withdrawal."[11] We might recall that John Keats, from whom Winnicott borrowed an epigraph for his famous essay on the "right not to communicate," writes of finding a contented hermetic repose "not in lone splendor" but "pillowed upon my fair love's ripening breast." The capacity for this erotic solitude has a history, of course. Bollas evokes the "silence of the small child before falling asleep," in reassuring proximity to his parent, but also "alone in [his] bed, eyes open, imagining [his] life."[12] Not surprisingly, maternal attention is the principal metaphor for this reliable yet unobtrusive presence upon which, or with which, the capacity to *be*—silent, alone, alive—is realized.

The "basis of the capacity to be alone is a paradox," explains Winnicott, precisely because it depends entirely on "the infant's awareness of the continued existence of a reliable mother."[13] To this paradox we might add a second: The analyst's interpretation of the patient's silence as a generative, animating experience of solitude presumes a penetrating, empathic recognition that, in *this* case, at *this* moment, with *this* patient, attending to the other requires maintaining rather than breaking silence. In such silent phases of treatment, the analyst "performs much the same function that the mother did with her infant who could not speak, but whose moods, gestures and needs were utterances that needed maternal perception."[14] Implicit in this hypothesis is not only the possibility of damaging misinterpretation (the kind of empathic failures that have presumably led the patient to treatment) but also, in the imagination of effective treatment, the assumption of a remarkable capacity for psychic attunement on the part of the analyst. The evocation of maternal presence in these post-Freudian interpretations of silence actually reintroduces an asymmetry between the

two subjects in the consulting room (wordless infant / patient; reliably present mother / analyst) that is nevertheless not a return to the much-criticized
"investigator-object" model of psychoanalysis.

Underlying what has been termed a "quiet revolution" in psychoanalytic
theory is a fundamental change in the epistemological model shaping the imagination of analytic practice, away from the ideal of acute interpretive detection
and toward an ideal of empathic sensibility.[15] The analyst's understanding is not
a penetrating power to see "inside" the patient but a power to encompass. In
Winnicott's well-known formulations of the diffuse, pervasive "holding" environment the analyst provides, the other upon whose presence the patient relies
becomes something less and something more than a companion subject. The
"patient is musing," writes Bollas (perhaps Winnicott's boldest student), "with
the analyst holding the space, the time, and the process."[16] In its most radical
articulation, the analyst's subjectivity is literally transformed into elemental life
support. Here is Michael Balint on the needs of patients who have entered what
he calls a "creative" phase of silence:

> [Their condition] presupposes an environment that accepts and consents to sustain and
> carry the patient like the earth or the water sustains and carries a man who entrusts his
> weight to them. In contrast to ordinary objects, especially to ordinary human objects,
> no action is expected from these . . . substances; yet they must be there and must—
> tacitly or explicitly—consent to be used. . . . Without water it is impossible to swim,
> without earth impossible to move. . . . The substance, the analyst, must not resist, must
> consent . . . must accept and carry the patient for a while.[17]

Balint's conflation of immersion in a sustaining environment with relationship
is unevenly upheld, however. The agency implicit in accepting and consent-
ing consists in the analytic act of understanding that what the other calls for
is an abnegation of will—not a withdrawal of presence but a release from the
responsiveness that the presence of a fellow subject seems always to demand.
Thus, he consents to or accepts a "two person relationship in which only one of
the partners matters."[18]

Balint, no less than Winnicott and Bollas, is theoretically committed to what
has come to be called an "intersubjective" view of the psychoanalytic process,
emphasizing that "all the events which lead ultimately to therapeutic changes
in the patient's mind are initiated by events . . . happening essentially *between*
two people and not inside only one of them."[19] The analyst who takes on the

sustaining power of earth and water does not dissolve into the atmosphere; rather, his protean diffusion is occasioned by the recognition that the patient is, at this moment, absolutely in need of someone that he "should in no way be obliged to take notice of, to acknowledge, or to be concerned about."[20] He needs to be left alone in the presence of another. "Emphatically, this does not mean that in these periods the analyst's role becomes negligible, or is restricted to sympathetic passivity," Balint insists, but the process does seem to require us to imagine the analyst providing precisely what the patient needs without saying or doing anything openly:

His presence is most important, not only in that he must be felt to be present but must be all the time at the right distance—neither so far that the patient might feel lost or abandoned, nor so close that the patient might feel encumbered and unfree—in fact, at a distance that corresponds to the patient's actual need; in general the analyst must know what are his patient's needs, why they are as they are, and why they fluctuate.[21]

This remarkably empathic calibration of silent mere presence (like Bollas's diffusion of "maternal care" into a holding of "space and time" for the other) presumes complete intersubjective attunement—at least on one side of this two-person relationship.

ROMANTIC SILENCE AND LYRIC MEDITATION

I want, for the moment, to defer consideration of the sympathetic acuity these theorists evoke in their interpretations of silence as a vitalizing, generative phase in psychoanalytic treatment and return to that basic paradox they all identify: the crucial presence of another, the sense that intimacy is the condition for the possibility of being alone. My proposal is that these psychoanalytic formulations help us recollect the intersubjective matrix implicitly sustaining many romantic lyric meditations that have been alternately celebrated and condemned for dwelling so exclusively on solitary self-experience. I have already mentioned the "sweet unrest" of Keats's erotic solitude, wherein the steadfastness of the self is both supported by and ever yielding to the "soft swell and fall" of the lover's breast in a silence that is not broken but rather reassuringly sustained by the wordless audibility of the other's "tender-taken breath." Insofar as Keats's "Bright Star" explicitly contrasts and prefers the pleasures of solitude in intimacy to the "lone splendor" of an invulnerably distant heavenly body, it thematizes a choice that poems like Wordsworth's "Tintern Abbey" or Coleridge's "Eolian Harp" seem to offer as halfhearted afterthoughts to meditative flight. So rigidly do we tend to differentiate solitude from sociality, the articulations of silent thought from the enunciated address to the other, that we risk missing the relational background sustaining these private meditations. Such poems do not directly concern the dynamics of intersubjectivity, but they do give voice to a form of subjective inwardness that is, paradoxically, made possible by intersubjective experience.[22] The peculiar grace of such intimacy is that the other need not be a preoccupation and hence allows for the spiritual "loitering" of silent musing.

The poem that has helped me to soften the opposition between being alone and being with another, and to reconsider the valences of romantic silence, is Coleridge's "Frost at Midnight"—a meditation that unfolds in a solitude inflected from the outset by inclusion of the silent, sleeping infant "cradled" beside the speaker.[23] In focusing on the phenomenology of meditation in this poem, I do not mean to discount recent appraisals of its important political contexts, nor am I alone in resisting the false critical dilemma such interpretations seem to pose, whereby privacy and self-reflection are necessarily viewed as an escape from social and political realities. The sense that self-involvement precludes, or seeks to evade, engagement with communal or civic life only duplicates the rigid opposition between solitude and sociality that a poem such as "Frost at Midnight" interrogates.[24] I want to draw attention to three movements in the poem. In the first movement, a dissonant note is introduced by the claim that this particular solitude—"calm indeed! So calm"—arouses and excites: it "disturbs / And vexes meditation with its strange / And extreme silentness" (8–10). What is marked as extraordinary here is precisely not silence as opposed to sound but *this* silence as compared to other more familiar, less intense experiences of silence. But what constitutes the estranging excess? What is so disquieting in this midnight calm? Thought is neither arrested nor agitated in the lines that follow. On the contrary, the self-conscious, alert but by no means anxious, reflections inspired by the film fluttering on the grate, "making it a companionable form" (19), seem to follow the mind at play.[25] The vexing of meditation does not seem opposed to spiritual idleness but rather names a liveliness only possible in the absence of anything, or anyone, calling for attention.

The boyhood recollection at the center of "Frost at Midnight" is the mirror image of this moment but not the echo of its silence. The fluttering film of ash called the "stranger" is present in each scene, but the second movement of the poem explicitly contrasts the projections of "idle thought," "transfus[ing] into all its own delights" with "fantastic playfulness" (20–25), to the earnest self-soothing of a child's brooding, expectant attention, a child "amus'd by no such curious toys" as those the "self-watching subtilizing mind" now enjoys (26, 27). The almost apostrophic "Ah me!" announcing the turn back to the oft-repeated experience memorably coalesced by the trembling film on the grate begins to specify the more familiar silence against which this midnight counts as extraordinary. Most remarkable about those late-night silences of childhood is their literal disquiet. The vague "numberless goings-on of life / Inaudible as dreams" (12–13) are attentive intensifications of silence in the present moment, quite different from the sharp ringing of the church-tower bells conjured by the child listening for "articulate sounds of things to come" in the music of his "sweet birth-place" (38, 34). The silence of childhood is broken by longings and expectations, yearnings away from the present. "Extreme silentness" by contrast inheres in the absence of clamorous desires.

The film on the grate is a portent the child, "with most believing superstitious wish" (29), takes in earnest. Its promise, summoned into tangibility by the willed recollection of those ringing bells, lulls him to sleep, prolonging the stirring, haunting, wildly pleasing dream that has already stolen his waking attention from the fluttering stranger before his eyes. Longing and expectation preoccupy him "all the following morn," yielding nothing to presence and wakefulness but disappointed anticipation: "mine eye / Fix'd with mock study on my swimming book: / Save if the door half-open'd, and I snatch'd / A hasty glance, and still my heart leapt up, / For still I hop'd to see the *stranger's* face" (41, 42–46). This brooding mind of childhood is not idle but all too busy with hopes shaped in the absence of longed-for others. Thought cannot become a toy for the preoccupied spirit, and silence is too unsettled by memory and desire to allow for the quiet excitation of meditation, the amusement of self-watching.

How appropriate then that the speaker turns from the mirror of the past and its image of anticipatory longing ever frozen by disappointment ("still my heart leapt . . . still I hop'd"), to the "Dear Babe," whose "gentle breathings heard in this dead calm" (49, 50) are the animating echo, the companionable hum of these silent musings in the present.[26] The heart that "leapt up" hopefully, expecting to see some longed-for, stubbornly absent other, now "fills . . . / With tender gladness" (53–54) at the child who is so beautifully, reassuringly present. Crucially, the audible breath "heard in this dead calm" should not be understood to interrupt the "extreme silentness" of the poem's opening. The gentle sound of the sleeping other at his side has been audible throughout. If the speaker can now attend to it as that which "fill[s] up the interspersed vacancies / And momentary pauses of the thought" (51–52), the reason is that his meditations have arrived at a more precise sense of what is so unfamiliar in this silence. The audibility of the infant's breath represents a refinement, rather than a rupture, of the speaker's initial meditations insofar as it identifies the condition for the possibility of this strange calm.[27] The compounded memories against which this silence seems so "strange and extreme" are filled with the noises of "my sweet birth-place" wishfully summoning "things to come," past and future impinging on and breaking a silence that is ultimately defined by the absence of others. "Strange and extreme," then, is the amplitude of a silence unbroken by the inner tolling of desire, the plenitude of a solitude held by the presence of another. Against the precisely determined longings that preoccupy the "presageful" mind of the child, the apparent sufficiency of the present might indeed seem to "disturb" and "vex" meditation. What is "idle Thought" to do when it feels no vacancy it needs to fill? It would seem it is free to play, to be "amus'd," and "Frost at Midnight" (in its original composition) closes with the "eagerness" of childhood excitement and arousal.

The last movement of the poem casts a final, highly reflexive projection of the "curious toys" created by "Idle thought" onto the image of the babe "stretch[ing] and flutter[ing]" from his mother's arms, reaching for novelty (84). Coleridge is habitually understood to be wishing for and pleasurably anticipating a future for his son different from his own past. The ardently willed contrasts are familiar: "Thou shalt learn far other lore, / And in far other scenes"; "I was reared . . . / pent mid cloisters dim," "but *thou*, my babe! Shalt wander like a breeze" (55–59). Coleridge's late revision of the poem settles on these imaginative wishes for the other ("therefore all seasons shall be sweet to thee"), extending them to, but also arresting them at, an indefinite future moment vaguely reminiscent of this midnight with its "silent icicles, / Quietly shining up to the quiet moon" (70, 78–79). I will cast my lot with those who prefer the 1798 version of the poem by dwelling on what the original final lines offer.[28] In recognizing those "silent icicles" of the future to be precisely "like those . . . which ere tomorrow's warmth / Have capp'd their sharp keen drops . . . / Will catch thine eye" (80–83), the speaker returns to his own midnight, "transfus[ing]" his "own delights" one last time onto the fluttering film. Immersion in the present, delight in a proximity that nevertheless leaves the subject "to that solitude which suits abstruser musings," evokes a companionable form in the child whose waking hours are play. The babe stretching from his mother's arms with a delighted "shout" of eagerness mimics the form of this generative meditation; his gesture echoes the "fluttering" the speaker turns into so many "curious toys" of thought. Rather than intruding upon the "self-enclosure of poetic imagination," the exuberant cry remains internal to the meditation; it breaks neither the silence nor the solitude but is the poem's culminating figuration of the free play of thought made possible by both. Held in his mother's arms, and therefore free to gaze and reach at what is novel and strange, the child is a fit emblem for the animating reflections of the speaker, held in the presence of his sleeping infant, and therefore free to muse in "fantastic playfulness" (25). (The child, one is tempted to suggest, becomes mother to the man.)

Certainly this generative silence—through which a vital subjectivity comes into being in the unattended presence of another—represents an idealized extreme in both romantic lyric meditation and psychoanalytic discourse. They are imaginations of authentic moments of self-experience for which the presence of another is absolutely necessary but in which there is no intersubjective tension and no thought of reciprocity. The absence of exchange or participation with the other seems, in fact, to strain the very sense of intersubjectivity, as the other seems to be present merely as an environment or playing field for the meditative subject. We typically recognize this "use" of the other as the crucial complicating feature of romantic lyric subjectivity, the problematic, symptomatic expression of an aggrandizing, illusorily autonomous ego. Dorothy stands alongside the speaker in "Tintern Abbey," but her presence is notoriously unacknowledged until the final movement of the poem, when the speaker seems not so much to address her as to project his hopes into her. Appreciation that "on the banks of this delightful stream / We stood together" seems decidedly subordinate to the exuberant celebration of the other as mirror and echo ("in thy voice I catch / The language of my former heart, and read / My former pleasures in the shooting lights / Of thy wild eyes!").[29] The touch of Sara's "soft cheek" resting on Coleridge's arm is a palpable condition for the tranquil musings of "Eolian Harp," though her presence is at once abstract and merely material. She belongs to the world that the poet gratefully possesses—"PEACE, and this COT, and THEE, heart honour'd maid"[30]—but is neither existentially distinct from the intangibly placid atmosphere nor phenomenally distinct from the solid object. I raise these famous instances not to rehearse familiar critiques of romantic subjectivity; in fact, I would argue that the way these poems make use of the other ought to expand our understanding of what intimacy can sometimes make possible and what it might sometimes entail.

Counting on the other to be there and yet not to matter: we have seen this as mystified, as objectifying, as presumptuous. But insofar as it evokes the dependencies and needs against which reciprocity can emerge as a relational ideal, such untroubled repose upon the other might compel us to take more seriously those expressions of gratitude that seem such inadequate mitigations of indulgent self-involvement. I noted earlier that we perhaps too rigorously distinguish silence from enunciated address to the other, too rigidly oppose isolation and attachment. While poems such as "Tintern Abbey" and "Frost at Midnight" seem to assume that there are moments in a relationship when only one person matters, might we not recognize their propositions as acknowledging reliance on the other, even in—perhaps even through—the indulgence of neglect? The others addressed in these poems are integral to the silent meditation, sustaining its composure and form. Apostrophic utterance in such compositions is an inward admission of the graceful fact that one is not alone—the precise opposite of the discomposing fear of finding oneself bereft of the other ("Oh mercy!" to myself I cried, / "If Lucy should be dead").[31] Such complacency—tranquil pleasure at once in someone and with oneself—*depends* on the other even as and precisely because there is no call for recognition.

I have suggested that the paradoxical intimacy Winnicott describes, where an experience of aloneness is predicated on the reliable presence of another, might allow us to look again, less suspiciously, at the relational environment supporting the silent meditations of the romantic lyric subject. The play of solitary self-reflection is not a flight from engagement but a cessation of intersubjective tension, a repose in the presence of another, an interregnum in preoccupation with the other. If that vision seems a disturbing fantasy of intimacy, presupposing and presuming upon another who "consents" to be "used," it is at least implicitly a fantasy involving both the desire and aspiration for intersubjective perfection. The one left alone to muse, to meditate, to experience the vital area of privacy dwells with another who, invaluably, does not interrupt this silence. The infant in "Frost at Midnight" is, in some ways, the best emblem of the rare exceptionality of nonimpinging intimacy. His sleep is a caesura in the attention his waking hours call for, his infancy a reminder of the simultaneously demanding and gratifying responsiveness that intimate involvement with others habitually entails. (The "father's tale" that closes "The Nightingale" reminds us, by contrast, of the sudden distress that typically interrupts a child's slumber, rousing the parent to hurry and hush and soothe.[32] It is precisely such habitual attendance that the "peaceful slumber" of "Frost at Midnight" fleetingly defers.)

In the perfect ease of intersubjective bliss ("pillowed on my fair love's ripening breast" or thrilled by the "gentle breathings" of the infant "cradled by my side"), the unintrusive yet comforting presence of the other is figured as—and can be mistaken for—the dissolution of a companionate fellow subjectivity into a mere object, abstraction, environment. I prefer to credit these poems for a self-consciousness in their use of the other, take more seriously their expressions of gratitude for the temporary reprieve or exemption from reciprocity that the other implicitly grants by remaining barely present, neither interrupting nor rebuking nor withdrawing. Gratitude here is not the condescending afterthought or inadequate substitute for a morally scrupulous respect, nor is it the first moment in a dialectic of recognition that would culminate in respect. The "strange and extreme silentness" of "Frost at Midnight" limns a suspension of the dialectical dynamic, a relaxation of the ethical drive to arrive at and sustain recognition, a pause in the tempo of intersubjective experience allowing for relational affects (appreciation, thankfulness, gratitude, humility) that exceed the logic of mutuality.

THE STRANGE INTIMACY OF AWKWARD SILENCE

The gracious silences I have been describing have their awkward counterparts, however. I now touch briefly on two romantic narratives in which silence does not hold the generative meditation of a self secure in the presence of another but instead dramatizes a mode of exchange that places two subjects in relation to one another without the achievement of shared confidence. These are examples of obtrusive intimacy, a disturbing proximity to the other that is palpable precisely to the degree that the desire and aspiration for sympathetic attunement are frustrated yet that, for this very reason, also serve as compelling representations of the intersubjective tensions and misperceptions that might ground rather than undermine the possibility of mutual recognition.

The first narrative—Wordsworth's account of his encounter with the "Discharged Soldier" in Book 4 of *The Prelude*—is one that I discussed earlier as a dramatic humbling of intersubjective expectations and a resolute dismantling of the connection between sympathy and charity that had been so central to the eighteenth-century ethical imagination. In returning to this poem, my aim is to refine the forms of intimacy distinctive of Wordsworthian encounter rather than to recapitulate the post-Enlightenment critique of sentimentalist ethical demands and presuppositions that shapes the disappointing arc of its narrative. Consider the uncomfortable silence that falls between the narrator and the soldier as they make their way toward the cottage that will lodge the traveler for the night. "Together on we passed / In silence" (480–481):[33] togetherness, at this point in the tale, only intensifies the awkwardness created by the repeated questions and stilted responses of their conversation. "Discourse had ceased" after several eager but unsatisfying efforts on the speaker's part to learn the soldier's "history," and the final silence is broken by a mildly scolding entreaty from the youth who recommends, on their parting, that the soldier henceforth "ask for timely furtherance and help / Such as his state required" (480, 491–492). Of course, for the reader, the soldier has been silent throughout. His words are, after all, withheld from us, as the speaker presents in their stead his own unspoken impressions, which are principally those of disappointment. The poem thus obliquely represents the soldier's resistance to the youth's inquiries. "Unmoved" and evidently unmoving in responding to the youth, asking no questions of his own, inviting no exchange of confidences, the soldier accepts the youth's assistance but also keeps him at a distance. Certain ambitions of the sympathetic imagination are thwarted even as the ethical obligation entailed by recognition of the other's need is fulfilled. What I now want to include in this account of the poem is its fantasy of animating the other, as if the other is not quite alive or needs to be restored to life by speaking.

Recall that the youth imagines his initial greeting as literally vitalizing the spectral stranger whose overheard utterances ("murmuring sounds, as if of pain"; "a murmuring voice of dead complaint"; "groans scarcely audible" [422, 431, 432]) are the only signs of life in the hauntingly motionless figure ("stiff in his form"; "still his form / Kept the same steadiness"; "at his feet / His shadow lay, and moved not"; "I wished to see him move, but he remained / Fixed to his place" [407, 423–424, 424–425, 429–430]). These evocative sounds of pain issuing from that petrified body combine to form the abstract impression of the stranger as "A desolation, a simplicity / That seemed akin to solitude" (418–419). So it is appropriate that, in hailing the stranger, the youth imagines a kind of resurrection: "Slowly from his resting-place / He rose" (437–438). Having made his presence known to the soldier, he has moved him to return the salutation, to show the life in him. But then his words turn out to be lifeless, as the speaker seems to encounter a dead soul. The audible "voice of dead complaint" falls silent in conversation. The stranger is "unmoved" when with "a quiet uncomplaining voice" he tells his "soldier's tale" (442–445); his "tone" is "as of one / Remembering the importance of his theme / But feeling it no longer" (475–478). Noting that "he traveled without pain," the youth now marvels at the "ghastly figure moving at my side" (466, 468), surprised by the inaudibility of the very pain that had moved him, "with a mingled sense / Of fear and sorrow" (420–421), to approach the man and ask his history. It is as if the disturbing stiffness and stillness of the stranger's body have been translated into the affectless composure the narrator (twice) names "indifference" (444, 476).

One might say that the youth's fantasy of bringing the other (back) to life, reviving him by inviting him to enter conversation, is frustrated by the soldier's reserve, but to do so would also be to simplify Wordsworth's representation of the youth's mingled surprise and disappointment at the other's failure to speak with feeling. I suggest that the initial fantasy of animating the other must also entail a fantasy about the possibility of others being dead-in-life, unreachable precisely insofar as they are unmoved to converse, affectively silent even in conversation. Certainly the disappointed expectations the poem invites us to question are registered in the soldier's failure to impress the youth as "solemn and sublime," but that almost dismissive evaluation is actually a striking characterization of what has been most consistent in the youth's experience of the stranger. The effort throughout has been precisely that of subliming and solemnizing a rather banal act of charity. The ambivalence of the initial approach and the awkwardness of the encounter are displaced by dramatic, creative misperceptions (the tall, thin man is a skeletal ghost, his muttering voice the complaint of pain, his weariness and reserve a "strange half-absence" of spirit). Appropriately, then, the only words directly attributed to the soldier describe the bare conditions of recognition that this encounter has in fact fulfilled, even as the youth has been absorbed in an elaborate evocation of the other as elusively unreachable. In reassuring the youth that "my trust is in the God of Heaven, / And in the eye of him that passes me" (494–495), the soldier blandly summarizes what the two have realized together. Words, in fact, need not be exchanged, nor confidences shared, nor sympathy achieved for the "help . . . his state required" to be proffered. This mild admonishment, the single break in the soldier's silence within the poem, prepares us to appreciate the achievement of their parting exchange.

On finally arriving at lodging for the night, the youth recalls that "the soldier touched his hat again / . . . and in a voice that seemed / To speak with a reviving

interest, / Till then unfelt, he thanked me" (498–501). The soldier voices his gratitude, and the youth returns his blessing, lingers, and turns "with quiet heart [to]
my distant home" (505). Certainly the ending of the poem is typical of Wordsworth's discomfort with the asymmetries of charity and is paradigmatic of the
strange sympathetic failings dramatized in many of the encounter poems. But
the "revival of interest" the youth now hears, or projects, into the soldier's voice
acknowledges an intimacy achieved between strangers who cannot be said to have
truly understood one another but between whom something might nevertheless be
understood to have transpired. We might say that in dwelling on his own impressions of an uncanny lifelessness about the soldier, the youth fails to attend to him,
but in so doing he also evokes him as an obtrusive, impressive presence, affectively
preoccupying precisely to the degree that he strikes the youth as "indifferent."

"Because we do not comprehend one another . . . we are therefore free to
invent one another. We change one another": Bollas would have us admit creative misperception of the other as a form of intersubjective experience rather
than a failure, a "being in touch with the other's otherness."[34] "Together on we
passed / In silence": The cessation of conversation here is surely uncomfortable;
the silence, a measure of both proximity and distance, a paradoxical intimacy.

A tale such as "The Discharged Soldier" presents a complex ethical phenomenology in which the imperative to recognize the other's need for "timely furtherance and help" also entails acknowledgment of a boundary, a point beyond
which the needy other neither invites nor welcomes an exchange of confidences.
The ostensible object lesson in such a poem redounds to the speaker as an admonishment of his empathic presumptions. To settle here, however, would be to
resolve the poetry of romantic silence into an opposed yet complementary set of
interpretive possibilities: silence as a reprieve from reciprocity; a vitalizing experience of the self in grateful repose upon the other, on the one hand; and silence
as a frustration of sympathetic striving, a disappointing failure of mutuality that
arises from intimate, awkward proximity, on the other hand. One last instance
of troubled intimacy illustrates the challenge to resolution of these matters.

Failures of sympathetic convergence that are nevertheless not failures of
attendance to others are typical of the Wordsworthian encounters. Ethics in
these poems turn on the uncomfortable absence of reciprocity, the troubling
intersubjective asymmetries of charitable action, and it is precisely here that we
might seek an intersection with the "paradoxical intimacy" conceptualized in
psychoanalysis.

"Resolution and Independence" distinguishes itself among Wordsworth's poems of encounter in explicitly presenting the narrator as its subject. Sympathetic failing is not the issue here (as it is in "The Discharged Soldier" or "The Old Cumberland Beggar") but rather receptivity to the other, a capacity to find or take or accept something from the other. The needy stranger in the poem does not appear as an occasion for charity but instead as "a something given" to the narrator, psychic balm for a disturbed state of mind.[35] This, after all, is what the poem's title retrospectively announces or proleptically claims: the narrator is changed, moved to resolution and independence through this encounter. It is almost too easy to read the poem as a tale of proto-therapeutic intervention. The narrator, a poet, is afflicted with "dim sadness," "dejection," "pain of heart" (28, 25, 35). "Fears and fancies thick upon me came," he confides, the kind of "fear that kills," he specifies (27, 113). He wonders in despair why he should expect "that others should . . . / Love him, who for himself will take no heed at all" (40–42) and openly concedes his "longing to be comforted" (117). It would seem that he is restored to graceful self-presence through the recollections, reveries, and self-mortifying insights generated in conversation with an old man working in a lonesome place. Although the success of the encounter in "giv[ing] me human strength" (112), as the narrator claims, has struck readers as troublingly, even laughably, inconsistent with the substance of the verbal exchange recorded, in many ways, the narrator's self-involved flow of association in the leech-gatherer's presence—from dreams, to former thoughts, to fantastic visions—is precisely what an analyst would hope to elicit from his patient.

Nevertheless, the impact of this encounter cannot so readily be assimilated to a therapeutic model. It would be difficult to maintain that the narrator's gloom, fear, and perplexity are decisively resolved by a meeting that might itself be only one movement in the variable succession of moods to which the mind is subject. The accidental happenstance of the meeting renders its "peculiar grace" unstable (50), vulnerable to unforeseeable, unsalutary future occurrences. Nothing in the encounter revises the poem's claim that the mind undergoes sudden, involuntary shifts in mood: "As high as we have mounted in delight / In our dejection do we sink as low" (24–25). There is no cure for the destabilizing subjection to affective highs and lows. Nor can we ignore the moralistic self-incrimination in the resolution of the speaker's mood. He is given "human strength, by apt admonishment," would "scorn" himself for infirmities he cannot see in "that decrepit man with so firm a mind" (112, 137, 138). The insight achieved here might be edifying, but it is also self-disciplining, even censorious. This is not a therapeutics of liberatory self-acceptance. And finally, that transformative flow of associations experienced in the leech-gatherer's presence is unspoken. The narrator greets the leech-gatherer, poses a question, and listens, or tries to listen. This is not a cure by talking.

I suggest that the poem's psychoanalytic substance does not lie in its ostensible narrative of mental infirmity and cure but rather in its representation of a paradoxical intimacy between strangers who cannot be said to truly come into contact with one another but between whom something might nevertheless be understood to have been communicated. The poem's insistent deflections away from dialogue to unspoken inward reflections that seem to distance the interlocutors at the very moment we would expect to hear them converse dramatize something peculiar, even peculiarly graceful, about the limits and possibilities of intimacy. How can the manifestly disappointing aspect of this encounter, in particular the narrator's distracted self-absorption, be construed as anything other than a failure of intersubjectivity? Is it possible to read the self-absorption of Wordsworth's narrator as a form of "creative misperception" that liberates a highly self-conscious imagining of the other?

Although the poem certainly invites us to see the narrator's melancholic anxiety dissipated or relieved through his chance encounter with the leech-gatherer, the salubrious turn away from the speaker's "untoward thoughts" (53) in fact occurs as soon as he glimpses the stranger, in the orderly procession of images and projections that *precede* their conversation. The "peculiar grace," the "leading from above," the "something given" that breaks the speaker's anxious ruminations is perhaps no more and no less than the mere sight of "a Man before me unawares" (50, 51, 55). The man's very heedlessness of the speaker fortuitously allows for a temporal interval between first sight and greeting that is also a propitious opening up of psychic space for the despairing poet who is suddenly hard at the creative work of figuration. The "Man before me" becomes "the oldest man . . . that ever wore gray hairs" (56); hyperbole gives way to a notoriously strange chain of similes attempting to capture, at one stroke, both the stillness of the man and the remarkable incongruity of his presence: "As a huge stone is sometimes seen to lie / . . . on the bald top of an eminence; / Wonder to all who do the same espy . . . / So that it seems a thing endued with sense: / Like a sea beast crawled forth, that on a shelf / Of rock or sand reposeth, there to sun itself" (57–63). These fantastic figurative elaborations return to their source now transformed into an uncanny phantasm: "Such seemed this Man, not all alive nor dead, / Nor all asleep" (64–65). Reanimation comes in the form of conjectural narrative as the man's "body . . . bent double" by old age inspires imagination of past suffering: "some dire constraint of pain, or rage / Of sickness felt by him in times long past, / A more than human weight upon his frame had cast" (66, 68–70).

Surely these unrestrained movements of figuration and fantasy suggest an attenuation of the "dim sadness and blind thoughts" that have darkened the poet's sunlit path. Indeed, his words of greeting to the leech-gatherer announce a change of mood: "This morning gives us promise of a glorious day" (84). Relief, or resolution, has, in some important sense, already occurred for the poet, in the auspicious occasion the man's mere presence has offered for an assertive resumption of imaginative work. This resolution occurs independently of the conversation he now initiates with the leech-gatherer and is, in some ways, undone by the failed effort to sustain dialogue with the stranger. The challenge of actually attending to the other is one the poet finds himself unable to meet: "The old Man still stood talking by my side; / But now his voice to me was like a stream / Scarce heard; nor word from word could I divide" (106–108). This heedlessness, the dissolution of the other's words, simultaneously distances the two strangers at the moment of their greatest proximity and propels a drift back into isolated inwardness. No sooner does the "whole body of the Man" dissolve into the immateriality of "one whom I had met with in a dream" than "my former thoughts returned: the fear that kills / And hope that is unwilling to be fed" (109–110, 113–114). However, they return to be reshaped—re-formed, as it were—by chastening reflection.

What gives the speaker "strength by apt admonishment" is neither wholly dependent on nor wholly independent of attention to the stranger who "still stood talking by my side" but is "scarce heard." Admonishment comes from the "whole body of the Man," not in his palpable proximity but in his *seeming* "like one whom I had met with in a dream." The leech-gatherer is distanced by the distraction that reconfigures him into an other within the speaker's psyche but is also obtrusive, impressive, bound to become a psychic preoccupation: "In my mind's eye I seemed to see him pace / About the weary moors continually / Wandering about alone and silently" (129–131).

As is typical in Wordsworth's poems of encounter, the narrator in "Resolution and Independence" oscillates unstably between three points of intersubjective orientation, two of them closely related and another entirely distinct. First, there is an ambition to know and a desire to be moved by the stranger in his presence, and, second, there is a self-conscious skepticism about those expectations. The question inspired by the poet's "longing to be comforted"—"How is it that you live and what is that you do?" (119)—elicits that infamous response about the scarcity of leeches, at once distracting from and frustrating the existential yearning for some comprehending edification. Sympathy and skepticism about sympathy give way to another form of encounter. The incommensurability between question and answer, the failure of dialogue, marks a troubled receptivity, showing us how the "mind's eye" fixes upon another who can be pursued only through the errant paths of "thoughts within myself" (129, 132).

CODA
Sitting with Strangers

The romantic forms of intimacy I have described in preceding chapters involve a deliberate frustration of the drive toward an identificatory equality and an often graceful suspension of the expectation of reciprocity. Recognition occurs even when, and sometimes precisely because, the prospect of mutuality recedes. Another makes an impression, becomes a preoccupation, without necessarily being fully known or heeded. Sympathetic aspirations are thwarted; ethical and epistemological aims are humbled. And in that clearing, other relational grounds appear, space for indeterminate and undetermined modes of attention and appreciation.

In devoting the conclusion of this study to the peculiar intimacies of psychoanalysis, I argue that contemporary reflections on this distinctively modern form of encounter involve a recuperation of eighteenth-century confidence in the efficacy of fellow feeling that coexists uneasily with efforts to account for the necessary asymmetries of affect, engagement, and disclosure within the relationship. As we saw previously, a significant body of post-Freudian theory harbors fantasies of intersubjective possibility that recapitulate the symptomatic tensions of eighteenth-century accounts of sympathy.[1] Psychoanalysts will speak confidently about the achievement of profound knowledge of other persons, of formative and transformative intimacy. Nevertheless, insofar as asymmetry is built into the very structure of the practice, psychoanalytic writing also attends to the nonreciprocal, elusive, at times estranging forms of intimacy that are characteristic of romanticism. To find these two strains within psychoanalysis involves recognizing, and distinguishing between, its genealogical debt to the sentimental psychologies of the Enlightenment and its strange inheritance of the unsettling but generative romantic eschewal of the ethical and epistemic presuppositions of sentimentalism.

THE MIRROR AND THE COUCH

The physician should be impenetrable to the patient and, like a mirror, reflect nothing but what is shown to him.

Sigmund Freud, "Recommendations for Physicians
on the Psychoanalytic Method of Treatment"

In the twentieth century the metaphor of the mirroring mind was influentially deployed by the founder of psychoanalysis to describe the profound self-knowl-edge supposed to arise through a sustained, peculiarly intimate form of rela-tion to another. An impenetrable surface reflecting the complex depths of the analysand's psyche, capturing truths otherwise invisible and unknown, Freud's mirror is meant to be one-sided. This is not, then, David Hume's famous image of sympathetic insight as a two-way glass, where the "minds of men are mirrors" to one another, though the history and the promise of that Enlightenment idea certainly belong to the genealogy of Freud's figure. In its one-sidedness, as much as in the clarity of reflection it promises, the impenetrable mirror is a condensed image for the positivistic commitment of classic Freudian analysis. The epistemic structure it assumes is one in which the analysand comes to be known as an ob-ject of the analyst's observation while the analyst never makes himself known to the patient as another, fellow subject. The analyst remains physically, figuratively, affectively out of the patient's sight, and the mirror thus conjured in the analytic space—conjured precisely by the analyst's remaining out of sight—eventually becomes the patient's unavoidable means to self-knowledge or, let us say, insight.

The material conditions for the emergence of the figurative one-way mirror are established in Freud's stipulations about the analytic space. In particular, the requirement that the patient "recline upon a sofa, while one sits behind him out of sight" makes it impossible for the analytic mirror to reflect anything except the sound of the voice met by the silence of an invisible presence in the room.[2] Freud's avowedly "personal motive"—"I cannot bear to be gazed at for eight hours a day or more" (*FR*, 354)—is supplemented but not altogether superseded by a theoretical rationale. Conceding that patients usually find the position as-signed them a "hardship," Freud nonetheless insists that "the intention and re-sult of it" are that "all imperceptible influence on the patient's associations" is thereby avoided (*FR*, 354). "Since, while I listen, I resign myself to the control of my unconscious thoughts," he writes, "I do not wish my expression to give to the patient indications which he may interpret or which may influence him in his communications" (*FR*, 354). "I do not wish" in this context means both that I do not want to be seen as I listen and that it is best for the patient not to see my response. Physical withdrawal from the patient's sight, like the emotional detachment Freud also prescribes, is intended to liberate the patient's thoughts and feelings by "isolating" him—by keeping him from reacting and responding to impressions of the analyst, ensuring that his is the only face reflected in the mirror. This assumes not only that thoughts and feelings uttered without regard for the other in the room are more revealing than whatever the patient might say to the analyst's face but also that keeping out of sight ensures an affectively neutral environment allowing for important temporal displacements—a kind of vacuous present to be filled by affects transferred from the patient's past. Nevertheless, Freud's demurral from pressing this theoretical rationale is itself uncharacteristic. Noting that "many analysts work in a different way" (most commonly sitting face-to-face with the patient), he admits that "I do not know whether the main motive of their departure is the ambition to work in a different way or an advantage which they gain thereby" (*FR*, 354–355). Although commitment to the couch—and with it commitment to sitting out of the patient's sight—remains a widespread psychoanalytic technique, it is remarkable how undertheorized the practice remains.[3] This is a point to which we will return; for the moment let us pause on Freud's admission of the "strain" of prolonged attention and extended exposure to the eyes of others. More than personal preferences, these are important acknowledgments of the awkward and unique discomforts of the intimate analytic situation for the analyst.

Apart from the theoretical justifications Freud offers, the consideration of the analyst's own needs and limitations in tolerating his exposure to patient after patient must also be seen as shaping the central—and still largely unquestioned—demand that the analyst remain affectively neutral. In one of Freud's most famous formulations of this tenet of classical practice, he writes: "I cannot recommend my colleagues emphatically enough to take as a model in psychoanalytic treatment the surgeon who puts aside all his own feelings, including that of human sympathy [*menschliches Mitleid*], and concentrates his mind on one single purpose, that of performing the operation as skillfully as possible."[4] Several questions come begging: How is sympathy different from (even opposed to) the unconscious attunement that Freud imagines the analyst to be capable of? (We might recall here Rousseau's figures of dispassionate penetration, such as the lawgiver of the *Social Contract* who "beholds all the passions of men without feeling any of them.") Isn't the analytic enterprise as a whole, the ambition and ideal of knowing another more deeply than he knows himself, at least partially premised on the possibilities of sympathy? "The justification for this coldness of feeling in the analyst," Freud explains, "is that it is the condition which brings the greatest advantage to both persons involved, ensuring a needful protection for the physician's emotional life and the greatest measure of aid for the patient" (*R*, 327–328). "The physician should be impenetrable to the patient," not only for the patient's own good but also as a way to keep an ever-shifting array of thoughts and feelings out of view, to "protect" the analyst's privacy in the midst of the other's revelations. It is tempting to say that Freud enjoins the analyst to appear other than he is: cool instead of sympathetic, aloof when perhaps frustrated by the patient's silence, withholding even though tempted to reveal himself. Ideally, for Freud, the analyst's training—his "psychoanalytic purification" (*R*, 328)—will enable him actually to be cool, aloof, withholding. But Freud's "Recommendations" also implicitly acknowledges the persistence of conflicting feelings beneath the impenetrable surface of neutrality. The potentially intolerable "strain" of successive, intensely intimate encounters attested to by the professed "personal" aversion to being continually "gazed at" by others contends with the ever-present temptation to meet the "demand" for intimacy that any sharing of confidence seems to make.

The couch on which the patient lies, exposed to the analyst who remains out of view, is a potent symbol of the strange distance separating theoretical acknowledgment of the subjectivity of the analyst—as a thinking, feeling presence in the room with the patient—from the practical implications of that acknowledgment. Given that contemporary discussions of the analytic relationship (and of countertransference in particular) emphasize the "mutual," "interpersonal," "reciprocal," and even "intimate" aspects of the process, it is at the very least surprising to find scant and often confused discussion—theoretical or clinical—of the physical position of the analytic partners.[5] Let me offer two recent reflections on the use of the couch that seem to lead in diametrically opposed directions.

Lewis Aron, a self-identified "relational" analyst, offers his typical introduction of the couch as an example of how "negotiation" and "mutuality" might be facilitated in the analytic setting. His reasons, like Freud's, are admittedly first and foremost personal: "I might say something like this," he reports: "I have a personal preference for the couch because it is easier for me to listen to you and to let myself relax and try to tune into what you are saying when I don't have the pressure of being looked at."[6] As with Freud, Aron's personal preference candidly forestalls justification on other grounds. More surprising is the admission that follows: "There have been times," Aron concedes,

> when patients have told me how isolated they have felt on the couch, and I told them that I found the couch to be a deprivation as well, since I missed not seeing them in the usual manner and had given up a more social position in relation to them. Patients have been quite surprised to learn not only that I might miss them, but that I have mixed reactions to the couch. Patients often assume that the analyst is free of conflict and ambivalence, and, while this fantasy needs to be analyzed rather than corrected . . . I believe that the usual anonymity and lack of personal reactions lend themselves to a notion that it is only the patient who has conflict. I do not see how this denial can be analyzed effectively if analysts collude with patients in conveying that they are conflict free. (142)

Aron's theoretical commitment to interaction and disclosure not only allows but actually requires that the analyst appear as a *particular* person to the patient, someone with preferences, reactions, conflicts even if these are neither openly expressed nor specified. For this clinical example to work in the service of that point, I suppose we must imagine that the patient's feeling of isolation on the couch is adequately addressed, perhaps even diminishes, with the revelation that the analyst also "misses not seeing them in the usual manner" and is thereby giving something up for the other rather than refusing to give something over. While Aron remains focused on the theme of heightening mutuality in analysis and creating the conditions for mutual recognition, he misses (considering) one obvious way to redress the "usual anonymity" of the analyst hidden out of sight. Surely the back and forth of the gaze might open up the very possibilities for "mutual disclosure" Aron is interested in; surely it is strange that the possibility that the couch itself might work against mutuality and recognition is ignored.

In fact, one of the most sustained contemporary defenses of the couch emphasizes a need for "privacy" in the analytic setting that seems to run counter to Aron's hope for "heightened mutual recognition." For Thomas Ogden, among the most innovative theorists of countertransference, the "structure of the analytic setting" is designed not only to facilitate the patient's free associations but also to render the analyst "as unconsciously receptive as possible."[7] Ogden does not take Freud's admission that "I cannot bear to be gazed at" as simply "personal idiosyncrasy" but as a recognition of the "privacy that [the analyst] requires to do his work" (113). The analyst's position behind the couch and out of sight helps "provide conditions of privacy in which the analyst might enter a state of reverie," he writes, just as "the analysand in using the couch . . . experience[s] similar respite from being stared at and might more easily give himself over to the drift of his own unconscious thoughts" (113).[8] For Ogden, the enjoyment of privacy, more than, or perhaps rather than, the feeling of being known and recognized, is what sets the analytic relationship apart from others. "Personal isolation" is protection against "the continuous strain that is an inescapable part of living in the unpredictable matrix of human object relations," he argues (122). If, for Aron, use of the couch offers an opportunity to disclose mutual feelings ("I told them that I found the couch to be a deprivation *as well*"), and if, for Ogden, use of the couch ensures that the analytic setting affords a "place of privacy" (128) for both analyst and patient, then these contrary implications crystallize that tension in post-Freudian writing between theoretical emphasis on affective attunement, on the one hand, and a competing conviction about the value of psychic privacy, on the other.[9] Jessica Benjamin at times maintains that the "analytic interaction" takes place face-to-face, involving "mutual gazing, gesturing, and vocalizing," and, at other times, invokes the couch as, metaphorically at least, a vehicle for the patient's experience of being "at once known and yet left alone."[10] Is the psychoanalytic relationship a space in which to discover and explore the possibilities of intimacy and recognition or a space in which the intimacy of being alone together affirms the essential solitude of the self?

THE FACE AND THE TELEPHONE: COUNTERTRANSFERENCE AND RECEPTIVITY

D. W. Winnicott reimagines Freud's mirror when he describes the analytic process as "a long term giving the patient back what the patient brings . . . a complex derivative of the face that reflects what is there to be seen."[11] The delicate awakening of what Winnicott calls a "sense of self" in analysis, as in every formative relationship, involves being "observed and mirrored back by someone who is trusted and who justifies the trust and meets the dependence."[12] Literalizing Freud's metaphor by making explicit that the mirror is a human face, Winnicott also turns its implications toward a generative form of communication, though still one that need not involve reciprocity.

Winnicott's analytic mirror hangs on two terms that establish the ethical and existential bases of the relationship between analysand and analyst: a "trust" counted on and justified and in that way established, and an unwilled "dependence." The terms call forth the earliest conditions of human relating as Winnicott understands them, even as they subtly evoke a different sense of what *happens* between patient and doctor than what is suggested by Freud's mirror of analytic insight. The Winnicottian analyst observes, to be sure. And in "reflect[ing] what is there to be seen," he seems to do no more than the Freudian analyst who "reflects back nothing but what is shown him." It is just that in meeting an "impenetrable" surface, the Freudian patient would seem to be alone with an object. The patient will *want* to trust and depend upon that object, and, of course, it is precisely upon that yearning demand of the transference that the therapeutic action of Freudian analysis works. What Winnicott adds to this picture is the idea that the patient must have a glimpse of the analyst as another subject, as one with whom exchange is possible, one who "gives back" what he receives.

Yet, practically speaking, in a typical session both the Freudian and the Winnicottian analysts are equally likely to remain silent and sit out of sight. What Winnicott and other theorists of a relational model press upon us is a new vision of the analyst as one who can never, must never, "put aside all his own feelings," including pity, compassion, and sympathy. Among the many post-Freudian revisions of psychoanalytic principles and practices, perhaps no concept has undergone as radical a transvaluation in recent decades as countertransference. The stray thoughts and feelings evoked in the analyst by his patient that were once regarded as an intrusive, potentially harmful failure of analytic technique, a dangerous breach of neutrality, are now more commonly viewed as a vital source of insight, a "new royal road to the unconscious," as a recent review of the literature suggests.[13] Freud, in whose writings the term rarely appears, defined "countertransference" as a damaging interference within a psychoanalytic treatment, a breakdown in detachment and neutrality, something that needs to be "kept in check" and that the analyst's own analysis ought to help him control. But "the theoretical step taken by psychoanalytic thought subsequent to Freud," observes Benjamin, takes countertransference to be an important analytic tool; the "analyst's countertransference recognition—empathy, attunement, and identification with the patient—[is seen] as decisive for change as . . . interpretation of unconscious processes."[14]

From a post-Freudian perspective, the analyst's silence itself involves a wide range of affective responses to the patient, the setting, and the treatment—including misgivings about that delicate attunement to the other upon which the treatment depends. Hans Loewald, for example, marvels at the "vast range of communicative interaction" in a clinical encounter (noting, without comment, that it "excludes only the visual eye-to-eye contact and grasp of facial expression"), but he then goes on to report his own dissatisfaction with a session conducted over the telephone.[15] The "funnelling of communication exclusively through voice and ear" strikes Loewald as impoverished, "although we are apt to think that this is what more or less happens in every analytic hour." "What was lacking was personal presence," he suggests, "the simple being together in the same room, whether visible or not."[16] What is striking here is the absence of reflection about the exclusion of "visual eye-to-eye contact," given Loewald's sensitivity to the power of physical presence. One might also wonder if the telephone session felt so different to the patient, who, after all, typically experiences the analyst's presence through the ear—precisely as silence occasionally broken by voice.

It cannot, in any case, be entirely accidental that Loewald uses Freud's most famous figure for the analyst's unconscious attunement to reflect on its potential failures and disruptions. The analyst, Freud writes, "has simply to listen and not trouble to keep anything in mind" (*R*, 325). In so doing, he "bend[s] his own unconscious like a receptive organ towards the emerging unconscious of the patient, as the receiver of the telephone to the disc. As the receiver transmutes the electric vibrations induced by the sound-waves back again into sound-waves, so is the physician's mind able to reconstruct the patient's unconscious" (*R*, 328). Freud's telephone evokes the marvel of that then-new technology to bring distant subjects into intimate communication. It is a figure that Christopher Bollas (unlike Loewald) repeatedly returns to in his descriptions of "unconscious communication." Bollas retains Freud's original emphasis on wonder by invoking pretechnological, quasi-supernatural figures of receptivity. The analyst is a "medium for the psychosomatic processing of the patient"; the dynamic between the analyst's silent, hovering attention and the analysand's free associations generates "a kind of spiritual communication" initiated "when we are receptive to the intelligent breeze of the other who moves through us."[17] The rhetoric appropriately and not accidentally hearkens back to romantic and sentimental figures of sympathetic response such as Hume's famous image of emotional diffusion and contagion: "As in strings equally wound up, the motion of one communicates itself to the rest; so all the affections readily pass from one person to another, and beget correspondent movements in every human creature." At the same time, as Bollas is well aware, to speak of our receptivity to one another as a "spiritual" capacity is to risk the charge of sentimental mystification.

The philosopher and analyst Jonathan Lear proposes a conceptual frame-work for the unbounded intersubjective accessibility implicit in Bollas's notion of "spiritual communication." Lear writes that "throughout philosophical an-thropology there runs the axiom that the possibility of interpreting others—as thinking, saying, doing anything—depends on interpreting them as being, more or less, like us. This 'principle of humanity' is *a priori* and non-optional: without it, an interpretation cannot get off the ground."[18] While this formulation cer-tainly draws on Freud's insistence that such identification is the "*sine qua non* of understanding," Lear's rhetoric evokes more abstract, but no less uncompromis-ing, assumptions about the possibilities of intersubjective recognition, notably those underlying the notion of respect in Kant (though it is feeling rather than reason that seems to be the universal underlying structure for the later writer).[19] In Loewald, an important psychoanalytic influence on Lear, "the essence" of analytic neutrality becomes a compound of "love and respect," emphasizing the affective involvement entailed by empathic identification. "Our object . . . is the other in ourselves and ourself in the other," he writes in a formulation that places the identifying analyst at the center of the practice, and thus "in our best moments of dispassionate and objective analyzing we love our object, the patient, more than at any other time, and are compassionate with his whole being."[20]

Jessica Benjamin usefully warns that a model of the analyst as "the one who empathically understands, who is emotionally attuned to me," threatens to "evoke longings for unattainable fulfillment" by inspiring the hope of being totally un-derstood by another. She suggests that "the same kind of idealization that crept into Freud's original formulations of the neutral, interpreting analyst might be embedded in formulations of the analyst's role as tender of the intersubjec-tive."[21] Benjamin is principally concerned with analyzing the desire to be fully known as an "erotics of transference," which, like the more familiar "passion of falling in love with the analyst," involves a "romantic fantasy" of intersubjectiv-ity. "At once known and yet left alone," the patient seems to be "floating in the reflection of the other's knowledge, which need not be distinguished from the self's knowledge."[22] In the strange coexistence of this ideal of unfettered "spiri-tual communication" with a seemingly opposed theoretical conviction in a vital area of privacy that places the "other ultimately beyond knowing,"[23] we might recognize an inheritance of, or return to, that eighteenth-century impasse be-tween confident claims of feeling for and akin to others and anxious doubts about our knowledge of others.

The evolving discourse on countertransference suggests rigid oppositions between sociality and solitude, between vitalizing sympathy and impregnable interiority, between remarkable claims for empathic access and insistence on an irreducibly private core of the self. Nevertheless, the most sophisticated explorations of the intersubjective dynamic in psychoanalysis contain both these possibilities without assuming them to be absolutely opposed or attempting a facile reconciliation between them. And it is within those complex accounts that I would locate a romanticist strain in contemporary analytic thought. If, as Bollas would have it, the "indisputable fact" that "the other is ultimately beyond knowing" is realized through deep exchange and exposure to the other ("spiritual communication"), then intimacy is something more and something less than mutual understanding and shared confidences. Admission of limitation and insuperable distance between subjects seems as theoretically crucial to the imagination of analytic intimacy as sympathetic attunement.

Even as Loewald relies on "deep mutual empathy" in the analytic process, imagining a profound and loving recognition of the "other in ourselves and ourself in the other," he argues that a successful treatment necessarily entails renunciation of these very possibilities. "The resolution of the transference at the termination of analysis," he writes, "includes the recognition of the limited nature of any human relationship."[24] Analytic practice seems to call for a quasi-telepathic understanding of the other but also to aim at an acknowledgment that such intersubjective perfection is illusory. Bollas brings these seemingly contradictory possibilities together when he writes that psychoanalysis entails "a deep mutual involvement in a process that deconstructs relational possibilities just as it joins two subjectivities in separate worlds of thought."[25] Subjectivities are joined, but worlds of thought are separate. Involvement is mutual, but the possibilities of relationship are unraveled. What might this look like in practice?

BREAKING SILENCE

Some of the boldest expositions of analytic intimacy explore frustration, boredom, sadness, and even hatred as affective responses indicating the success, rather than the breakdown, of "unconscious communication" between analytic partners. The increasing theoretical centrality of countertransference is often reflected in the writing of psychoanalytic reports in which narrative trajectory is driven by the analyst's record of experience and response.[26] I touch briefly on one case history in which the tension between remarkable claims of empathic power on the part of the analyst and the acknowledgment of the existential fact of relational failure and disappointment are foregrounded.

Nina Coltart's essay "Slouching towards Bethlehem" (1986) has achieved a kind of mild notoriety in analytic circles as the piece in which the analyst screams at her patient. The work is an intriguingly candid account of her effort to treat a patient through a long period of deliberate silence and is distinctive in clinical literature of this kind for eschewing a conceptual preface or frame. One does not know, as one embarks on the narrative, what theory (of transference, resistance, regression) the case will illustrate. In the second year of her work with this patient, Coltart reports that "he suddenly ground to a halt, and fell violently silent, exuding ever stronger black waves of hatred and despair."[27] Coltart will ultimately interpret this sudden violation of the therapeutic alliance as the patient's effort to re-create earlier trauma by evoking hatred and despair felt with and toward one whose presence is otherwise inescapable. But her account of the case dwells on the long phase prior to that interpretive surmise. "Technical maneuvers that I had learned over the years for approaching and entering silence [proved] to no avail," she reports, leaving her repeatedly and increasingly vulnerable to his silence.

> He never failed to attend. . . . He slouched and humped himself grimly and disjointedly up and down my stairs and in and out of my room. His gaze, when he glanced at me, was shifty, evil, and terrified. . . . When I spoke about what I saw and felt, he glowered, grunted and sank further into an ungainly heap. . . . I carried dark and heavy projective identifications, to put it one way, which I tried in vain to decode to him, until I was almost as saturated in despair as he was. (9–10)

The Kleinian term "projective identification," the theoretical key to Coltart's diagnosis, appears late and almost as an aside ("to put it one way") in an account that remains focused on emotionally charged sense perceptions. The patient trudges heavily up "my stairs and in and out of my room": possessive pronouns remind us that we are following the responses of the analyst as shaped by the patient's occupation of her physical and psychic space.

To speak "about what I saw and felt" in this context is to attempt to articulate the space between herself and the other by reminding them both of the distance words are intended to traverse. Coltart's speech is an ineffectual effort to restore distance, to break the oppressive affective proximity generated by his silence. The patient's refusal to speak, in this case, seems paradoxically an imposition of intimacy, an insistence that the analyst feel the encumbrance of his presence, which is only intensified by her effort to introduce words between them. The "glowering," "grunting" and "[sinking] further" her words elicit are not, after all, failures to respond. The climactic admission, "I was almost as saturated in despair as he was," speaks precisely to the odd notion that sympathetic perception might simultaneously involve "an act of unconscious evocation that parts the subjects and announces the solitude of the self" and "an act of intelligent comprehension" (*BC*, 45). The analyst's apprehension of the other's despair includes and coexists with an isolating immersion in her own despair. The silence between them generates an estranging intimacy, a highly attentive sensitivity to the other that relates but does not join the subjects in a reassuring mutuality of feeling.

The dramatic climax of Coltart's account eludes theorization. Certainly the spontaneous rupture that breaks the relational impasse between herself and the patient cannot be termed a "technical maneuver" for handling silence. The analyst's sudden outburst seems a violation of both Freudian and post-Freudian principles of technique (neither a resolute insistence on the transference nor a deliberate calibration of nonintrusive silence). "One day, without really thinking it out clearly," she reports, "I simply and suddenly became furious and bawled him out for his prolonged lethal attack on me, and on the analysis. I wasn't going to stand for it a second longer, I shouted, without the remotest idea at the moment of what I was proposing!" (10). Proceeding not so much to explain as to elaborate on the thoughtlessness of this moment, Coltart recalls: "I had given up trying to 'understand' this patient, given up theorizing and just sat there . . . attending only with an empty mind to him and the unknowable truth of himself . . . until such a moment as I was so at one with it that I knew it for the murderous hatred it was, and had to make a jump for freedom—his as well as mine, though I did not think that out at the time" (10). The claim of empathic attunement here ("I was so at one with it," where "it" refers both to the "unknowable truth" of the other and ultimately to the aversive recognition of that unknowability as "murderous hatred") is framed and qualified by the analyst's initial renunciation of that very possibility ("I had given up trying to 'understand'"). Who, or what, has been comprehended here? "The word 'counter' . . . establishes the fact of the separateness of the analyst from that which he is . . . empathizing with," observes Masud Khan; "any blurring of boundaries in this context leads merely to a clinical confusion of psychic realities."[28] I take it that this confusion is marked when Coltart accuses the patient of a "lethal attack against me and the analysis," given that her violent utterance of the charge is a wild deviation from analytic decorum and itself possibly lethal to the analysis.

Coltart eschews the distinction between spontaneous emotional response and analytic technique in her work with the silent patient: "I was pushed by introjected and/or subjective frustration . . . into a display of affect . . . consistent with the content of what I was interpreting." Introjected and/or subjective (his feelings or mine?): Coltart's narrative admits the confused interfusion of these possibilities because it dwells on the phenomenological present of the encounter. The case is not retrospectively structured by analytic resolution and interpretation; rather, what the case illustrates is a breakdown in the asymmetry between analytic partners that has been so persistently presumed in psychoanalytic theories from Freud onward, including those whose rhetoric is inflected with the idealizing intersubjective egalitarianism of finding "oneself in the other and the other in oneself."

A later essay, "The Silent Patient" (1991), dwells precisely on the overturning of analytic expectations, the intellectual and affective confusion created when the other offers no words to work with:

First . . . we have to face the fact of silence itself . . . a strange and unwelcome shock. . . . One's training . . . goes out the window. We have no words from the patient, and can think of none of our own. . . . What is this? Not what we were led to expect. Where is the chatty, desperate, seemingly open patient . . . ? Instead of searching sensitively for an opening in the patient's material . . . we are presented with almost endless openings, with . . . nothing in-between! So the whole question of the timing of what we say becomes . . . more, not less, urgent. . . . Do we open the next session? Do we say something after half an hour? At the end? Or not till next week? What is our countertransference telling us? Do we feel amazed, anxious, interested, peaceful, or irritable?[29]

The "strange and unwelcome shock" of being faced with silence is set apart from the reflections Coltart categorizes as "countertransference" because the introduction of the theoretical term would misrepresent the leveling proximity of the encounter. Professional training has "gone out the window"; there is no "material" for the analyst to work with. The intersubjective space created by the analytic compact has dissolved, leaving "nothing in-between" the two subjects but the uncomfortable intimacy of awkward silence. Under the guise of exploring "technical questions" about clinical approaches to such patients, Coltart effectively undermines the distinction between the analytic partners. No finely honed empathic insight allows for confident interpretation. The other's silence frustrates the aspiration toward perfect attunement (the sensitive search for "an opening" to the other), compels recognition that intimacy involves discovery of the other's elusiveness ("almost endless openings"). Yet ironically, appropriately, the acknowledgment of a desperate sense of intersubjective ignorance ("what is this?") emerges as possible ground for identification with the patient—the critical insight that the "analyst's own silence . . . occasionally may feel persecutory to the patient" (88).

The impulsive, hostile outburst Coltart describes in "Slouching towards Bethlehem" as a "jump for freedom" loosens the intimate clutch of the other's silence but does not drive the analyst and her patient into a "hopeless remove" from one another. In subsequent sessions, she reports that "we came to see how much, to his own surprise and horror, this man had needed to live out, and have experienced and endured by another person without retaliation, his primary hatred of a genuinely powerful mother" (10). Details of the patient's history follow, but what deserves notice is Coltart's use of the first-person plural to convey the analytic resolution: what "we came to see" suggests understanding arrived at by two persons, not through the attunement of dialogue but through the estrangement of being "together in silence."

. . .

The "spiritual communication" Bollas evokes, that receptivity to the "intelligent breeze of the other," is not an overcoming of separateness but an intimate, shared experience of separateness. The practice of maintaining a silent, neutral demeanor before the patient is, according to Bollas, "a representation of the essential feature of all human relations: that the other is beyond hearing and knowing." Psychoanalysis is then "a place" set apart "for the experiencing of essential aloneness" but is not, for that very reason, essentially different from all other relational experience. Solitude felt in the presence of the other is somehow constitutive of intimacy. The work of analysis unfolds in the "profound but deeply generative aloneness of the psychoanalyst [and] his patient," writes Bollas, affirming the existential fact that "in our true self we are essentially alone."[30] At the same time, these assertions of insuperable isolation are not meant to "serve a rhetoric of despair" representing us as "hopelessly removed from one another" (*BC*, 186).

Mutual involvement in the deconstruction of mutuality: It is not that the psychoanalytic relationship (or any other) oscillates between moments of intersubjective attunement and moments of incommunicable privacy. Intimacy with and estrangement from the other are simultaneously realized conditions. The paradoxical intimacy of psychoanalysis turns out to be paradigmatic of an "extraordinary paradox" in intersubjective experience as such for Bollas: "Because we do not comprehend one another (especially in the discreet, momentous conveying of the contents of our inner world) we are therefore free to invent one another. We change one another. We create and recreate, form and break our senses or understandings of one another, secured from anxiety or despair by the illusion of understanding and yet freed by its impossibility to imagine one another." "Creative misperception" in this account is a form of "perceptive understanding" of the other (*BC*, 186, 190). Forsaking confidence in sympathetic apprehension of the other, this approach challenges the ideal of reciprocity implicit in the equivalences and identifications between subjects presupposed by sympathy in order to affirm rather than undermine the generative force of intimate experience.

THE AESTHETICS OF INTIMACY

It has been my argument that romantic-era texts engage with and challenge the aims and presuppositions of philosophical inquiries and treatises by reshaping ideas of sympathy, passion, and fellow feeling in lyrical and narrative forms that involve an immersion in the phenomenological dynamics of intimacy. I have suggested that these transformations are liable to be lost if their aesthetic qualities are subsumed within—and implicitly subordinated to—the explanatory categories and frameworks of contemporary sciences of the mind. Wordsworthian encounter, Austenian sociability, Coleridgean meditation all may be adduced in relation to findings in contemporary theories of mind reading, mirror neurons, facial recognition, and the basic emotions, but such a procedure will inevitably gloss over deviant specificities that not only do not correspond to those findings but also, in their very noncorrespondence, constitute an alternative mode of inquiry. In the meticulous rendering of instances, the dilation of particular moments, the admission of emotional vicissitude and unsettling thoughts, romantic-era literature at once affirms the generative psychic force of intimacy and refuses to abstract that force into a law or theory of relational experience. What I mean by this might perhaps be conveyed by a final example of the irreducibly particular forms of intimacy that come into view under aesthetic scrutiny.

. . .

Marina Abramović's 2010 performance "The Artist Is Present" at New York's Museum of Modern Art involved a sustained series of silent encounters with strangers. At the center of the museum's atrium, the artist sat for seventy-five days as a stream of visitors waited their turn to occupy the seat opposite her and to stay for as long as they remained motionless, wordlessly meeting her gaze.

The structure of these encounters can be described only as asymmetrical. The artist is one; the visitors are many (1,545 during the two and a half months of the performance). The artist is "known" to the visitors (as creator of this piece and of the large body of work on display in the galleries above the atrium); the visitors are strangers to the artist. The artist undergoes the strain of the duration of the performance, hour after hour, day after day; the visitors tolerate the frustration and anticipation generated by long lines and the uncertainty of being summoned to that seat.[31] But embedded within that asymmetrical structure is the ostensibly leveling austerity of face-to-face proximity, of mutual gazes held in silence. Moreover, the spectators, some waiting their turn to sit but many simply there to watch the mutual gazers, might also be understood to have participated in creating the piece, constituting by their very presence the aesthetic form of the work. "The Artist Is Present" becomes performance art by virtue of creating, summoning, and receiving its audience.

Marina Abramović, "The Artist Is Present." Museum of Modern Art, New York, NY, 2010. Photograph by David Balliano, in Marco Anelli, *Portraits in the Presence of Marina Abramović* (Bologna, Italy: Damiani, 2012).

Marina Abramović, "The Artist Is Present." Museum of Modern Art, New York, NY, 2010. Photograph by Marco Anelli in *Portraits in the Presence of Marina Abramović* (Bologna, Italy: Damiani, 2012).

In sitting with the artist, each visitor also sat for a portrait, and the collection of these photographs, posted daily and building cumulatively into a remarkable gallery of highly differentiated facial expressions, at the time and in retrospect may be understood as a documentary record of the performance, a collaboration in the artwork, a separate artistic project.[32] The photographs capture the affective portrait of the sitter drawn (out) by the artist and, at the same time, document the co-creation of the piece: the artist is made present by all those who sat with her.

I want to draw attention to the conjunction between the irreducible particularity of emotional expression recorded in the 1,545 portraits and the remarkable consistency of sitters' reports of their experience, which attest, almost

Thumbnail portraits of sitters. Photograph by Marco Anelli, in *Portraits in the Presence of Marina Abramović* (Bologna, Italy: Damiani, 2012).

unanimously, to a paradoxical, powerful dynamic between communication, self-reflection, affective impact, and projection. "I sit for 28 minutes with Marina and in this time, the whole flux of the pain and beauty of my life thus far passes through me," writes one; "the flux of the experience of life flows between us quite smoothly."[33] "I felt I got something from her. I felt there was an actual moment of connection. I felt we communicated for a split second. Whether or not what I felt was something real or not, I'm not sure," writes another.[34] Such avowals of the emotional intensity of the experience—"I was overwhelmed by such an effusion of feelings with each moment that passed"—do not preclude candid reflection on the uncomfortable coincidence of attention to another and the inward drift of thoughts and feelings: "The act of participating became deeply self-reflective [because] staring constantly at someone whom you do not know without the interceding act of speech ... is uncomfortable and awkward."[35] "Everything you feel is your own," one sitter reported. "It's not really because of her, but facilitated by her. She provides something like a mirror, a moment to reflect and be introspective about your life."[36] Abramović herself, in a postperformance interview, described the encounters as generative occasions for self-experience: "Very soon, while you're having this gaze and looking at me, you start having this invert and you start looking at yourself. So I am just a trigger, I am just a mirror and actually they become aware of their own life, of their own vulnerability."[37] Perhaps most saliently, in relation to the intimacies explored in this book, is the sense in which introspection may take the form of preoccupying reflection on the limits and possibilities of experience with others. "The overwhelming feeling I had was that you think you can understand a person just by looking at them," concluded one visitor, "but when you look at them over a long period of time, you understand how impossible that is."[38] Yet that understanding arises only in exposure to another.

In the terms of this study, the conceptual and experimental shape of "The Artist Is Present" not only presupposes the affective impact of mere proximity to another; it also so restricts the form of that proximity as to evoke and yoke together two seemingly opposed meanings of intimacy. The attention and close engagement with another that we call intimate cannot but coexist with private, perhaps incommunicable feelings that nevertheless depend on and are elicited by the virtually constant presence of others in our lives.

NOTES

1. The vexed relationship between the terms "sympathy" and "empathy" has been the subject of numerous discussions. As is well known, the contemporary English word "empathy" is a twentieth-century translation of the German neologism *Einfühlung* (used first by art historian Robert Vischer in 1873) and has come to designate the capacity by which we enter into and understand the thoughts and feelings of another person. Eighteenth- and nineteenth-century English usage of the term "sympathy" certainly includes this sense of identification of another, along with connotations of pity and compassion. The possibility of distinguishing empathy from pity, the interdependence of these concepts, and their frequent conflation are precisely what makes the intellectual history of the term "sympathy" so complex. In the context of the history of psychoanalysis, the current ubiquity of "empathy" (and the relative absence of "sympathy") in theoretical accounts of analytic practice is singularly ironic given James Strachey's avoidance of the term in his translations of Sigmund Freud. Strachey renders *Einfühlung* variously as "sympathetic understanding," "have the feelings of," "feel his way into," and "feel our way into" (George W. Pigman, "Freud and the History of Empathy," *International Journal of Psychoanalysis* 76 [1995]: 244–246). Looking back to eighteenth-century usage of sympathy, one psychoanalyst notes that "our loss of [this] meaning ['picking up the feelings of others'] leaves us floundering in a welter of technical terms," including intersubjectivity, projective identification, mirroring, "none of which is fit to fulfill the elementary and general role" of sympathy (David M. Black, "Sympathy Reconfigured: Some Reflections on Sympathy, Empathy and the Discovery of Values," *International Journal of Psychoanalysis* 85 [2004]: 582). The points of coherence and divergence between sentimental, romantic, and psychoanalytic imaginations of "feeling for others" receive sustained attention in Chapter 5 and the Coda. I use the term "sympathy" because the implications and contradictions of its varied usages are at issue throughout this study.

2. Although her argument is aimed at describing different forms of collectivity, Lauren Berlant's effort to define intimacy against the predictable or normalizing narratives associated with sentiment shares, with this account, an interest in "encounters . . . which might take place on the street . . . or in fantasy . . . but rarely register as anything but residue" in accounts of modern sociability. I attend to what Berlant calls the "minor intimacies" that "generate an aesthetic of attachment" without any "inevitable forms or feelings attached to it." "Intimacy: A Special Issue," *Critical Inquiry* 24 (Winter 1998): 281, 283, 285.

3. Frances Ferguson, *Solitude and the Sublime: Romanticism and the Aesthetics of Individuation* (New York: Routledge, 1992); Marshall Brown, *Preromanticism* (Stanford: Stanford University Press, 1994); Adela Pinch, *Strange Fits of Passion: Epistemologies of*

Emotion, Hume to Austen (Stanford: Stanford University Press, 1996); Julie Ellison, *Cato's Tears and the Making of Anglo-American Emotion* (Chicago: University of Chicago Press, 1999). See also Gavin Budge, ed., *Romantic Empiricism: Poetics and the Philosophy of Common Sense, 1780–1830* (Lewisburg, PA: Bucknell University Press, 2007); Vivasvan Soni, *Mourning Happiness: Narrative and the Politics of Modernity* (Ithaca, NY: Cornell University Press, 2010).

4. James Chandler, "The Politics of Sentiment: Notes toward a New Account," *Studies in Romanticism* 49 (Winter 2010): 553–575.

5. Christopher Bollas, *The Mystery of Things* (New York: Routledge, 1999), 10.

6. Ludwig Wittgenstein, *Philosophical Investigations*, trans. G. E. M. Anscombe (New York: Macmillan, 1953) §§ 108–109.

7. Max Scheler, *The Nature of Sympathy* (1913), trans. Peter Heath (London: Routledge and Kegan Paul, 1954), 49.

8. Francis Hutcheson, *An Inquiry into the Original of Our Ideas of Beauty and Virtue* (1729), in *British Moralists, 1650–1800*, ed. D. D. Raphael, 2 vols. (Oxford: Clarendon, 1969); David Hume, *An Enquiry concerning the Principles of Morals* (1751), ed. Charles Hendel (New York: Macmillan, 1957), 120. "This universal benevolence towards all men can be compared to the force of gravitation . . . and is strongest when bodies come to touch each other" (Hutcheson, *An Inquiry*, 1:290).

9. Anthony Ashley Cooper, Third Earl of Shaftesbury, *The Moralists* (1709), in *Characteristics of Men, Manners, Opinions, Times* (1711), ed. Lawrence Klein (Cambridge: Cambridge University Press, 1999), 326.

10. John Locke, *An Essay concerning Human Understanding* (1689/1706), ed. Peter Nidditch (Oxford: Oxford University Press, 1975), 145, 633–636.

11. David Hume, *A Treatise of Human Nature* (1739–1740), ed. David Fate Norton and Mary J. Norton (Oxford: Oxford University Press, 2000), 236, 368.

12. William Wordsworth, "Strange Fits of Passion" (1798), in *William Wordsworth: The Poems*, ed. John O. Hayden (New Haven, CT: Yale University Press, 1977), 1:366–367. Hereafter cited parenthetically by line number.

13. On the primacy of fear in Hobbes, see especially Alan Ryan, "Hobbes' Political Philosophy," and Bernard Gert, "Hobbes' Psychology," in *The Cambridge Companion to Hobbes*, ed. Tom Sorrell (Cambridge: Cambridge University Press, 1996), 157–175, 208–245.

14. Stanley Cavell, *The Claim of Reason: Wittgenstein, Skepticism, Morality and Tragedy* (Oxford: Oxford University Press, 1979), 372–383, 420–432. See also "What Is the Scandal of Skepticism?," in Stanley Cavell, *Philosophy the Day after Tomorrow* (Cambridge, MA: Harvard University Press, 2005), 132–154.

15. Mary Wollstonecraft, *A Vindication of the Rights of Men* (1790), in *The Works of Mary Wollstonecraft*, ed. Janet Todd and Marilyn Butler (New York: New York University Press, 1989), 5:30, 53.

16. Immanuel Kant, *Groundwork of the Metaphysics of Morals* (1785) (hereafter cited parenthetically as *GM*), in *Immanuel Kant: Practical Philosophy*, trans. Mary J. Gregor (Cambridge: Cambridge University Press, 1996), 44. All parenthetical citations of the original German text are drawn from *Kants gesammelte schriften*, Prussian Academy Edition, 28 vols. (Berlin: Walter de Gruyter, 1902—). Volume and page numbers found in the margins of most translations refer to this edition.

17. Vivasvan Soni offers the most recent version of this indictment, concluding that "sympathy . . . which promised to serve as a bridge between self and other, betrays its promise and leaves the self embroiled with its own emotions" (308–309). Soni's argument is largely focused on a reading of Adam Smith's *Theory of Moral Sentiments* (1759), the paradoxes of which are certainly germane to Shaftesbury as well. Other theorists in the sentimental tradition, especially Hutcheson, Hume, and Rousseau, are, however, acutely aware of the problem of "affective narcissism" and so do not readily fit Soni's broad diagnosis (309). Chapters 1, 2, and 3 address the important and generative divergences among these writers.

18. Pinch, *Strange Fits of Passion*, 107–108.

19. Ibid., 109–110.

20. Thomas De Quincey, "Literature of Knowledge and Literature of Power" (1848), in *Prose of the Romantic Period*, ed. Carl Woodring (Boston: Houghton Mifflin, 1961), 447. De Quincey describes the affective mediation of knowledge in the "literature of power" as necessarily passing "on and through that *humid* light which clothes itself in the mists and glittering *iris* of human passions, desires, and genial emotions."

21. On the distinction between moral and pathological feeling, see *GM*, 55; and in the same volume, *Critique of Practical Reason* (1788) (hereafter cited parenthetically as *CPR*), 198–201; and *The Metaphysics of Morals* (1797) (hereafter cited parenthetically as *MM*), 528–529.

22. Ruth Leys, "The Turn to Affect: A Critique," *Critical Inquiry* 37:3 (2011): 443. See also Constantina Papoulias and Felicity Callard, "Biology's Gift: Interrogating the Turn to Affect," *Body and Society* 16:1 (2010): 29–56.

23. Brian Massumi, *Parables for the Virtual: Movement, Affect, Sensation* (Durham, NC: Duke University Press, 2002), 28; and Eric Shouse, "Feeling, Emotion, Affect," *M/C Journal* 8 (2005): 1. Also quoted in Leys, "The Turn to Affect," 437, 442. For a similar approach, see Teresa Brennan, *The Transmission of Affect* (Ithaca, NY: Cornell University Press, 2004).

24. Antonio Damasio, *The Feeling of What Happens* (New York: Houghton Mifflin, 2000), 172–173. See also Paul Griffiths, *What Emotions Really Are* (Chicago: University of Chicago Press, 1997). On Damasio's use by cultural theorists, see Papoulias and Callard, "Biology's Gift," 39–41.

25. Hume, *Treatise*, 228.

26. Accessible syntheses of the "basic emotions" view include Griffiths, *What Emotions Really Are*; Joseph LeDoux, *The Emotional Brain* (New York: Simon and Schuster, 1996); Paul Ekman and Richard J. Davidson, eds., *The Nature of Emotions: Fundamental Questions* (Oxford: Oxford University Press, 1994). Excellent accounts of the cultural formation of eighteenth-century sensibility include Lynn Hunt, *The Family Romance of the French Revolution* (Berkeley: University of California Press, 1992); David Marshall, *The Surprising Effects of Sympathy* (Chicago: University of Chicago Press, 1988); G. J. Barker-Benfield, *The Culture of Sensibility* (Chicago: University of Chicago Press, 1992).

27. On the "capture" of affect, see Massumi, *Parables for the Virtual*, 28. William Reddy makes an admirable effort to synthesize universalist theories of emotion developed in evolutionary and cognitive science with constructionist approaches in his study of eighteenth-century sentimental culture, *The Navigation of Feeling: A Framework for the History of the Emotions* (Cambridge: Cambridge University Press, 2001).

28. John Savarese and Colin Jager offer a related criticism in "Cognition, Culture,

Romanticism: A Review Essay," *Romanticism and Victorianism on the Net*, no. 57–58 (2010), http://www.erudit.org/revue/ravon/2010/v/n57-58/1006519ar.html. For an extended defense of an "aesthetic perspective" against the prevailing "stress on the cognitive and moral dimensions" of the emotions, see Charles Altieri, *The Particulars of Rapture: An Aesthetics of the Affects* (Ithaca, NY: Cornell University Press, 2003), 1–36.

29. Jesse Prinz, "The Emotional Basis of Moral Judgments," *Philosophical Explorations* 9:1 (2006): 29–43. Prinz's engaging body of writing consistently amasses and synthesizes research in neuroscience, cognitive psychology, and evolutionary biology and is unabashed in subordinating philosophical concepts of mind and motivation to those findings.

30. Stephen Darwall, "Empathy, Sympathy, Care," *Philosophical Studies* 89 (1998): 262.

31. Ibid., 263. Experimental findings are presented throughout, but see especially 264–274.

32. Blakey Vermeule, *Why Do We Care about Literary Characters?* (Baltimore: Johns Hopkins University Press, 2010), 249. See also Suzanne Keen, *Empathy and the Novel* (Oxford: Oxford University Press, 2007).

33. Lisa Zunshine, *Why We Read Fiction: Theory of Mind and the Novel* (Columbus: Ohio State University Press, 2006), 10.

34. Alan Richardson, *The Neural Sublime: Cognitive Theories and Romantic Texts* (Baltimore: Johns Hopkins University Press, 2010), xi, 12.

35. Ibid., 82.

36. Ibid., 95–96. For an engaging critique of the reductive preconceptions shaping current theory of mind, see Alva Noë, *Out of Our Heads: Why You Are Not Your Brain, and Other Lessons from the Biology of Consciousness* (New York: Hill and Wang, 2009), 25–46.

37. Paul Hernandi, "Literature and Evolution," *SubStance* 30 (2001): 55–71, quoted in Zunshine, *Why We Read Fiction*, 166. Jonathan Kramnick offers a challenging critique of this view in "Against Literary Darwinism," *Critical Inquiry* 37:2 (2011): 327, 337–338.

38. Wordsworth, "Preface to *Lyrical Ballads*" (1802), in Hayden, *William Wordsworth: The Poems*, 1:881. Hereafter cited parenthetically by page number.

39. My thinking about differences in methodology has been helpfully shaped by Andrew Miller's useful distinction between "conclusive" and "implicative" criticism in *The Burdens of Perfection* (Ithaca, NY: Cornell University Press, 2009), 26–32.

40. It is worth noting, however, that at a phenomenal level of description, the moral law is grasped as immediately and irresistibly as sentimentalist moral feeling: "When I think of a categorical imperative, I know at once [*sofort*] what it contains." Subsequent examples of the self-evidence of the imperative involve the immediacy of "seeing at once [*sogleich*]" what is required in each case (*GM*, 73–74).

41. Emmanuel Levinas, "Is Ontology Fundamental?" (1951), in *Basic Philosophical Writings*, ed. Adriaan Peperzak, Simon Critchley, and Robert Bernasconi (Bloomington: Indiana University Press, 1996), 10; Emmanuel Levinas, *Totality and Infinity*, trans. Alphonso Lingis (Pittsburgh: Duquesne University Press, 1961), 208. On the face, see especially *Totality and Infinity*, 194–219, and "Ethics and Spirit," in *Difficult Freedom: Essays on Judaism*, trans. Sean Hand (Baltimore: Johns Hopkins University Press), 8. On the relationship between Kant and Levinas, see Darin Crawford Gates, "The Fact of Reason, and the Face of the Other: Autonomy, Constraint, and Rational Agency in Kant and Levinas," *Southern Journal of Philosophy* 40 (2002): 493–522.

42. Jean-Jacques Rousseau, "On the Social Contract" (first version, commonly called "The Geneva Manuscript"), in *The Collected Writings of Rousseau*, ed. Roger Masters and Christopher Kelly (Hanover, NH: University Press of New England, 1994), 4:79. Kant famously credited Rousseau for a powerful transformation of his own regard for others in a series of handwritten annotations to his copy of *Observations on the Feeling of the Beautiful and Sublime* (1764): "There was a time when I believed that [the thirst for knowledge] constituted the honor of mankind, and I despised the people, who know nothing. Rousseau set me right about this. This blinding prejudice disappeared. I learned to honor humanity, and I would find myself more useless than the most common laborer if I did not believe that this attitude of mine can give worth to all others in establishing the rights of humanity." Immanuel Kant, *Observations on the Feeling of the Beautiful and the Sublime and Other Writings*, ed. Patrick Frierson and Paul Guyer (Cambridge: Cambridge University Press, 2011), 96.

43. Christine Korsgaard, *Creating the Kingdom of Ends* (Cambridge: Cambridge University Press, 1996), 190.

44. Ibid., 189.

45. Ibid., 193, 195.

46. As with friendship in the *Metaphysics of Morals*, so with the commandment to "love your neighbor as yourself" in the *Critique of Practical Reason*, which Kant interprets as a command to aspire: because it "presents the moral disposition in its complete perfection . . . it is not attainable by any creature but is yet the archetype which we should strive to approach and resemble in an uninterrupted and endless progress" (*CPR*, 207).

47. Stanley Cavell, *Cities of Words: Pedagogical Letters on a Register of the Moral Life* (Cambridge, MA: Harvard University Press, 2004), 124, 142–143.

48. Wittgenstein, *Philosophical Investigations*, §§ 109, 129; Levinas, *Totality and Infinity*, 215.

49. See, for example, Jonathan Lear's observation that "the form of life itself seems to be a missing object" in the *Investigations*. Consequently, "the meaning of a present act is partially determined by a context that does not yet fully exist. The individual acts are themselves helping to constitute the form of life." "On Reflection: The Legacy of Wittgenstein's Later Philosophy," *Ratio*, n.s., 2 (June 1989): 37.

50. Ferguson, *Solitude and the Sublime*; Thomas Pfau, *Romantic Moods: Paranoia, Trauma, and Melancholy, 1790–1840* (Baltimore: Johns Hopkins University Press, 2005); Mary Favret, *War at a Distance* (Princeton: Princeton University Press, 2010); William Galperin, *The Historical Austen* (Philadelphia: University of Pennsylvania Press, 2003), and "The History of Missed Opportunities: British Romanticism and the Emergence of the Everyday" (unpublished ms., 2010, print). See also Jacques Khalip, *Anonymous Life: Romanticism and Dispossession* (Stanford: Stanford University Press, 2009); and David Collings, *Wordsworthian Errancies* (Baltimore: Johns Hopkins University Press, 1994). Pfau's proposal that "romanticism can become an object of knowledge only if, at every turn of the analysis, the intellectual and aesthetic heritage of the romantic era is recognized as both the driving motivation and the abiding conceptual framework shaping the critical results" (14) calls for awareness of our own implication in the long intellectual historical *durée* to which our interpretations belong. Such a commitment allows the "counterfactual dissenting strains" within a particular historical moment to

emerge with and against the "fixity and coherence of so-called 'actual' history" (25). Exemplary in this regard is Favret's investigation of the "wanderings of mind, the interruptions and lapses—of time, knowledge, and feeling—that compose the everyday" and are constitutive of romantic-era writing understood as a literature of wartime (4). Galperin's suggestion that a "slowing down" of interpretation that allows literature to become "text and context at once" will unfailingly "prove a complication" to prevailing historical generalizations is borne out by his sustained examination of the "resistant or uncanny character" of Austen's realism ("History of Missed Opportunities," 7–8; *Historical Austen*, 216). Frances Ferguson's relatively early critique of the reductive presupposition that "romantic internalization is equated with privacy, and specifically with a commitment to privatization" (152), has most recently been picked up by Khalip, who pursues the possibility of "reconceiv[ing] the literary text as the site of abstentions that evoke 'identity' as always an unmade and undone thing" (14).

51. Martin Heidegger, *Being and Time* (1926), trans. John Macquarrie and Edward Robinson (New York: Harper and Row, 2008), 155, 157. Hereafter cited parenthetically by page number.

CHAPTER 1

1. Levinas, *Totality and Infinity*; Giorgio Agamben, *Homo Sacer: Sovereign Power and Bare Life*, trans. Daniel Heller-Roazen (Stanford: Stanford University Press, 1998).

2. David Clark's readings of Kant, Frances Ferguson's work on Bentham, and Adam Potkay's study of eighteenth-century moralists are exemplary instances of literary critical engagement with central texts in the history of ethics. See David Clark, "Kant's Aliens: The *Anthropology* and Its Others," *New Centennial Review* 1:2 (Fall 2001): 201–289; Frances Ferguson, *Pornography, the Theory: What Utilitarianism Did to Action* (Chicago: University of Chicago Press, 2004), 1–33; Adam Potkay, *The Passion for Happiness: Samuel Johnson and David Hume* (Ithaca, NY: Cornell University Press, 2000).

3. I cannot recall the precise phrasing of the example Parfit used in his course "Recent Ethical Theory" (at Harvard University in spring 1995). A related thought experiment appears in his *Reasons and Persons* (Oxford: Oxford University Press, 1984), 494–495. In the appendix, "What Makes Someone's Life Go Best," if "one of my strongest desires was to be a successful parent" and "my children's lives fail . . . in part [as] the result of mistakes I made" but their "lives go badly only after I am dead," it nevertheless remains an open question for Parfit whether or not "death makes a difference" in assessing whether my desires have been fulfilled.

4. Francis Hutcheson, "Reflections on the Common Systems of Morality," in *On Human Nature*, ed. Thomas Mautner (Cambridge: Cambridge University Press, 1993), 100. The essay, signed "Philanthropos" and originally published in the *London Journal* (nos. 277 and 278, 1724), previews and abstracts arguments from the soon-to-be-published *Inquiry concerning the Original of Our Ideas of Beauty and Virtue* (1725).

5. The anti-Kantian argument for moral sentiment is well developed by Annette Baier. See especially, "Hume, the Women's Moral Theorist?," in *Moral Prejudices* (Cambridge, MA: Harvard University Press, 1994), 51–75. Christine Korsgaard offers a counterintuitive argument that places Hume's sympathy in relation to Kant's respect in "The General Point of View: Love and Moral Approval in Hume's Ethics," *Hume Studies* 25:1–2

(1999): 3–41. See also her *Sources of Normativity* (Cambridge: Cambridge University Press, 1996), 51–66.

6. Candace Vogler's criticism of the ahistorical "habits of scholarship and analytic interpretation" within the discipline of philosophy is a useful caution in this context. "The Moral of the Story," *Critical Inquiry* 34 (Autumn 2007): 9–10.

7. The centrality of Adam Smith for literary critics has been largely influenced by David Marshall's work. See, for example, "Adam Smith and the Theatricality of the Emotions," *Critical Inquiry* 10:4 (1984): 592–613. More recently, Vivasvon Soni treats Smith's *Theory* as "the most programmatic" version of eighteenth-century sentimentalism, and his indictment of sympathy as "an ethical attitude . . . that presupposes no identification with the other as its object" rests largely on a reading of Smith. *Mourning Happiness* (Ithaca, NY: Cornell University Press, 2010), 294, 308.

8. Adam Smith, *The Theory of Moral Sentiments*, ed. Knud Haakonsen (Cambridge: Cambridge University Press), 11. Hereafter cited parenthetically by page number.

9. J. B. Schneewind, *The Invention of Autonomy* (Cambridge: Cambridge University Press, 1998), 523.

10. Hutcheson, "Reflections," 100.

11. Anthony Ashley Cooper, Third Earl of Shaftesbury, *An Inquiry concerning Virtue or Merit* (1699), in Klein, *Characteristics of Men, Manners, Opinions, Times*, 179. Hereafter cited parenthetically as IVM.

12. Shaftesbury, *The Moralists*, 324–325. Hereafter cited parenthetically as M. Shaftesbury famously turned against the philosophical methods and conclusions of Locke, who superintended his early education, associating the moral implications of Locke's *Essay* with what he called the "poison" of Hobbes. In a letter to his protégé, Michael Ainsworth, Shaftesbury warned, "'Twas Mr. Locke that struck at all Fundamentals, threw all *Order* and *Virtue* out of the World, and made the very *Ideas* of these . . . *unnatural* and without Foundation in our Minds." Quoted in Robert Voitle, *The Third Earl of Shaftesbury* (Baton Rouge: Louisiana State University Press, 1984), 119 (original emphasis). On Shaftesbury and Locke, see ibid., 60–70, 118–126; and Stanley Grean, *Shaftesbury's Philosophy of Religion and Ethics* (Athens: Ohio University Press, 1967), 204–218.

13. Thomas Hobbes, *Man and Citizen (De Homine and De Cive)* (1642/1658), ed. Bernard Gert (Indianapolis, IN: Hackett, 1991), 110–111.

14. Bernard Mandeville, *The Fable of the Bees* (1714), ed. Irwin Primer (New York: Capricorn, 1962), 195–200. Hereafter cited parenthetically by page number.

15. Mandeville's denial of the moral value of "natural affections" is typically taken as a radically negative assessment of ethical competence. That "which might seem to prove that there is virtue even in the vilest is converted to a proof that there is *no* virtue even in the most excellent," according to Leslie Stephen's still valuable interpretation. Other readers find Mandeville's definition of virtue as a necessarily self-denying "rational ambition of being good" to anticipate Kant's separation of "good will" from merely contingent inclinations toward kindness. Leslie Stephen, *English Thought in the Eighteenth Century* (1876) (London: Smith, Elder, 1902), 2:37. See also Basil Willey, *The Eighteenth Century Background* (London: Chatto, 1953), 95–97.

16. Hume, *Treatise*, 312–317 (hereafter cited parenthetically as *T*). In his introduction to the *Treatise*, Hume names Shaftesbury (along with Locke, Mandeville, Hutcheson, and

Butler) among the "late philosophers in England who have begun to put the science of man on a new footing" (5).

17. The disturbing disjunctions between sympathy and justice in Hume are taken up at length in Chapter 3.

18. Shaftesbury, *Sensus Communis, an Essay on the Freedom of Wit and Humour* (1709), in *Characteristics*, 51. The same point is made in *The Moralists*, where it is also proposed that complex forms of political and cultural organization—such as moral regard for the "complete society"—evolve naturally from reproduction and parenting: "Is it possible [man] should pair and live in love and fellowship with his partner and offspring and remain still wholly wild and speechless and without those arts of storing, building and other economy as natural to him, surely, as to the beaver or to the ant and bee? . . . That it began thus . . . and grew into a household and economy is plain. Must not this have soon grown into a tribe, and this tribe into a nation?" (*M*, 287).

19. Locke, *Essay concerning Human Understanding*, 389. Kenneth Winkler has recently traced the persistence of Lockean assumptions in Shaftesbury, noting in particular the absorption of the "skeptical structure" of Locke's argument. "'All Is Revolution in Us': Personal Identity in Shaftesbury and Hume," *Hume Studies* 26:1 (2000): 9–10.

20. Hume, *Enquiry*, 93.

21. Ibid., 97; see also Hume, *Treatise*, 228. Compare Hume's image of justice as the work of many hands to the individually designed, self-supporting ethos promoted by Theocles. In Hume, the "social virtue of justice" is like "the building of a vault where each individual stone would, of itself, fall to the ground" without the "mutual assistance and combination of its corresponding parts" (*Enquiry*, 121). In *The Moralists*, Theocles describes the "wise and able man" as one who becomes "in truth the architect of his own life and fortune by laying within himself the lasting and sure foundations of order, peace and concord" (*M*, 332).

22. In a characteristic view of the opposed philosophical tendencies of the period, Stephen Cox argues that the sentimentalist emphasis on natural sociability arises in response to an "anxiety about the self-closed subjectivity of the individual mind" implicit in empirical psychology but finds that anxiety redressed by the espousal of a fundamentally "social self." I am arguing that while the anxieties associated with "self-closed subjectivity" are personified in, and ostensibly confined to, Shaftesbury's figure of the misanthrope, that same structure of mind evidently shapes Theocles's untroubled admission of radically individuated perception ("what is pain to one is pleasure to another"). *"The Stranger within Thee": Concepts of Self in Late Eighteenth Century Literature* (Pittsburgh: University of Pittsburgh Press, 1980), 19, 24.

23. The best recent discussion of *The Moralists* is Michael Gill, *The British Moralists on Human Nature and the Birth of Secular Ethics* (Cambridge: Cambridge University Press, 2006), 100–118. Thomas Pfau reminds me that, given Shaftesbury's experimentation with literary forms, especially the dialogue with its long philosophical history, one must be wary of imposing conceptual coherence on the works collected in *Characteristics* (personal correspondence). My own efforts are directed toward identifying the explicit and implicit philosophical positions that consistently appear in his writings and that are directly addressed by the contemporary philosophical interlocutors who attempted to assimilate his ideas within their own more systematic expositions.

24. Michael Gill identifies a related impasse. Shaftesbury's hypothesis that virtue is "proper and natural to humans" collapses "if we cannot take for granted that there is an external world." The naturalist foundation of moral sense is eroded by admission of the skeptical possibility that "all our perceptions could be illusory." "Shaftesbury's Two Accounts of the Reason to Be Virtuous," *Journal of the History of Philosophy* 38:4 (2000): 539, 543.

25. Soni's argument that, for Smith, the affect of the other does not matter in the "sympathetic relation" (*Mourning Happiness*, 308) is in accord with mine. But it is a mistake to characterize sentimental ethics *tout court* as the paradox of an "identificatory ethics in which the self remains wrapped up in its own affections" (ibid.). This implication in the works of both Smith and Shaftesbury provokes complex responses within the tradition of sentimentalism itself; it is less a paradigmatic feature of sentimentalism than a threatening consequence that some writers in the tradition strive to avert, others fail to avoid, and most understand as a crucial dilemma to resolve.

CHAPTER 2

1. Hume, *Enquiry*, 120.

2. Jean-Jacques Rousseau, *Julie, or the New Heloise*, trans. Philip Stewart and Jean Vaché (Hanover, NH: University Press of New England, 1997), 608–609. Hereafter cited parenthetically by page number. Original French text from Jean-Jacques Rousseau, *Oeuvres complètes*, 5 vols., ed. Bernard Gagnebin and Marcel Raymond (Paris: Gallimard, 1959–1995).

3. Shaftesbury, *Inquiry on Virtue and Merit*, 229.

4. The definitive treatment of the conflict between being and appearance in Rousseau remains Jean Starobinski, *Jean-Jacques Rousseau: Transparency and Obstruction*, trans. Arthur Goldhammer (Chicago: University of Chicago Press, 1988); originally published as *Jean-Jacques Rousseau: La Transparence et l'obstacle* (Paris: Gallimard, 1971).

5. Shaftesbury, *The Moralists*, 287.

6. Hume, *Treatise*, 309, 312.

7. Jean-Jacques Rousseau, *On the Social Contract*, in *The Basic Political Writings*, trans. Donald A. Cress (Indianapolis, IN: Hackett, 1987), 142. Hereafter cited parenthetically as *SC*.

8. On the discontinuities between the "natural" and the "social" in Rousseau, see Victor Goldschmidt, *Anthropologie et politique: Les Principes du système de Rousseau* (Paris: Librairie Philosophique J. Vrin, 1974), 175–219, 261–274; and Victor Gourevitch, "Rousseau's Pure State of Nature," *Interpretation* 16 (1988): 23–59. I treat this topic at length in *Isolated Cases* (Ithaca, NY: Cornell University Press, 2004), 63–95.

9. Jean-Jacques Rousseau, *Discourse on the Origins of Inequality* (1755), in *The Discourses and Other Early Political Writings*, trans. Victor Gourevitch (Cambridge: Cambridge University Press, 1997), 216. Hereafter cited parenthetically as *DOI*.

10. On the radical contingency of the transition from the state of nature to society in the second *Discourse*, see Gourevitch, "Rousseau's Pure State of Nature," 7.

11. Hobbes, *De Cive*, 212–213.

12. Jean-Jacques Rousseau, *Emile, or On Education* (1762), trans. Allan Bloom (New York: Basic Books, 1979), 46. Hereafter cited parenthetically as *Emile*.

13. Jean-Jacques Rousseau, "On the Social Contract, or Essay about the Form of the Republic" (commonly called the "Geneva manuscript"), in *The Collected Writings of Rousseau*, vol. 4, trans. Judith R. Bush, Roger D. Masters, and Christopher Kelly (Hanover, NH:

University Press of New England, 1994), 90. Hereafter cited parenthetically as "Geneva." Wherever Rousseau attends to legitimacy, secure transmission of property is not his principal concern. Rather, emphasis is placed on the need to redress emotional vulnerabilities to which only men are subject. Because "the wife . . . has no such thing to fear," she "does not have the same right" to oversee her husband's behavior. The attenuation of fear is as important as deterrence of infidelity. On the relationship between sexual difference and deception in Rousseau, see Ingrid Makus, "The Politics of 'Feminine Concealment' and 'Masculine Openness,'" in *Feminist Interpretations of Jean-Jacques Rousseau*, ed. Lynda Lange (Philadelphia: Pennsylvania State University Press, 2002), 187–211.

14. Jean-Jacques Rousseau, *Letter to d'Alembert* (1758), in *Collected Writings*, vol. 10, trans. Allan Bloom et al., 313. Hereafter cited parenthetically as *LA*. Recent feminist interpretations of sexual difference in Rousseau emphasize the analysis of the interdependence and asymmetry between domestic and public spheres in his work. See Leah Bradshaw, "Rousseau on Civic Virtue"; Susan Miller Okin, "The Fate of Rousseau's Heroines"; Lori Marso, "Rousseau's Subversive Women," in Lange, *Feminist Interpretations of Rousseau*.

15. On the imbrication of gender, romantic love, and "the aporetic nature of human relations" more generally in Rousseau's work, see Rebecca Kukla, "Rousseau and the Problem of Gender Relations," in Lange, *Feminist Interpretations of Rousseau*, 346–381.

16. René Descartes, *Meditations on First Philosophy* (1641), trans. Donald A. Cress (Indianapolis, IN: Hackett, 1980), 57.

17. Jean-Jacques Rousseau, *Emilius and Sophia; or, The Solitaries*, anonymous translation (London: H. Baldwin, 1783), 22. Further reference to this first English translation of Rousseau's posthumously published, unfinished work is cited parenthetically as *ES*. Written largely in 1762 and left unfinished, *Emile et Sophie* was first published in 1780. On the composition and projected shape of the work, see Charles Wirz, "Note sur *Emile et Sophie, ou Les Solitaires*," *Annales de la Société J-J Rousseau* 36 (1963–1965): 291–304.

18. Pierre Burgelin traces how the novelistic sequel exposes the failure (*échec*) of the perfect female education described in *Emile* in "L'Éducation de Sophie," *Annales de la Société J-J Rousseau* 35 (1959–1962): 113–130. Equally germane are interpretations emphasizing the connection between what Anthony Skillen calls the "fatal logic of love" in Rousseau and his "dismal dialectic of social life" more broadly conceived ("Rousseau and the Fall of Social Man," *Philosophy* 60 [1985]: 111).

19. Jean-Jacques Rousseau, *Discourse on the Arts and Sciences*, in *The Discourses and Other Early Political Writings*, 8.

20. Mary Wollstonecraft, *Vindication of the Rights of Woman* (1792), in *The Works of Mary Wollstonecraft*, ed. Janet Todd and Marilyn Butler (New York: New York University Press, 1989), 5:161.

21. Rousseau, *Discourse on the Arts and Sciences*, 7–8.

22. Jean-Jacques Rousseau, *The Confessions* (composed 1764–1770), trans. J. M. Cohen (New York: Penguin, 1953), 398.

23. The passage is repeated almost verbatim in *La Nouvelle Héloïse*: "Marriageable persons" attend gatherings "where the eyes of the public [are] constantly focused on them," ensuring that they appear as they are to "people whose interest it is to know us well before taking on the obligation of loving us" (375–376).

CHAPTER 3

1. In Hayden, *William Wordsworth: The Poems*, 1:399. Hereafter cited parenthetically by line number. The fragment appears in an important manuscript of 1798–1800 including versions of "Salisbury Plain," "The Ruined Cottage," and "The Discharged Soldier." For details, see Stephen Gill, "Wordsworth's Poems: The Question of Text," in *Romantic Revisions*, ed. Robert Brinkley (Cambridge: Cambridge University Press, 1992), 51–52.

2. William Wordsworth, *The Prelude, 1799, 1805, 1850*, ed. Jonathan Wordsworth, M. H. Abrams, and Stephen Gill (New York: Norton, 1979), Book 12, ll. 186–188, 197–199 (1805 version). Hereafter cited parenthetically by line number.

3. Hume, *Treatise*, 368. Hereafter cited parenthetically as *T*.

4. Mary Wollstonecraft, *A Short Residence in Sweden, Denmark and Norway* (1796), ed. Richard Holmes (New York: Penguin, 1987), 99; Samuel Taylor Coleridge, "Effusion XXXV" (1795), in *Coleridge's Poetry and Prose*, ed. Nicholas Halmi, Paul Magnuson, and Raimonda Modiana (New York: Norton, 2004), 18–19.

5. On the implicit "argument against the privacy of consciousness" in Hume's moral philosophy, see Korsgaard, *Sources of Normativity*, 144–145.

6. In "Of Skepticism with Regard to Reason," Hume distinguishes between "sensitive" and "cogitative" judgments. "All the rules of logic require a continual diminution, and at last a total extinction of belief and evidence," he argues, but at the same time "Nature, by an absolute and uncontroulable necessity has determin'd us to judge as well as to breathe and feel" (*T*, 123). Consequently, although "skeptical doubt arises naturally from a profound and intense reflection," we do not live reflexively but rather "embrace by a kind of instinct or natural impulse" the very world that dissolves in thought (*T*, 142, 144).

7. See, for example, Hume's famous reduction of causal necessity to the mind's "propensity, which custom produces, to pass from an object to the idea of its usual attendant" (*T*, 112). Similarly, given repeated interruptions in our perception, only by "illusion" and "a fiction of the imagination" are "broken appearances united" so that common objects (the sun or ocean, mountains, houses, tables) appear to have a continued existence (*T*, 131–133).

8. Hume, *Enquiry*, 52. Hereafter cited parenthetically as *E*.

9. The affections that bind individuals to one another also threaten cohesion in a broader community, according to Hume (*T*, 316). His emphasis on partiality has often been understood as a mere extension of the motivating principle of self-love, albeit broadened to include friends and relations within the ambit of the self's interests. But Hume himself resists such a reductive analysis, arguing that insofar as "common language and observation" plainly distinguish "love, friendship, compassion, gratitude" from the "selfish passions," the "former affections" cannot be "modifications of the latter" (*E*, 90). Hume's "sentimentalism" consists precisely in this admission of a concern for others as coeval with human sociality.

10. On the "progress" from natural, partial sympathy to the "extensive sympathy" associated with a "general point of view," see Baier, *A Progress of Sentiments*, 181–182; and M. Jamie Ferreira, "Hume and Imagination: Sympathy and 'the Other,'" *International Philological Quarterly* 34:1 (1994): 39–57.

11. Critique of the moral value of sentiment proceeds from the conviction that to ground morality in innate feeling is to degrade both morality and the dignity of the human being as a deliberating agent. Criticizing Burke specifically and sentimentalism broadly,

Mary Wollstonecraft argues that moral relations cannot be derived from the "common affections and passions [that] equally bind brutes together," nor can "active exertions of virtue" be reduced to "mechanical instinctive sensations." Kant's derogation of sentimental motives is well known: "There are many souls so sympathetically attuned that . . . they find an inner satisfaction in spreading joy around them and can take delight in the satisfaction of others so far as it is their own work. But I assert that . . . however amiable it may be [an action of this kind] has no true moral worth, but is on the same footing with other inclinations." Mary Wollstonecraft, *A Vindication of the Rights of Men* (1790), in Todd and Butler, *Works of Mary Wollstonecraft*, 5:53; Kant, *Groundwork*, 53.

12. The generality and inflexibility of civil laws in Hume would surely be legible to a Kantian: all such laws "regard alone some essential circumstances of the case, without taking into consideration the characters, situations, and connexions of the person concerned, or any particular consequences which may result from the determination of these laws" (*E*, 94). On the confluence between these thinkers, see Korsgaard, "General Point of View," 3–41.

13. Hume frequently insists that sympathy depends on the immediate presence of the other and is necessarily weakened and diminished by distance (*T*, 248–249).

14. "Every thing contiguous to us, either in space or time . . . [is] conceiv'd with a peculiar force and vivacity, and excels every other object in its influence on the imagination" (*T*, 274). Thus, when "uneasiness is either small in itself, or remote from us, it engages not the imagination" (*T*, 250).

15. Natural sympathy and justice collide over inequalities of wealth because justice— and the broad social cohesion it ensures—almost exclusively concerns the security of property ("such possessions as we have acquir'd by our industry and good fortune"). It is against the "instability of their possession" in a world where material goods are scarce that Hume explains the development of justice as a convention "bestow[ing] stability on the possession of those external goods" (*T*, 313–314).

16. Influential new historicist studies by James Chandler, Marjorie Levinson, and David Simpson typically find Wordsworth's renderings of the poor to be complicit in a conservative social politics that could at best only sentimentalize the reality of material need and are broadly symptomatic of an evasion or occlusion of history. James Chandler, *Wordsworth's Second Nature* (Chicago: University of Chicago Press, 1984); Marjorie Levinson, *Wordsworth's Great Period Poems* (New York: Cambridge University Press, 1986); David Simpson, *Wordsworth's Historical Imagination* (New York: Methuen, 1987). Ironically, for his contemporaries, Wordsworth's sentimental attention to poverty implied a radical politics. Charles Burney (in the *Monthly Mirror* of June 1801) complained that the *Lyrical Ballads* appear "calculated to diffuse the seeds of a general dissatisfaction" by spreading "a wayward spirit of discontent." Francis Jeffrey (in the *Edinburgh Review* of October 1802) famously accused Wordsworth of promoting Rousseau's "antisocial principles" and "discontent with the present constitution of society." *William Wordsworth: The Critical Heritage*, ed. Robert Woof (New York: Routledge, 2001) 144, 154. See William Christie's examination of the "relationship . . . at once analogical and genealogical, between certain assumptions and strategies characteristic" of Wordsworth's contemporary critics and recent romantic historicism. "Francis Jeffrey in Recent Whig Interpretations of Romantic Literary History," *ELH* 76:3 (2009): 577–597.

17. "Beggars," in Hayden, *William Wordsworth: The Poems*, 1:516, ll. 16–17.

18. Thomas Pfau identifies the self-conscious effort to negotiate between the "immediacy" of feeling and its "communicability as social value" as the defining problematic of Wordsworth's 1802 Preface to *Lyrical Ballads*. "'Elementary Feelings' and 'Distorted Language': The Pragmatics of Culture in Wordsworth's Preface to *Lyrical Ballads*," *New Literary History* 24:1 (1993): 136. Examples of the renewed interest in the ethical complexities of Wordsworth's poetic practice include Adam Potkay, *Wordsworth's Ethics* (Baltimore: Johns Hopkins University Press, 2012); Stuart Allen and Jonathan Roberts, "Wordsworth and the Thought of Affection," *European Romantic Review* 16:4 (2005): 455–470; David Collings, *Wordsworthian Errancies* (Baltimore: Johns Hopkins University Press, 1994); Simon Jarvis, *Wordsworth's Philosophic Song* (Cambridge: Cambridge University Press, 2007); Clifton Spargo, "Begging the Question of Responsibility," *Studies in Romanticism* 39 (2000): 51–80.

19. Don Bialostosky's study of the tensions between narrative and narratorial personae in Wordsworth remains useful. *Making Tales: The Poetics of Wordsworth's Narrative Experiments* (Chicago: University of Chicago Press, 1984).

20. As the youth perceives him, the soldier certainly embodies that "inertia and apathy" that Mary Favret has identified as emblematic of wartime experience in the era. But the composition of the episode as a whole tends toward the more complex "poetic response" Favret describes, specifically the effort to register "the felt distance from crucial events, the limits of knowledge in a mediated culture . . . the difficulty of finding sounds or forms to which feeling can attach itself." *War at a Distance* (Princeton: Princeton University Press, 2009), 10–11.

21. Smith, *Theory of Moral Sentiments*, 14. For Smith, sympathy *follows* from, rather than prompts, "inquiry" into the "situation" of the stranger. Knowing the other's story allows for that imaginative transport whereby I take the other's place, feeling what I would feel (and not necessarily what she feels) under like circumstances. Indeed, we may very well "feel for another a passion of which he himself seems incapable" (14). Wordsworth insists on the dynamics of encounter as potentially producing an estranging misalignment of affect between two persons who are, at least for a moment, intimately proximate. The encounter yields neither Hume's contagious congruence of feeling nor Smith's vicarious sympathy—it tells an altogether different story.

22. Rather like the chance meeting of "Resolution and Independence," this encounter at a "sudden turning" typifies what Pfau identifies as Wordsworth's self-conscious use of "serendipity" as the "enfeebled successor to the once rugged metaphysical idea of providence." Only in the "simultaneously aesthetic and social" practice of recounting and repeating "can we hope to articulate why a seemingly incidental narrative should continue to haunt us with intimations of an antecedent, more capacious, knowledge." *Romantic Moods* (Baltimore: Johns Hopkins University Press, 2005), 211–212.

23. Cavell, *Claim of Reason*, 438.

24. Early versions of both "The Old Cumberland Beggar" and the discharged-soldier episode (originally drafted as an independent poem) appear together in the Alfoxden notebook and were probably composed in early 1798. See Mark Reed, *Wordsworth: Chronology of the Early Years, 1770–1799* (Cambridge: Cambridge University Press, 1967), 28–30. The line numbers cited parenthetically from "The Old Cumberland Beggar" are in Hayden, *William Wordsworth: The Poems*, 1:262–268.

25. David Bromwich, *Disowned by Memory: Wordsworth's Poetry of the 1790's* (Chicago: University of Chicago Press, 1998), 38.

26. In the frequently cited Fenwick note to this poem, Wordsworth recalls writing the poem at a time when "the political economists were . . . beginning their war against mendicity in all its forms, and by implication, if not directly, on alms-giving also." *The Poetical Works of William Wordsworth*, ed. E. de Selincourt and Helen Darbishire (Oxford: Oxford University Press, 1940–49), 4:445–446. These comments of 1843 cast a disproportionate shadow over interpretation of the poem composed four decades earlier and in which critique of policy toward the vagrant poor is but one element of the speaker's elaborate effort to defend against the implications of his own description.

27. William Wordsworth, "A Letter to the Bishop of Llandaff," in *The Prose Works of William Wordsworth*, ed. W. J. B. Owen and Jane Smyser (Oxford: Oxford University Press, 1974), 43. This early, unpublished essay remains remarkable in Wordsworth's oeuvre for its strident faith in the ameliorative possibilities of the "science of civil government" to "counteract that inequality among mankind which proceeds from the present *forced* disproportion of their possessions" (43). The young Wordsworth agitates for the very "extinction" of the class of mendicants that the speaker of "The Old Cumberland Beggar" laments because he imagines the possibility of extinguishing poverty itself. This latter possibility of radical change—the prospect of a world without beggars—is altogether absent in "The Old Cumberland Beggar." The speaker presents us with a choice of where the beggar might be "confined"—either to a "stated round in their neighborhood" on "fixed days" or to the "house, misnamed of industry"—a choice that itself reflects a confinement, or dulling, of imagination, a foreclosure of the idea of futurity.

28. In the *Groundwork*, Kant writes of our "interest" in the moral law as "moral feeling," allowing that there is a "feeling of pleasure or of delight in the fulfillment of a duty" (106).

29. Wordsworth, "The Convention of Cintra," in Owen and Smyser, *Prose Works*, 339.

30. Addressing the use of repetition in his poetry in the "Note to 'The Thorn'" (1800), Wordsworth explains that as long as the "craving" to "communicate impassioned feelings" is accompanied by a "consciousness of the inadequacies of our own powers," we "cling to the same words." Such words become "*things*, active and efficient, which are of themselves part of the passion" rather than "symbols of the passion." If we keep this in mind, it would be a mistake to say that weight is Wordsworth's recurrent figure for the inability to salvage the "dignity of individual man" from "our animal wants and the necessities" (*Prelude*, 12:83, 94), but it does seem to mark the *feeling* of that incapacity. See, for example, in *The Prelude*, "life's mysterious weight / Of pain and fear" (5:443–444); "the weight / Of that injustice which upon ourselves / By composition of society / Ourselves entail" (12:102–105); "the heavy and weary weight / Of all this unintelligible world" (39–40) in "Tintern Abbey"; the soul's "earthly freight" in the "Intimations" ode ("custom lie upon thee with a weight / Heavy as frost, and deep almost as life!") (127, 128–129). Wordsworth, "Lines Composed a Few Miles above Tintern Abbey" and "Ode: Intimations of Immortality from Recollections of Early Childhood," in Hayden, *William Wordsworth: The Poems*, 1:357–362, 1:523–529.

31. William Wordsworth, *The Borderers*, in Hayden, *William Wordsworth: The Poems*, 1:163–241, ll. 2119–2124. Hereafter cited parenthetically by line number.

CHAPTER 4

1. William Wordsworth, "Simon Lee, the Old Huntsman; with an Incident in Which He Was Concerned" (1798), in Hayden, *William Wordsworth: The Poems*, vol. 1, ll. 95–96. Hereafter cited parenthetically by line number.

2. Recall the famous defense of the "language really used by men" in the Preface to the second edition of *Lyrical Ballads*: "Such a language ... is a more permanent and a far more philosophical language, than that which is frequently substituted for it by Poets, who think that they are conferring honour upon themselves and their art in proportion as they separate themselves from the sympathies of men, and indulge in arbitrary and capricious habits of expression" (870).

3. Kant, *Metaphysics of Morals*, 577. Hereafter cited parenthetically as *MM*.

4. See also Immanuel Kant, *Lectures on Ethics*, trans. Peter Heath (Cambridge: Cambridge University Press, 1997), 197.

5. Jacques Derrida, "Given Time: The Time of the King," trans. Peggy Kamuf, *Critical Inquiry*, 18:2 (1992): 161–188, esp. 166–172.

6. Pierre Bourdieu, *The Logic of Practice*, trans. Richard Nice (Stanford: Stanford University Press, 1992), 105.

7. Jane Austen, *Pride and Prejudice* (New York: Norton, 2001) 125. Hereafter cited parenthetically by page number.

8. As when Elizabeth awkwardly resists Sir William's "gallant" effort to partner her in a dance with Darcy. Though Darcy is "not unwilling to receive" her hand on this occasion, Elizabeth draws back, insisting "with some discomposure" that she must not be supposed "to beg for a partner" (18). The pride wounded on their first meeting briefly disturbs Elizabeth's characteristic social facility in this second encounter. Similarly, at the Netherfield ball, feelings of "displeasure," "sharpened by immediate disappointment" at Wickham's absence, make it impossible for her to "reply with tolerable civility" to Darcy's conversational overtures (61).

9. "My own sex, I hope, will excuse me," writes Wollstonecraft, "if I treat them like rational creatures" so as to argue that "true dignity" consists in "obtain[ing] a character as a human being, regardless of the distinction of sex." *Vindication of the Rights of Woman*, 81.

10. Claudia Johnson, *Jane Austen: Women, Politics, and the Novel* (Chicago: University of Chicago Press, 1988), 89.

11. See especially William Galperin, *The Historical Austen* (Philadelphia: University of Pennsylvania Press, 2003); and Mary Favret, "Everyday War," *ELH* 72:3 (2005): 605–633.

12. Kant, *Groundwork*, 98–101 (hereafter cited parenthetically as *GM*). Christine Korsgaard offers a compact and lucid exposition of the two worlds Kant imagines us to inhabit in the *Groundwork* in *Creating the Kingdom of Ends* (Cambridge: Cambridge University Press, 1996), 200–205.

13. On the experience of love "in the absence of reciprocity," see Jean-Luc Marion, *The Erotic Phenomenon*, trans. Stephen E. Lewis (Chicago: University of Chicago Press, 2007), 67–101.

14. David Miller, *Jane Austen, or The Secret of Style* (Princeton: Princeton University Press, 2005), 46. "The days of wit and retorts simply pass away," Miller writes, leaving a "self of which, in the very first moment of coming to know it, she is 'absolutely ashamed'" (46–47).

15. Thomas Pfau, *Romantic Moods* (Baltimore: Johns Hopkins University Press, 2005), 12. "Far from constituting a psychological miscellany, mood establishes a quasi-cognitive relation to the world in the specific modality of *emotion*, that is as an intrinsically evaluative experience." See also Marion, *The Erotic Phenomenon*, on the "affective tonality" of the lover (95).

CHAPTER 5

1. Sigmund Freud, "Recommendations for Physicians on the Psychoanalytic Method of Treatment" (1912), in *Collected Papers*, trans. Joan Riviere (London: Hogarth Press, 1953), 2:330.

2. Freud rejects the "affective technique" of mutual disclosure on a number of grounds: It "verges upon treatment by suggestion," "achieves nothing towards the discovery of the patient's unconscious," and risks unproductively intensifying the transference. A practice of personal revelation from the physician "fails on account of the insatiability it rouses in the patient" to know more and more of the analyst. Freud readily concedes that a silent patient will start speaking when encouraged by the analyst's candor ("it will induce the patient to bring forward sooner and with less difficulty what he already knows and would otherwise have kept back for a time" [124]), but this "gain" is "cancelled in the end" by desires that the analyst cannot control or moderate. As with Freud's other recommendations for practice (including attending to the patient while seated out of his sight), the prescribed detachment of the analyst is justified on theoretical grounds but also meets a particular need of the analyst's—for "protection of his emotional life" from the demanding impingements of the patient's appetite for an *exchange* of intimacy.

3. Sigmund Freud, "The Dynamics of the Transference" (1912), in *Collected Papers*, 2:318.

4. Jessica Benjamin, *Like Subjects, Love Objects* (New Haven, CT: Yale University Press, 1995), 3, 24. Jonathan Dunn observes that "in the current psychoanalytic literature the concept of intersubjectivity constitutes a major epistemological and clinical challenge" to the "positivistic scientific orientation" of classical theory. "Intersubjectivity in Psychoanalysis: A Critical Review," *International Journal of Psychoanalysis* 76 (1995): 723.

5. M. Masud Khan, "To Hear with Eyes: Clinical Notes on Body as Subject and Object," in *The Privacy of the Self* (New York: International University Press, 1974), 246.

6. D. W. Winnicott, "Communicating and Not Communicating Leading to a Study of Certain Opposites" (1963), in *The Maturational Processes and the Facilitating Environment* (London: Hogarth Press, 1972), 179, 187.

7. Christopher Bollas, *The Shadow of the Object* (New York: Columbia University Press, 1987), 270.

8. Winnicott, "Communicating and Not Communicating," 192. Adam Phillips describes the "new kind of silence" theorized by Winnicott as a "secret metabolism of the self." While it is not my intention to take up Winnicott's evocative but problematic use of the term "true self" in his late work, it is worth noting that the notion binds together qualities of vitality, animation, authenticity: it entails the "experience of aliveness," "gives the feeling of real," is "the source of what is authentic in a person," and is emblematized by "the spontaneous gesture." As Masud Khan is not alone in observing, Winnicott's "true self" is a "conceptual ideal that is known most concretely by its absence," in the observation of inhibition, anxiety, lack of affect, rigidity, and reticence. See D. W. Winnicott, "Ego

Distortion in Terms of True and False Self" (1960), in *Maturational Processes*, 140–153; Adam Phillips, *Winnicott* (London: Penguin, 2007), 150, 133–135 (originally published 1988); M. Masud Khan, "The Finding and Becoming of Self," in *Privacy*, 294.

9. Winnicott, "On Communicating and Not Communicating," 187.

10. D. W. Winnicott, "The Capacity to Be Alone" (1958), in *Maturational Processes*, 31.

11. Ibid., 31.

12. Bollas, *Shadow*, 263.

13. Winnicott, "The Capacity to Be Alone," 31. "At the start is an essential aloneness," writes Winnicott, but "at the same time this aloneness can only take place under maximum conditions of dependence." The paradox is vitally constitutive in that it is both originary and available for reliving, "the fundamental state to which every individual, however old . . . can return in order to start again." *Human Nature* (New York: Brunner / Mazel, 1988), 131–132.

14. Bollas, *Shadow*, 235.

15. See, for example, Arnold Cooper's identification of a "'romantic' and intersubjective emphasis" in contemporary theory and the related clinical emphasis on "the effort of two people to connect affectively." *The Quiet Revolution in American Psychoanalysis* (New York: Brunner-Routledge, 2005), 222.

16. Bollas, *Shadow*, 271.

17. Michael Balint, *The Basic Fault* (Evanston, IL: Northwestern University Press, 1992), 179 (originally published 1969).

18. Ibid., 23. Describing this "use" of the analyst as a "capacity to be with oneself, unintruded upon by the need to relate," Bollas emphasizes that such "aloneness [is] not equivalent to isolation" because it is necessarily "underwritten by the presence of the other." Benjamin goes further, arguing that when "the subject has a space to become absorbed in internal rhythms" in a "solitude provided by the other," he has in no sense withdrawn from involvement with the other. "Loving the other," she suggests, might at times involve "tak[ing] a position quite inimical to intersubjective recognition." Bollas, *The Mystery of Things*, 11; Benjamin, *Like Subjects, Love Objects*, 161, 8.

19. Balint, *The Basic Fault*, 9.

20. Ibid., 180.

21. Ibid., 179.

22. Noel Jackson makes a related argument, contending that "such poems conceive community as the very medium of self-consciousness . . . as a constitutive outside that structures perception imperceptibly from within." "Critical Conditions: Coleridge, 'Common Sense,' and the Literature of Self-Experiment," *ELH* 70 (2003): 137.

23. Samuel Taylor Coleridge, "Frost at Midnight" (1798), in *Coleridge's Poetry and Prose*, ed. Nicholas Halmi, Paul Magnuson, and Raimondo Modiano (New York: Norton, 2004). Hereafter cited parenthetically by line number. Unless otherwise noted, all citations to Coleridge's poetry are from this volume.

24. Paul Magnuson and Judith Thompson offer arguments typical of an admonitory historicism, implicating interiority in an evasion of social and political concerns. Paul Magnuson, "The Politics of 'Frost at Midnight,'" *The Wordsworth Circle* 22 (1991): 3–10; Judith Thompson, "An Autumnal Blast, a Killing Frost: Coleridge's Poetic Conversation with John Thelwall," *Studies in Romanticism* 36 (1997): 427–456. Jackson offers a salutary

corrective when he suggests that insofar as poems like "Frost at Midnight" question "the notion that consciousness is truly private at all," they are implicitly "efforts to articulate the ground for politics in the first place" (139). See also Laura Quinney's defense of "psychological experience" as itself "one of the forms and manifestations of historical experience" in the period, in "'Tintern Abbey,' Sensibility and the Self-Disenchanted Self," *ELH* 64:1 (1997): 152.

25. Observing that the speaker "cannot comprehend the strange dreamlike vacuity," Magnuson reads the disturbance of the poem's opening as an obstacle to reflection, arguing that the "puzzling calm frustrates his musings." I see the "vexing" of meditation as an animating arousal, a stirring of thought rather than a hindrance. Paul Magnuson, *Coleridge's Nightmare Poetry* (Charlottesville: University of Virginia Press, 1974), 30.

26. One might argue that the disturbing childhood memory Coleridge revives here is itself a clamorous interruption of the present. Like Rei Terada, I understand the perceptual poesis of the speaker's musing as affectively distinct from the "most-believing" mood of the child "at the mercy of hopes that were not going to be fulfilled." The recollected disturbance of childhood is, however, continuous with meditative observation in the present. Bollas remarks that the patient who is creatively musing or "study[ing] in silence" is not only "aimlessly lingering amidst perceptual capacities" but also "remembering" something known but hitherto "unthought." In this sense, memory need not be a temporal displacement into the past nor a "return of the repressed" but genuinely evocative "news of the self" taking shape in the present (*Shadow*, 272). Rei Terada, "Phenomenality and Dissatisfaction in Coleridge's *Notebooks*," *Studies in Romanticism* 43 (Summer 2004): 268.

27. Like Jackson, I do not read the turn to Hartley as rebuking or transcending the reflexive self-consciousness of the silent thinker ("Critical Conditions," 135). Although it is "largely experienced and expressed in silence," what Khan names the "fallow mood" of alert quietude "needs an ambience of companionship in order to be held or sustained. . . . Someone—a friend, a wife, a neighbor—sitting around unobtrusively, guarantees that the psychic process does not . . . become morbid." M. Masud Khan, *Hidden Selves* (London: Maresfield, 1989), 185.

28. On the textual history, see Matthew Vanwinkle, "Revision in 'Frost at Midnight,'" *Studies in Romanticism* 43 (2004): 583–599.

29. Wordsworth, "Lines Composed a Few Miles above Tintern Abbey," in Hayden, *William Wordsworth: The Poems*, ll. 150–151, 116–119.

30. Samuel Taylor Coleridge, "Effusion XXXV (The Eolian Harp)," in Halmi, Magnuson, and Modiano, *Coleridge's Poetry and Prose*, 17–20, ll. 1, 56.

31. Wordsworth, "Strange Fits of Passion," ll. 27–28.

32.   . . . once when he awoke

In most distressful mood . . .

I hurried with him to our orchard plot,

And he beholds the moon, and hush'd at once

Suspends his sobs, and laughs most silently.

Samuel Taylor Coleridge, "The Nightingale: A Conversational Poem," in Halmi, Magnuson, and Modiano, *Coleridge's Poetry and Prose*, 102–105, ll. 98–103.

33. Line numbers refer to Book 4 of the 1805 edition of Wordsworth's *Prelude*.

34. Christopher Bollas, *Being a Character: Psychoanalysis and Self-Experience* (New York: Hill and Wang, 1992), 186.

35. "Resolution and Independence," in Hayden, *William Wordsworth: The Poems*, vol. 1, l. 51. Hereafter cited parenthetically by line number.

CODA

1. It is, I hope, abundantly clear that psychoanalytic work is present in this study not as an interpretive framework but as body of writing that merits interpretive attention in its own right, especially in relation to philosophical and literary imaginations of intimacy. It is worth noting that because the British Psychoanalytical Society (unlike the American) has never required a medical degree for admission, many of its trainees—and many of the writers I discuss in this chapter—have an academic background in the humanities. Masud Khan and Nina Coltart both read English (at the University of Punjab and Oxford, respectively), as did Adam Phillips; Christopher Bollas completed a PhD in English before immigrating to the United Kingdom for psychoanalytic training. Literary texts appear frequently in their writings as examples, evocations, or alternative articulations of conceptual arguments, and sensitivity to narrative and interpretive complexity shapes their case histories. This intellectual formation attests to genealogical links between literary and psychoanalytic work and reopens a question I raised in the Introduction about the relationship between romantic-era literature and the psychologies (sentimental and empiricist) that were the prevailing sciences of mind at the time.

2. Sigmund Freud, "Further Recommendations in the Technique of Psychoanalysis" (1913), in *Collected Works*, 11:354. Hereafter cited parenthetically as *FR*.

3. In a recent case history of a patient's "phobia" of the couch, Nancy Kulish is surprised to discover how "few writers have examined in depth the meaning of the couch to the patient and in the analytic relationship." Her review of the sparse literature on the subject indicates both theoretical flexibility ("the couch does not in itself define psychoanalysis") and practical attachment to the couch as "a badge of analytic identity" with a "magical quality for the analyst." "A Phobia of the Couch," *Psychoanalytic Quarterly* 65 (1996): 468, 488–491.

4. Freud, *Collected Papers*, 2:327. Hereafter cited parenthetically as *R*.

5. On the "relational" assumptions uniting diverse postwar psychoanalytic theorists, see Jay Greenberg and Stephen Mitchell, *Object Relations in Psychoanalytic Theory* (Cambridge, MA: Harvard University Press, 1983). See also Benjamin, *Like Subjects, Love Objects*, 2–15.

6. Lewis Aron, *A Meeting of Minds: Mutuality in Psychoanalysis* (Hillsdale, NJ: Analytic Press, 1996), 142. Hereafter cited parenthetically by page number.

7. Thomas Ogden, "Privacy, Reverie and Analytic Technique," in *Reverie and Interpretation* (London: Karnac, 1999), 113. Hereafter cited parenthetically by page number.

8. As Aron notes, Ogden is "quite conservative technically" (*A Meeting of Minds*, 71). Indeed, in defending the couch, Ogden transposes Freud's image of the analyst as detached surgeon onto the analytic setting, comparing the "area of privacy" created by the couch to "the surgeon's requirement for a sterile field in which to operate" ("Privacy," 114).

9. See the discussion of post-Freudian interpretations of silence in Chapter 5.

10. Benjamin, *Like Subjects, Love Objects*, 160, 170.

11. D. W. Winnicott, "The Use of an Object and Relating through Identifications," in *Playing and Reality* (London: Tavistock, 1971), 89.

12. Ibid., 61.

13. Jeanne Wolff Bernstein, "Countertransference: Our New Royal Road to the Unconscious?," *Psychoanalytic Dialogues* 9:3 (1999): 275–299.

14. Benjamin, *Like Subjects, Love Objects*, 155–156.

15. Hans Loewald, "Psychoanalytic Theory and the Psychoanalytic Process" (1970), in *Papers on Psychoanalysis* (New Haven, CT: Yale University Press, 1990), 286.

16. Ibid.

17. Christopher Bollas, *Forces of Destiny* (London: Free Association Books, 1989), 59, and *Being a Character* (New York: Hill and Wang, 1992), 63 (hereafter cited parenthetically as *BC*).

18. Jonathan Lear, *Love and Its Place in Nature: A Philosophical Interpretation of Freudian Psychoanalysis* (New Haven, CT: Yale University Press, 1990), 191.

19. Cf. Freud: "Consciousness makes each of us aware only of his own states of mind; that other people, too, possess a consciousness is an inference which we draw by analogy from their observable utterances and actions, in order to make this behavior of theirs intelligible to us. . . . Without any special reflection we attribute to everyone else our own constitution and therefore our consciousness as well, and this identification is a *sine qua non* of our understanding." "The Unconscious" (1915), in *The Standard Edition of the Complete Psychological Works of Sigmund Freud*, ed. James Strachey (London: Hogarth, 1957), 14:168.

20. Loewald, "Psychoanalytic Theory," 229, 297.

21. Benjamin, *Like Subjects, Love Objects*, 159–160, 165.

22. Ibid., 172.

23. Bollas, *The Mystery of Things*, 13.

24. Loewald, "Psychoanalytic Theory," 354.

25. Bollas, *The Mystery of Things*, 66.

26. In his 1997 plenary address to the American Psychoanalytic Association, Robert Michels argues, "Writing a case history . . . is at least in part a countertransference theme or enactment" and thus "reveal[s] how the meaning of the analysis is incorporated into the analyst's personal and professional life." Adrienne Harris notes that the "lines between documentation and creative fiction are increasingly blurred" in psychoanalytic case reports due to "intensified interest in the subjectivity of the analyst." Theodore Shapiro, on the other hand, characterizes contemporary interest in the intersubjective dynamics of analysis as "a shift . . . toward a romantic vision of the practice" and worries that "we will find ourselves in the ranks of other artists of the mind, such as novelists." Robert Michels, "The Case History," *Journal of the American Psychoanalytic Association* 48:2 (2000): 372; Adrienne Harris, "The Analyst as (Auto)biographer," *American Imago* 55:2 (1998): 257; Theodore Shapiro, "Empathy: A Critical Reevaluation," *Psychoanalytic Inquiry* 1 (1981): 427, 437.

27. Nina Coltart, "Slouching towards Bethlehem . . . or Thinking the Unthinkable in Psychoanalysis," in *Slouching towards Bethlehem* (New York: Guilford, 1992), 9. Hereafter cited parenthetically by page number.

28. Khan, *Privacy*, 206.

29. "The Silent Patient," in Coltart, *Slouching towards Bethlehem*, 85.

30. Bollas, *The Mystery of Things*, 11–13.

31. Although most visitors sat for an average of twenty minutes, because each was invited to remain as long as he or she chose, some sat for hours and some for just a moment or two. Many of those who ultimately took their place before the artist described the waiting period as an unexpected but important aspect of the experience. Stephanie Gumpel's comment is typical: "Although at first I want a better place in line, I realize that 8 hours of waiting makes the piece itself so much richer. It is an 8 hour meditation of why I want to be here, and . . . I transcend my fear of being in this performance." Stephanie Gumpel, "Day 6—Marina Abramovic—The Artist Is Present," May 21, 2010, http://www.stephaniegumpel.com/archives/185. For details of the performance, see "The Artist Is Present: Marina Abramović," http://www.moma.org/interactives/exhibitions/2010/marinaabramovic/.

32. To view a full set of the photographs by Marco Anelli, see "Marina Abramović: The Artist Is Present—Portraits," March 9–March 12, 2010, http://www.flickr.com/photos/themuseumofmodernart/sets/72157623741486824/. They have recently been gathered in a monograph: Marco Anelli, *Portraits in the Presence of Marina Abramović* (Bologna, Italy: Damiani, 2012). As a collection, Anelli's portraits both belong to and mount a challenge to the historical archive of drawings and photos used as illustrations of emotional expression by scientists from Charles Darwin to Paul Ekman. On the problematic use of "posed" photographs by Ekman in particular, see Ruth Leys, "How Did Fear Become a Scientific Object and What Kind of Object Is It?," *Representations* 110:1 (Spring 2010): 66–105.

33. Gumpel, "Day 6."

34. Dimitri Chrysanthopolous, *themetree*, May 6, 2010, http://themetree.tumblr.com/post/577337725/yup-heres-my-flickr-portrait-from-the-marina.

35. Jeffrey Bussmann, "The Agony and the Ecstasy of Waiting for Marina Abramović," Post-Nonprofalyptic, May 1, 2010, http://postnonprofalyptic.blogspot.com/2010/05/agony-and-ecstasy-of-waiting-for-marina.html.

36. Posted comment by Jeffrey, May 10, 2010, at "Visitor Viewpoint: MoMa's Mystery Man," *Inside/Out*, http://www.moma.org/explore/inside_out/2010/05/10/visitor-viewpoint-momas-mystery-man.

37. "Marina Abramović: The Artist Speaks," *Inside/Out*, June 3, 2010, http://www.moma.org/explore/inside_out/2010/06/03/marina-abramovic-the-artist-speaks.

38. Dan Visel, quoted in Jim Dwyer, "Confronting a Stranger, for Art," New York Times, April 2, 2010, http://www.nytimes.com/2010/04/04/nyregion/04about.html.

INDEX